KELTON KING

Freedom Road

PUBLISHING HOUSE
SWEENEY

First published by Sweeney Publishing House 2024

Second edition

ISBN (paperback): 978-1-967583-01-0
ISBN (hardcover): 978-1-967583-00-3

Editing by Demi Rouhani
Cover art by Maddock Merlot

This book was professionally typeset on Reedsy.
Find out more at reedsy.com

Contents

Acknowledgments

Thank you to Maddock Merlot for illustrating the hardcover and Demi Rouhani for taking the time to edit these essays, both free of charge. Any further typos or errors found in the text are my own fault.

Preface: 1st Edition

Dear Reader,

The following is a selection of essays written over approximately two years from 2022-2024. I will say that I am not an expert on any of the topics in these essays. I have not run any businesses nor organized a workers' union, my history of activism includes attending a handful of protests, and at the time of writing this, I've only earned my AA degree in pursuance of a bachelor's in Economics (In fact, a large chunk of these essays were written outdoors in the FSCJ courtyard). Despite all this, I've always found history to be a fascinating subject, and observing the history unveiling right before our very eyes is my biggest driver to pursue my studies. For those of you who are also interested in politics and economics, you'll know the double-edged sword of talking about it in everyday life. You have a lot of topics and ideas you want to discuss, but every conversation starts at a surface level, and many times you're unable to reach the depths of conversation you want to get into.

I've written these essays for a few reasons. First and foremost, to share with those in my life who are interested in learning what I believe in without having to listen to me jump around from point to point. Secondly, it serves as a foundation on which I can continue to build as I learn more through studying and organizing. For example, there are pieces within this text like my analysis of culture and the oversimplification of capitalism arising out of feudalism that I plan on tackling in more detail in a book of its own. Third and finally, sort of in tandem with point two, the book serves as a timepiece in my life! As I deepen my understanding of economics and run into more and more walls and questions (as I did throughout the process of writing these essays), there is no telling how this foundation might evolve. However, being able to reflect on my early ideas in the future and compare how they've shifted, whether they be further into socialism or possibly rightward into a more 'mixed' economy, will be invaluable to me.

Whether you find these essays interesting enough to begin your own studies or scoff at their stupidity, I thank you for taking the time to read them!

Kelton King

June 28th, 2024

Preface: 2nd Edition

Dear Reader,

After much deliberation between my bouts of boredom with writing additional books, I decided to revisit this text, update it, and revise it. At the bottom of this letter, I'll leave a brief change log for your ease of access.

I decided to treat this text as a living document for the time being, and in doing so, I wanted to narrow the scope of my message. To do that, I have removed the additional selected essays following Part II: 'On Revolution' as they are quite broad in regard to topics ranging from critiques of religion, unions, and books. I have also edited down other parts of the book, in particular, the vast majority of my analysis of the 2024 U.S. Presidential Election. My prediction was obviously wrong with Donald Trump winning the presidency. Perhaps, with hindsight, I shouldn't have overvalued the anti-Trump vote, but truthfully, the election is rather meaningless in the grand scheme of things. A bourgeois politician is a bourgeois politician, after all. I am not removing this section to hide my analysis and prediction; I believe it to be a simply unnecessary 1,500 words in the context of answering the electoral question. An essay has been added to Part II: 'On Revolution' titled 'On Fascism & Trumpism' that seeks to analyze the rise of both historic Fascism in Europe and 'Trumpism' around the globe today, comparing their similarities and differences.

Furthermore, I have replaced these removals with the addition of a new part: Part III: 'Topics on the International.' In this part, we look at scaling the system detailed in the earlier parts to the international level by questioning how federalism can be used to bind the international proletariat together in the stage of the revolution. The essay 'The Tie That Binds' investigates the necessity of upholding the primacy of class struggle by analyzing 'The Federalist Papers,' the failed socialist federation of Yugoslavia, and Abdullah Ocalan's ideology of 'Democratic Confederalism.' 'The Gradient Scale' serves to scale the political-economic model detailed in Phases One and Two to the international level in a deeper theoretical model than that left in the first edition. The final two essays have recycled parts of the first edition along with a new and deeper analysis of both the national and religious questions within the context of an international proletarian federation.

This will be the final edition of Freedom Road for the foreseeable future. In between classes at UNF, I have been researching and writing the first draft of a companion text called Captured Culture, which could be referred to as an 'Exit' on Freedom's Road. It will be a three-to-four-part analysis of cultural supremacy, cultural narcissism, cultural control, and possibly cultural revolution.

Kelton King

February 18th, 2025

Introduction

Throughout these essays, we will critique the capitalist system and theorize a possible alternative and the process of establishing that alternative. Our arguments have been adapted and developed by the theories of others just as they adapted and developed the theories of those who came before them. This work is entirely subjective and should be treated as such. Read it. Criticize it. Take the parts you like and discard the parts you don't. We only ask that when you absorb the material, you do so with an open mind!

"The history of all hitherto existing society is the history of class struggles." These words by Karl Marx were not sophistry, they have opened the eyes of generations of people – still 141 years since his death – to the seemingly eternal conflict that plagues humanity, the class war. The first thing one must understand is that capitalism is not an 'evil' system. It is certainly a fundamentally exploitative one, sure, but to call it evil is to ignore its historical relevancy. When looking at human history as a constant war of attrition between economic classes, capitalism's purpose becomes clear.

For the first several thousand years of humankind, we practiced what we call today, primitive communism. People were nomadic, hunter-gatherers, traveling from one area to the next living off the land and collectively sharing resources for the survival of their family or community. Eventually, these groups began to domesticate animals and cultivate farmlands. The ability to sustain themselves allowed them to settle and expand, often close to water sources. As these groups expanded, they came into contact with one another and trade between tribes occurred. At first it was bartering, but eventually to simplify things, a universal measure of exchange was created in the form of currency. As these societies grew, they consisted not just of one family or community, but of several different tribes. They didn't share the same communal spaces and as the land spread, so did they, which led to the first real emergence of private property and class divisions. And with class division and private property comes conflict. These separate societies soon went to war with one another, the strongest prevailed and subjugated the weaker ones through the form of slavery. As these 'strong' societies continued to expand their land and power, so did their class divides. This eventually developed into the period we refer to as Feudalism. At the top, there were nobles who acquired their positions through wealth, power, inheritance, and in some cases apparently God revealed that they were special in a dream. Below them were their vassals or smaller lords who helped maintain the vast lands of their rulers. These vassals of course wouldn't want to toil the land all day themselves, so they used the peasantry or serfs who worked for their landlords in return for food and shelter. And when the peasantry wasn't enough, extra labor could be brought in in the form of slaves captured through conquest. For over a thousand years this was the way of the world, and of course, there were peasant revolts, but a small, unarmed, and unorganized squabble was easily put down by the lords' mercenaries and trained soldiers. Through constant war, the need for innovation to get an edge over the competition drove societal industrialization. It is here we saw the rise of capitalism, first in the form of mercantilism, or merchant capitalism, and later in the form of industrial capitalism. During the rise of mercantilism, guilds of artisans formed. These were small producers who mainly operated at the local community level but also produced for export to other nations. These artisans and guilds formed what is called the middle class. The middle class as we use it in this article is very different from the way it is used in the modern day. In our use of the word, the middle class refers to another component of the bourgeoisie, the petite bourgeoisie, or small business owners, whereas today most people who use the term middle class are referring to the working class, what we call the proletariat. With increasing power due to primitive accumulation, this middle class of merchants and artisans grew tired of being under the thumb of the lords and noblemen, and it is here we began to see the first clashes of class conflicts between the feudal lords and the capitalists. As with the peasant revolts, these revolts were also doomed to failure – that was until the capitalists were able to team with the peasantry to overthrow the feudal class once and for all. As industrialization continued, the capitalist class grew with wealth, power, and influence. Their new factories needed laborers and so finally, the proletariat was formed.

The Industrial Revolution set the stage for the next contradictory classes, but first, the old and outdated governance had to be abolished, and so it was. With the assistance of the peasantry and the proletariat, the capitalist class was able to overthrow feudalism and establish itself as the new ruling class. This started at the end of the eighteenth century in Great Britain and quickly spread across Europe, which would soon forcefully spread it to the rest of the world through colonialism like they were spoon-feeding babies. Whether they liked it or not, the free market was coming! Along with expanding its economic power, the new world order expanded its political power. Kings were axed and replaced with 'democratic' parliaments, which were of course structured in a way to preserve the power of the ruling class and limit that of the workers and the peasantry. These revolutions are referred to as bourgeois revolutions.

The new ruling class of capitalists exploits the classes below them, constantly expands its influence through imperialism abroad, and strips the earth of its finite resources in hopes of short-term profit regardless of the long-term environmental impact, however, these revolutions for all the bad they do are still considered progressive. They are progressive because they have carried us on to the next step in the evolution of humanity and the evolution of class struggle. With the feudal lords gone and the peasantry becoming more and more a part of the proletariat as the world develops, two classes remain, the bourgeois capitalists and the proletariat working class. The inherent contradictions between these two classes will always put them into conflict. To put it simply, if the capitalist at home exploits his workers too heavily, their own conditions will drive them to revolt against the capitalist. If the capitalist at home treats his workers well, his enterprise will fail due to not being profitable enough to compete with his competitors who continue to heavily exploit their workers. If the entire nation of capitalists treats their workers well to make up for lost profit, they will have to send their exploitation elsewhere through the act of economic colonization and outsourcing. To stop the threat of revolutions at home the capitalists have taken this road. They treat their workers just well enough that they are content to run on the hamster wheel until they grow too old to fight and are replaced. The hard jobs, the back-breaking labor – manufacturing, in particular – are shipped across the sea to exploit the labor of maldeveloped nations whose corrupt bourgeois governments rely on foreign capital to maintain their own power. With the hard labor sent abroad to workers paid dirt poor wages in even poorer working conditions, there is no big threat of organized unionization and mass strikes on the home front. The capitalist is free to accumulate more and more wealth, continue to bribe politicians, pollute the air, and continue to expand the growing wealth gap between owner and worker.

The workers have overthrown the divine kings of the past and have been wowed into believing they are now the masters of their own fate because they get to cast a vote at the ballot box. They have been lied to. The workers will not be the master of their fate until they realize they've merely replaced one supreme ruler for a small band of equally corrupt oligarchs. The issue of feudalism wasn't just that lords and kings had complete say over the nation's political policy, but also that they had complete control over its economic policy. The workers allowed the capitalists to take over those responsibilities and in return, the capitalists did their part. They further expanded and developed the means of production around the world, at least in the areas that were profitable to them, but now they have outlived their usefulness as the ruling class. The means of production have been developed, the world has been mapped and charted, and there is no further need for expansion and environmental damage. It is time for the working class, the proletariat, to pull the wool from their eyes and see the path to true democracy, to true freedom, is only possible through direct conflict with the ruling class of capitalists. True freedom can only be won through the dismantling of the fake bourgeois democracy and the exploitative capitalist mode of production. Only when the workers themselves – not under the influence of politicians or bureaucrats – control the means of production across society at large will they be able to direct their own future, to be the masters of their own fate. When asked why socialist revolutions have failed everywhere they've been tried, one might want to first answer, how many slave revolts were crushed before societies began abolishing the practice? How many people claimed God ordained their rulership and were turned away and exiled by the people? How many peasant revolts were squashed by the lord's soldiers? And how many attempts were there by capitalists to overthrow their monarchs? As a matter of fact, you could spend your entire life studying the failed bourgeois revolutions of France alone. The point of these questions is to understand that our lifetimes are short, but our history of class struggles is not. There has never been a clean transition from one ruling class to the other and to expect the first attempts at overthrowing the most powerful ruling class to ever exist to succeed (especially from extremely underdeveloped nations) is completely asinine! Every attempted transition will be marked by failures. The entire point is to study each movement, analyze their conditions of success and ultimate failure, and then continue on the struggle. To ignore the past, to write it off as a complete failure, is to walk into future conflict with no plan of battle, no armor, no weapons – just the pig-headed belief that you are somehow smarter and better fitted to overthrow a system that you know nothing about. It's foolish!

With the brief and extremely oversimplified history of how the capitalist system came to rule, we can take a closer look at how it exploits the workers. Starting with private property and wage labor. Anyone who wants to scare you away from learning about what the movement of communism is will leave you with this quote from Karl Marx's Communist Manifesto, "The theory of Communism may be summed up in one sentence: Abolish all private property."[1] They will not explain this quote to you. Instead, they will jeer that the communists want to steal your toothbrush and your home and send you to labor to death in the gulags. As always, fear and ignorance are the biggest weapons the ruling class utilizes against the socialist movement

[1] Marx 1848, p. 22

today. They refuse to differentiate between what socialists deem private property and personal property. Private property, put simply, is productive property. Any property that is used for production, in other words, the means of production that are privately owned and thus expropriating the labor of workers through the wage system is to be abolished. This would refer to things like factories, farms, mines, power plants, stores, etc. The abolition of private property doesn't mean we all pile in the community bulldozer and roll over these buildings, what is being abolished is the private owner's relation to the property and hence also his relation to his employees and society. With the transition from private productive property to socially controlled productive property, the owner no longer profits off the labor of the workers, he no longer owns the property but becomes a worker, a member of the proletariat.

You might ask, what's the problem with owning private property and profiting off the work of labor? There are several issues. First and foremost, the profit expropriated from the workers. The surplus value is left in the hands of the owner or shareholders and although they didn't produce it, they get 100% of the say in its distribution. This surplus value is the most powerful tool of the capitalist. He can reinvest it in his business, speed up production, cheapen production costs to beat out his competition on the way to dominating the market share, continue accumulating capital through investments or bank accounts, and he can shape society how he sees fit through bribing (or lobbying as we sugarcoat it) politicians at all levels of society. The accumulation of surplus value leads to corruption and monopoly. It is not a defect or a bug of capitalism or liberal democracy, but a feature. One might go so far as saying it's the entire point! There is no other path for capitalism but expansion. The owner must expand his business because if he doesn't, he will lose his market share to his competitors and be driven out of business. The more he expands, the more capital he receives. The more surplus value he extracts, the more political power he gains until eventually, as we see today, entire industries are in the hands of a handful of companies and their shareholders. As capitalism continues to develop, we see the return of kings. Except this time they are shielded from the angry mob of proletarians who instead throw their blame at the feet of politicians who have already been bought by the kings of industry. Liberal or bourgeois democracy is the strongest foundation for the ruling class of capitalists because when the going gets tough for the workers and they are looking for heads to roll, they'll be given a ballot that promises a fix to their problems if they just shade in a box, and that will hold them over until the next election, the next imperialist war, or the next culture war talking point.

The exploitation of the worker is carried out through the wage system. What the capitalist calls a free and voluntary contract is in reality nothing more than signing your soul to a new master. To live and provide for their families, people need food, water, clothing, shelter, and healthcare. These things are, of course, locked behind a paywall. The necessity of accessing these items compels them to find work. If your sustenance of life depends on another person giving you a work contract there is an extreme power imbalance, that action is by definition coercive. The owners of businesses know this and utilize it to their advantage, the worker needs work to survive so they will accept low wages. The long length of the workday with minimal breaks, of course, allows the capitalist to buy the labor power of the worker for longer than is needed to provide an adequate exchange of labor for the money required for the workers' immediate sustenance. Therefore, the worker provides more labor than is required for their continued sustenance for no extra compensation! Capitalists argue that competition inside the industry will cause businesses to have to compete for laborers, thus raising their wages. But in reality, it is quite the opposite. Businesses, by nature of their competition, are always trying to drive one another out of the industry. The ultimate goal is to become the sole monopoly power. To do this they will do everything they can to maximize profits, finding ways to increase production speed and cheapen production costs, cutting loose ends, producing lower or higher quality goods to try and earn more of the market share, etc. That is if they are on equal footing. If there is one business that has a larger share of the market compared to its competition, it can temporarily raise wages or lower prices to price out the competition. In doing so, it dominates the market and now has total control to set wages and prices wherever they want because it is now next to impossible to threaten their monopoly over the industry. You can see this take place when any big department store moves into an area with local businesses – the small businesses cannot compete with the power of the big businesses' capital. The workers themselves are then stuck with low-wage jobs where they are convinced by the propaganda of capitalist society to not discuss wages with each other and to not even consider the possibility of unionizing. Unionizing is the owner's biggest fear. If the workers negotiate their contract as a collective instead of individuals, the power imbalance weakens. Together the workers are stronger than separate, and the owner knows that and will fight their unionization with every weapon in his arsenal. Here, once again, we see the power of the wage system. If the workers begin to unionize and attempt a strike, the owner can fire them and bring on new workers for the same low wages, because as long as people's livelihood relies on that work contract, someone will fill that position. This also brings us to the myth of meritocracy under capitalism. The belief that if you work hard you will rise up the ladder. The wage system has nothing to do with merit. Workers' wages are paid as a part of the production process and to the capitalist that's all they are – another tool, another factor to take into account when trying to maximize profits.

The private ownership of production and the exploitation of the laborers through the wage system is the process through which the capitalist produces their commodities to be brought to market and sold for profit. This is the foundation of capitalism. The profit gained through exploitation corrupts politicians, keeps people impoverished, destroys the environment, drives imperialism and exploitation abroad, and focuses on short-term profit and economic growth over long-term societal growth. That is the reason we need to embrace socialism. We must begin this transition in order to free ourselves from a system designed to keep us subservient to capital for the enrichment of the ruling class. We must abolish the capitalist class by tearing down every leg that it stands on from private property, to wage labor, to the base unit of capitalism, the commodity!

The road to freedom is long and arduous. It is lined with potholes, military checkpoints, bad drivers, and plenty of false exits. And though traveling this road takes a lot of mental and physical fortitude, it is a necessity for the survival of our species. As we have for all of human history, we will travel the road to freedom and liberation or we will get off on a wrong exit and find ourselves right back on the road. Socialism or barbarism is an endless cycle so long as we continue to pick barbarism! We will finish this article with a quote from the great Albert Einstein's *Why Socialism?*

"It is important to understand that even in theory the payment of the worker is not determined by the value of his product. Private capital tends to become concentrated in few hands, partly because of competition among the capitalists, and partly because technological development and the increasing division of labor encourage the formation of larger units of production at the expense of smaller ones. The result of these developments is an oligarchy of private capital the enormous power of which cannot be effectively checked even by a democratically organized political society. This is true since the members of legislative bodies are selected by political parties, largely financed or otherwise influenced by private capitalists who, for all practical purposes, separate the electorate from the legislature. The consequence is that the representatives of the people do not in fact sufficiently protect the interests of the underprivileged sections of the population."[2]

[2] Einstein 1949

I

Foundations of Cooperative Federocracy

1

Phase One

Introduction

From this point forward we will refer to the system of which we are describing during the transition from capitalism to socialism as Cooperative Federocracy. Cooperative meaning an economy based upon cooperation and Federocracy meaning a federalized democratic government. This system is built upon the phrase "Life, Liberty, and the pursuit of happiness" written by Thomas Jefferson in the US Declaration of Independence, but this time we will build a system true to these promises, not one built to protect the rule of capital. Our system is designed from the bottom up to provide all citizens the right to life – the necessities being access to shelter, food, water, housing, healthcare, and energy. Liberty – the freedom to direct their own life, to be their own master. And the pursuit of happiness – an increase in freedom through more leisure time from work and the current economic conditions we live under. These promises made by liberalism hold true for the bourgeois participants of the capitalist system at the expense of the working class. Through a rejection of the capitalist system and the liberal ideology, these can become the foundations of the transition that could build a new world that is freer for all.[3]

Before we get into the basics of the economic structure, we should take a look at the political sphere. Currently, the U.S. is controlled by the dictatorship of the bourgeoisie, the rule of the capitalist class. This rule is upheld by the bourgeois democracy we are faced with, or as I will describe it henceforth, pseudo-duopoly. Before we can talk about replacing the system, we must go over the current one. The pseudo-duopoly we face in America is the strongest inhibitor to a growing class consciousness today. The country is divided into two parties, the Democrats and the Republicans, or the progressives and conservatives. These parties are nothing more than controlled opposition. The political system they play in was handcrafted by the founding fathers to protect the rule of the capitalist class, as can be seen by their choice to only give voting power to white, land-owning men. By allowing only white, male landowners to vote, from the foundation they were able to adapt and construct a system that was designed to uphold the rule of white male capitalists, or in other words, race, patriarchy, and capital. Only through centuries of civil movements did other groups of people finally achieve suffrage, but by the time everyone was finally given a voice, the system was already complete and strong enough to stop the threats to race, patriarchy, and capital.

As we mentioned previously, the accumulation of capital allows the capitalists to use our political sphere as another tool for production. Political influence is used to pass pro-business policies, deregulate industries, regulate competition, bail them out during economic crises, use public funding to enhance their own technologies, cut their taxes, and most of all

[3] Although we refer here to Thomas Jefferson and the 'US Declaration of Independence,' we do so only in an attempt to appeal to the hardcore constitutionalist American proletarian. Marxism and Communism are not another branch of Liberalism nor do they proclaim to achieve the aims of liberalism for in reality, they seek to abolish them as they are very much the present state of things! We have made clear at many points in these essays what Marxism and Communism truly entail, however, it is not a lie that the liberation of the proletariat would provide the people with better access to life, liberty, and the pursuit of happiness. The only difference is between what those words mean in the liberal and communist world!

to use as a shield against the working class. Whenever the economy stagnates and falls, the public throws the blame at the politicians and replaces them with another politician funded and groomed by the capitalist class to serve their interests And on the off chance an outsider or independent creates a big enough grassroots movement to get themselves into a political office, they either compromise on their ideas to stay in power, telling themselves they are still the voice of the voiceless, or decide to become just another capitalist reformer. If they stand true to their principles, they will quickly find themselves out of office by scandal, assassination, or by being out-funded during the next election cycle. By any means necessary. The system cannot be changed from within because both parties, however different they try to make themselves seem to the public, are capitalist parties. They stand for the same economic system. Their disagreements, while vitaly important, are always over social issues like abortion, LGBTQ+ rights, racism, gun rights, education, etc. This is not to say these issues are not related to class and economics, they are integral to both, however, under a system of two capitalist parties all social or cultural victories by the liberal party will only serve to embolden and further radicalize the conservative party until it is eventually transformed into a fascist party – all of which are capitalist parties.

This is an unavoidable phenomenon under liberal bourgeois rule. As long as society strides to be socially progressive but remains fiscally 'conservative' (capitalist), the conservative opposition will increasingly be propagandized by a rising reactionary populist that all the problems in society are caused by some minority group. And that this minority group is secretly a cabal of Marxists trying to influence the minds of their children. As Hitler referred to the Jewish people as agents of "Cultural-Bolshevism," Republicans today claim that 'woke' people (LGBTQ+) are agents of "Cultural Marxism." This is not unique to America; however, you can find this happening in every liberal bourgeois country in the world because progress will always be attacked by tradition. The rise of fascism is a natural process of capitalism. This is because a liberal bourgeois society is merely the placeholder for society to transform to freedom – through socialism or to state-controlled masters through fascism. This cycle will continue until humanity destroys itself or finally evolves to the next political-economic stage.

So, we face an endless cycle of political corruption built on the accumulated wealth of capitalists that is used as a tool to keep the working class divided into two blocks cheering their party on like it's their favorite sports team. They learn their names, donate to their campaigns, champion their slogans, and go to verbal war with the other side. But when it comes to economics, neither side has any idea about anything. And why would they? Their parties don't talk about economics outside of vague references to trade wars, reports on inflation, and once again the social actions of corporations. Since Reagan brought "trickle-down" economics to popularity nothing meaningful has been done by either party economically, and yet both sides are convinced the other is ruining the economy. Nothing has changed, nothing will change. But the media news cycles will pump the propaganda of each party into their voter's heads and send them off to vote in "the most important election of their lifetime." How do we fix this? We attack the issue on two fronts, politically and economically.

PHASE ONE:

Preface:

At the start of phase one, the first phase of transition, we will assume through whatever powers may be that the workers have successfully wrested power away from the capitalist ruling class. It is in the first phase that we will lay the foundation. The fundamental building blocks to another world begin here and to do that we must start from the bottom up. What are our immediate goals? Establishing the dictatorship of the proletariat, the rule of the working class over the capitalist class in both the political and economic spheres of society. To do this, we will start the process of attacking society's capitalist structure one step at a time. Piece by piece, we will tear that capitalist structure down upon itself. As each structure of capitalism falls a new building and a new society will take its place. That society is one built upon the principles of socialism. In this phase, the foundations of capitalism we will chip away at are the private ownership of the means of production, wage labor, and commodity production. That is not to say all these things will be completely eradicated during the first phase. That won't be the case. Some things are easier to evolve out of than others, and the conditions for each could be different for differing societies. We do not claim that the first phase is socialist, it is merely setting up the foundations for the socialist mode of production we will discuss in phase two.

ECONOMY:

Economic Introduction:

The fundamental building block of any economic system is the shop or the enterprise. It is here where workers gather at the local level to produce goods and services, so it is here we must begin. In the first stage, we will mainly be targeting private ownership of the enterprise as well as diminishing the pain of wage labor. At this stage, the capitalist market will not be abolished, but we will work to regulate and control it through proper structure and worker control, not by the influence or orders of the party and its officials. To start, we will take the principles of worker cooperatives and expand on them exponentially. In our critique of worker cooperatives, we noted the main issue was not with the model itself, it was with those who claimed that by just implementing worker cooperatives alone, socialism would be achieved. We are not making that claim. We intend to use the worker cooperative model as a basic foundation to build a cohesive and productive economic system that furthers the construction of a socialist society, without neglecting to give the direction of industry to the workers themselves.

Under the current capitalist organization of enterprises, we see a firm hierarchy within the shop itself. There is the owner of the business, and in many cases, the shareholders he is beholden to. Then there is middle management, those that oversee the workers. These management positions are in most cases chosen by the shop's ruling class, the owner. Without a say in choosing their management, the workers are stuck with whoever is placed above them. Their new ruler is assigned to them, and they are to obey or face repercussions. In larger enterprises where the owner doesn't work alongside their employees, this decision is often made without knowing if the new manager is liked by the staff or a good technical fit, and in some cases, they even bring in outside help. In that case, an outsider or worse, the owner's friend or family, a complete stranger to the workers is made their direct overseer. This is very rarely ever a good outcome. While these are more common events in larger enterprises, they can and do occur in smaller enterprises. Furthermore, by the rights of being the private owner of the business and its means of production, the owner and shareholders directly hold the power over the allocation of the business's surplus value - its profit. We previously went over the issue of capital accumulation, but we'll briefly summarize it again. Capital accumulation into the hands of the few increases the divide in wealth between owner and worker, or the bourgeois capitalists and the proletarian working class. As the capitalist becomes richer and accumulates more capital to invest with, he can expand his operations and bring on more workers to exploit the labor of, giving himself access to even more capital. Once large enough, this allows the capitalist to shape society to his image. Politicians can be bribed, the state can be used to crush opposition, media can be bought and used for propaganda, competition can be bought out or destroyed, or it can continue to accumulate through investments or savings accounts where the money never 'trickles down' to the rest of society.

You may ask if worker cooperatives are still a capitalist organization of the enterprise, then how will these issues be solved? The answer is simple, not every issue with capitalism can be eliminated in one fell swoop, but by moving the power of the enterprise from the hands of a sole owner or board of shareholders into the hands of the enterprise's entire workforce; the power is diluted. There is internal democracy over the decision-making, and the accumulation of capital is diluted between all the workers. A collective group of workers is less likely to lower their standards of living compared to a sole owner, less likely to pollute their own towns, and less likely to cut staff during hard times (among other things). However, it's not all sunshine and rainbows. The next step is to solve the issues we've noted with worker cooperatives. Namely, as shares dilute with each new member, they tend to not expand well and they still face the same conditions forced on a business with sole ownership. That being they still operate in a capitalist market based on profit-driven competition. We must now work to evolve the cooperative model to deal with these threats, and in doing so, continue to build a socialist reconstruction of the economy.

But before we can begin to play with the building blocks, the individual enterprises, we must first address the issue of private property. This is the first major differentiation we will make from the capitalist system and as discussed before, it sounds a lot scarier than it works in practice. What the abolition of private property means is the removal of private ownership of the means of production. This includes but is not limited to stores, factories, farms, rental housing, energy plants, etc. It is also here we make our first distinction from the worker-cooperative model. The abolition of private property does not mean the transition of ownership from the owner to the enterprise workers. We are transferring enterprise control to the workers, not ownership. The difference may seem minute, but it's an important distinction to make. Our goal is to eventually transition from a profit-driven economy to a social-driven economy. To do so, the economy must be run for the benefit of society. Currently, the economy is run for the accumulation of profit for a sole owner or shareholders. By transferring ownership to the workers, the economy is then run for the accumulation of profit for the many owners. As mentioned in the section *'Critique of Cooperatives & Syndicalism,'* this transfer of power from sole owner to many owners does a lot of good in that it dilutes the accumulation of capital into more hands instead of the few, but it doesn't change the inherent issue of capital accumulation itself. By establishing worker control, not ownership, of the economy, the groundwork for a future based on social production is set, although the full transition to social production does not occur in the first phase, merely the framework for it.

A key factor in taking the fear away from the policy of private property abolition is to clearly make the distinction between personal and private property in a way that is understandable to the common person. To do that we will break the terms down further. Private property consists of the land and tools owned by an individual or group of individuals that are used for the production of goods and services to sell for profit. As previously mentioned, this includes things like factories, farms, machinery, rental housing, etc. As the private owner, the individual or group controls the means to produce goods and services that society needs. The factories and machines are sitting there ready to produce whatever society needs, but they cannot be used without the permission of the private owner, the capitalist. They give their permission through the form of wage contracts to workers, as we discussed earlier. This unnecessary middleman hoarding over the means of production is what we seek to abolish. We are not seeking to abolish personal property. Personal property is an object directly in use by a person. A family who lives in a house is directly using the property as shelter that is, therefore, their personal property. The car a person uses as transportation is in their direct use; a backyard garden is directly used and consumed by the gardener; a person directly uses their toothbrush, watch, phone, cooking pots, etc. Therefore, these by nature of their direct use is their personal property. If a person converts their personal property, an item in their direct use, into a means of creating a good or service to sell for profit (for example hiring farmers to work a garden or land-lording), they have converted their personal property into private property. A landlord is a person who rents out a house to those seeking shelter. By renting out a home, the landlord has converted their personal property into private property, which under this new system would not be allowed. By forming a monetary contract, they have sold the direct use of the home to someone else, meaning they have transferred their personal property to someone else. With the abolition of private property, the field of land-lording collapses as its market immediately vanishes.

Phase one is marked by the transition of all enterprises, whether they be stores, farms, factories, gyms, car dealerships, office buildings, etc — from private ownership to social ownership. All enterprises. This idea may sound utopian. Some may argue it's too soon in the process to abolish private property or that 'society' owning everything means state control, or in a different direction, total anarchy. We are going to make the case that the abolition of private property[4] can be done from the outset without handing the economy to party officials and without devolving into unorganized and decentralized communes. How is this possible? The plan is simple, a federated system of cooperative councils.

The first step is simple. Transitioning from private ownership to social ownership can be done as soon as the working class comes to power, whether that be through revolution, reform, or some other means. As capitalism develops, it expands and industrializes the land it rules over, that is its most beneficial attribute. It is through this development that the transition is made possible. In a developed nation, there is no need for a vanguard party to directly oversee the economy through periods of rapid industrialization because the buildings are already built. The factories, machinery, and offices - the means of production, are already built. Not only are they built, but they are also already staffed with workers. With this understanding, the transition becomes remarkably easier to foresee. All that must happen is the removal or the abolition of private ownership rights over the enterprises. The ownership class including shareholder boards are simply removed. The workers do not join the ownership class or form the new board of shareholders. Instead, simply by their role as workers, they become the direct users of the enterprise or means of production, giving them the right to collectively direct those means of production. The owner is not thrown in a prison cell or put "on the wall." The owner's role, if accepted by the majority of the workers, transitions from owner to worker. Not above, but equal to all other workers in the enterprise. Again, it's important to note that transitioning to public ownership doesn't mean that all workers are removed from their jobs and reallocated to new areas. The enterprises are

[4] The alteration of private property as discussed in the first phase is the abolition of private property of the individual. The abolition of private property of the class cannot be done until socialism has been realized, which we do not get to until phase two.

already running, collaboration between co-workers already exists, and the production of goods and services doesn't end because of the elimination of private ownership, all that changes is the social relationship between owner and worker and between the enterprise and society. Social ownership doesn't mean a person can walk off the street into a factory and start messing with the machinery. The person will still have to go through a hiring process, and that process is to be decided on and run by the workers themselves. By nature of being direct users, the workers self-manage the enterprise similar to the worker cooperative model. Party oversight is not needed at this level. To quickly summarize, the transition from private ownership to public ownership is marked by the abolition of the ownership class and the transfer of enterprise direction to the collective decision-making of the workers.

Local Enterprises:

In this section, we will be setting the foundational piece upon which the entire society's economy will be built. As stated before, the individual enterprises are the basic building blocks of the economy. They, by their nature, are the furthest decentralized productive unit at our disposal. Every city, state, and nation is built up of them. The buildings are already built and the workers are already there, so it is at the individual enterprise at the local level of a town or city that we begin our societal reconstruction. We will begin with a brief overview of our theory of the organization of the enterprise, which will include structure, democratization, wage laws, and meritocracy. We will then look at the implementation of this model in specific industries, and lastly, we will address the issues of scaling a cooperative economy by introducing part of our version of workers' councils; local Industrial Syndicates.

With the abolition of private property, the ownership of the enterprise is given to society as a whole, and control of directing the enterprise is turned over to the enterprise workers themselves. There are no shares of the business to be transferred to the workers, as the enterprise is no longer something to be purchased and owned. Therefore, the first decision the workers must make is to decide on the future of the former owner. If the owner was good or fair to their workers there is a good chance they will be allowed to join the workforce. Also, owners as people have their own strengths, weaknesses, and skill sets. For example, an owner may have good managerial skills and then be elected to a managerial position if needed, or an owner may be a poor manager, but personally charismatic, so they may join the workforce as a salesperson. If the owner was particularly unliked and unskilled, the workers may not offer them a position in the enterprise at all. In that case, the owner joins the ranks of the unemployed and must seek a job elsewhere. With the owner accepted into or rejected from the workforce, the transition to full worker control is complete. The workers are now free to collectively decide on what goods or services they produce, how they're produced, (quality of resources, tools, production process,) setting workdays, hours, paid time off, sick days, and forming and electing internal managerial positions if needed. With these decisions made, the workers can begin production again, but this time through self-management, in the way they see fit. If the enterprise is running slowly and needs more workers, they are free to run their own hiring process, but once a worker joins the enterprise, they become a direct user of the means of production and therefore have an equal say in decision making. If the enterprise has too many workers, the workers will have to confront that issue as a collective to work around it, fire a worker, or attempt a worker transfer, as we will dive into in the Syndicate section.

The enterprise, while in control of the workers, is still beholden to the laws of the nation. This is where the institution of a national wage law will infringe upon enterprise democracy for the betterment of society and meritocracy. This national wage law will apply to all enterprises regardless of field. The wage law requires all workers to receive pay based on productivity compared to the average socially necessary labor time required per hour in the specific enterprise. We will use an example for ease of understanding. Assume an enterprise produces shoes. The average worker in the enterprise produces five pairs of shoes an hour. If a worker produces ten pairs of shoes, they have doubled the enterprise average and therefore will receive a proportionally larger cut from the enterprise profit. Hence if a worker underperforms and produces two pairs of shoes an hour, they will receive a proportionally smaller cut of the enterprise profit. If all workers produce the average of five shoes an hour, then all workers will receive the same share of the profits. There will of course be accommodations for disabled workers as their productivity is further limited by said disabilities. The purpose of the wage law is to ensure a fair allocation of payment to the workers while incentivizing production through a truly meritocratic system. This stops one worker from developing a mind control device and convincing their co-workers to give them the largest share of the profit and deals with the complaint of workers making the same salary while performing unequal work. This meritocratic structure of pay is necessary until society has completely abolished commodity production and the money form because society has not yet evolved from profit-driven to socialized economics. After production, the commodities (goods and services) are sold on the market. The surplus profit is then taxed by the assemblies, paid in a small fee to the syndicate, proportionately compensated to the workers based on productivity, and finally distributed by the workers' collective decision-making. They may decide to give themselves bonuses, reinvest in the enterprise with new equipment or better resources, bring on more workers, donate to or fund local projects, etc.

In this phase, we have abolished the relationship of owning the means of production, but the enterprise still runs under the capitalist model of producing commodities to be sold on the market for profit. This is a necessity in a gradual transition out of capitalism, and recognizing it is just the starting phase and not the end goal, marks the program as fundamentally different from those whose models end at the abolition of private property. By taking our time and further socializing, democratizing, and decommodifying the economy step by step, the nature of humans living under capitalist rule slowly evolves alongside it. It is directly through the act of the workers themselves taking control and collectively directing production across all facets of society that the argument of human nature being one of greed and opportunism withers away in place of the evolution of solidarity, comradery, and compassion. Through every evolutionary struggle, human nature has evolved alongside the changing economic modes of production and religions rise from the 'heretical' peasantry until they are co-opted by the ruling class to be used as a constraint or tool of control against their antagonist class, whether they be tribe vs tribe, lord vs serf, or capitalist vs laborer. At this level, most proponents of worker-cooperatives or 'market socialism' agree on these principles, but those models stop here. They entrust that these regulations on the market will stop the steady corruption of society from capital. They argue that the market is no longer a capitalistic entity or that commodity production under socialist oversight is socialist commodity production. These ideas are farcical. A market is run on commodity production. Commodities are goods and services produced to directly be sold for profit. Therefore, a market selling commodities for profit is a capitalist model no matter the rhetorical knife used to slice it. Two quotes from Anton Pannekoek ring true here, first, *"Instead of clearly seeing the situation and resisting, blindfolded by the dear traditional slogans, they go into new slavery."*[5] You can call your economic model a great liberator of humanity, it may raise half the world out of abject poverty, and it may rapidly industrialize a nation's means of production, but as long as your program ends with the production of commodities to be sold for profit through the market, capital will accumulate alongside political power, democratic institutions are corrupted, and in the end, *"What has been gained by hard fight in times of prosperity is often lost in times of depression."*[6] In the first phase, our model seeks to take a step forward past previous models of economic democracy by further attacking the issues of competition, monopolization, and capital accumulation. You may ask if the market is operating under capitalistic principles how can the steady expansion of one enterprise over a market share be stopped? The answer? Institute a monopoly of the industry from the outset.

---

[5] Pannekoek 2003

[6] Pannekoek 2003

Industry Syndicates:

Under a capitalist mode of production, the issue of one enterprise consolidating a monopoly over a particular industry is a constant threat. This issue is somewhat tamed through economic democracy because the power of a sole owner or group of shareholders is distributed into the hands of more people, but these democratic enterprises are still in a perpetual state of economic war with competing democratic enterprises. They are still beholden to the principles of capitalism, expand or be subjugated, cut costs, or be cut off. With enough time, one enterprise could absorb the others or run them out of their industry.

The logical constraint on this is that the more members the enterprise absorbs the more the profit share and voting power divides among all members. The problem with this sole enterprise monopoly is that, even while democratic, the enterprise will now be representing the entirety or vast majority of a local industry. That increase in market share means more work to be distributed to the workers, and increased workloads lead to people being too bogged down with their actual labor to have the time to think about doing their other roles of management. This will inevitably lead to particularly ambitious members convincing stressed and overworked members to trust their word and vote alongside them. These members acting more like politicians than comrades will form a new form of bureaucracy that will infect the system from the bottom and spread through all levels of the economy. The solution is a modification of the Mondragon experiment. There, cooperative enterprises across multiple industries are lumped under a representative body called a federation, a federation of democratic enterprises in principle. In our view, this is a positive step, but one that can easily be transformed into a fully functioning federalized council system.

Here is the difference, firstly, our model does not clump enterprises together across industries, the workers perform different jobs and therefore their representative bodies should individually represent them. Secondly, our model acts under the idea of federalism, meaning that on the regional level, the enterprises of City A will not be directly represented by the enterprises of City B, even if they are a part of the same industry. For example, manufacturing enterprises in City A will be represented by a Manufacturing Syndicate in City A, and manufacturing enterprises in City B will be represented by a Manufacturing Syndicate in City B. In our use, the definition of a syndicate is a group of organizations or enterprises combined to promote their common interest. The syndicates operate on the local level of every economic sphere, meaning cities. To function, a city requires the operation of a large range of industries like, but not limited to, agriculture, energy, manufacturing, logistics, construction, engineering, technology, healthcare, housing, communications, water management, retail, hospitality, etc. The list of industries is extensive and varies from city to city as well as the size of each industry in varying cities. For example, some cities have lots of farmland, hence their biggest industry is agriculture there are manufacturing cities, energy-productive cities, etc. The point is that local economies are very variable. After the enterprises of these industries have been democratized, they will be organized under the Syndicate of their specific industry. Manufacturing enterprises under a manufacturing syndicate, construction enterprises under a construction syndicate, agricultural enterprises under an agricultural syndicate, etc.

These syndicates organize the enterprises under them, but it does not rule over them. They are not institutions that direct production, for now, they are simply representative bodies or councils. The differences between a syndicalist union structure of the economy and the syndicate council system will become evidently clear as the model scales. The local syndicates are not bodies that petition the local government to institute workers' rights. The syndicate acts almost like a governmental body of its own, except it's not a government of a local population of people, but a government of the workers of a specific industry. The role of the local syndicate is to promote cohesion, comradery, and prosperity between the enterprises of its industry. They promote healthier competition and inter-industry cooperation, as well as handle industry reinvestment, research and development, worker transfers between enterprises, the expansion of new enterprises, the closing of existing enterprises, and set the rules of regulations for operating within the industry. The syndicate is solely made up of workers from the local industry. By nature of operating within the industry, every enterprise will elect one member to the syndicate, to account for proportional representation rules may be instated to represent industry population. For example, Construction Enterprise A has 50 workers, Construction Enterprise B has 30 workers, and Construction Enterprise C has 10 workers. Each enterprise will elect members to their local Construction Syndicate. To start each member will elect one representative. Following a rule of one additional representative per ten workers would lead to the following syndicate organization: Construction Enterprise A sends 6 representatives, Construction Enterprise B sends 4 representatives, and Construction Enterprise C sends 2 representatives. In total, the Construction Syndicate will consist of 12 representatives who represent the interests of an industry of 90 workers. It's important to remember these twelve representatives do not now dictate where, how, and what is produced. They don't decide on individual enterprise management, policies, or practices. Nor do they control the act of selling products or services and the surplus value accumulated from doing so. Their job strictly serves two roles, the first being oversight of the industry and the second being industry reinvestment from funds allocated to them by their local Economic Chamber, which we will get into later.

Enterprises are relegated to their local industry syndicate. This means that enterprises cannot join out-of-area syndicates, for example, a construction enterprise in City A cannot join the construction syndicate in City B. Conversely, a syndicate has no oversight or reinvestment ability in any industry but their own. This means any policies or practices applied in the enterprises of City A do not apply to those under the syndicates in City B, as well as the Construction Syndicate of City A cannot reinvest in the construction enterprises of City B. The funds provided to a local industry must be used for the local industry. Once the syndicate receives its allocated funds from its Economic Chamber, the representatives will meet and collectively decide on how to reinvest those funds into their industry.

The representatives may decide to distribute those funds to the enterprises equally, by proportion, or by some other means, for direct reinvestment by the enterprises themselves, this being items like upgraded tools, equipment, and technology. The representatives may also decide to allocate funds to research and development within their field like better machinery for factories, better pesticides for farms, etc. What they cannot do is distribute the funds to themselves or the workers as bonuses, the funds allocated to the syndicate must be reinvested in the industry. Any unused funds are returned to the Economic Chamber for reallocation to another Syndicate for reinvestment.

Syndicate representatives are nominated and elected by their enterprise. The only qualification they require for candidacy is to be an active member of the enterprise, former members, and outsiders cannot be elected to the Syndicate. How the election is held is up to the enterprises to decide, the only rule is one worker one vote. Once the representatives are elected, we reach two scenarios on how the Syndicate process works. The first and preferable option is that the representatives remain as workers in their enterprise, working alongside their members, hearing their concerns, and bringing them to the Syndicate meetings which would be held at scheduled times, most likely quarterly. This method stops the representatives from becoming isolated from those they represent, they aren't free from hearing their concerns, and in fact, by continuing to do labor the representatives themselves will understand their concerns firsthand. The second method would be that once elected, the representatives leave the enterprise and work full-time as Syndicate members, most likely in an office of their own. This method allows the syndicate to operate constantly and quickly respond and adapt to concerns, but it threatens to grow into a bureaucracy of isolated and ambitious politicians. If maintainable, the first method is preferred.

Once elected, the representatives will begin handling their duties. They will still operate as a member of their enterprise and they will bring the concerns of their enterprise to the Syndicate meeting. Issues between enterprises will be confronted and hopefully settled at these meetings. For example, large enterprises may transfer workers to smaller enterprises in a mutually beneficial exchange, the large enterprise members increase their share of the profits and individual voting power, and the smaller enterprise members receive needed assistance and possibly an increase in Syndicate voting power. There are no terms or limits for being a Syndicate representative. If the enterprise is happy with their representation, the representative may perform their duties indefinitely. However, the representative position is revocable by a majority vote of the enterprise at any time. If a representative is recalled, they remain a full member of the enterprise but vacate the role of representative once a new election is held. A recalled member cannot be immediately re-elected to the Syndicate, but they may vote for their replacement. Voting for representatives is a mandatory act one agrees to when joining an enterprise, it is not an optional choice. As the model scales it may be necessary to put a ceiling on the number of representatives allowed in a Syndicate for the sake of efficiency, in that case, once a limit is established a system would have to be installed to keep proportional representation fair for all enterprises while still accounting for individual enterprise size. In that same breath, to ensure no enterprises go unfunded a precedent may be set that each enterprise must receive a minimum allocation of funds for reinvestment based on size and proportional productivity. It is still entirely possible that one enterprise manages to expand and consolidate a monopoly over the Syndicate, but the manufactured monopoly stops it from expanding any further. By the rules of the system, even if one enterprise controls the entirety of a local industry and therefore the Syndicate, they cannot expand into City B's industry, nor can they invest in City B's industry to profit from stocks because they don't exist. The largest portion of the economy they can control is a singular local industry. That singular local industry still operates under the principles of democratic organization, one worker one vote, as well as the fact that the accumulation of capital is significantly stifled by distribution to all members, the fee to maintain the Syndicate representatives, the capital assets tax, and the corporation tax on their profit. These Syndicates allow for all industries of a city to be democratically run and organized in a way that promotes further cooperation and solidarity, as well as sets the pathway for a system of decentralized centralization. With a Syndicate over every local industry, the next council is ready to be formed, the centralizing force of the local economy, the Economic Chamber.

Local Economic Chamber (LEC):

With the democratized individual enterprises organized under their respective Industry Syndicates and the issue of monopolization limited to that of one local sector, we must establish the body from which the Syndicates receive their funds for reinvestment. Other models, like Professor Wolff's and Schweickart's, as well as models put in practice, like worker self-management under Tito's Yugoslavia, relied on funds allocated by banks, particularly central banks. They of course apply their own constraints on these banks to keep them working in the public's interest, but it is in our belief that the centralization of power to allocate funding for economic development and innovation into the hands of bankers instead of the workers themselves is a catastrophic misstep. The basis of our belief is decentralized centralization, which may sound like an oxymoron, but allow us to explain. We seek to democratize the power of both the political and economic spheres of society into as many hands as possible. To do this, we distribute that power to the workers as a class, the proletariat. However, while we distribute this power to the workers, we recognize that an economy run entirely by worker-cooperatives is one, inefficient, and two, still beholden to all the principles of capitalist production and distribution. So, while we decentralize the power to the workers themselves, we then create a federal system of economic councils to collectivize these enterprises and their industries together to work closer together, promote cohesion and healthier competition, work in the public interest of all workers, and to further lay the foundation for a socialist mode of production and distribution. Hence decentralized centralization.

The first council system we implement is on the local or city level, this is called the Local Economic Chamber (LEC). A city's LEC is comprised of representatives from every Industry Syndicate in said city. For example,

City A's LEC may be comprised of but not limited to representatives from City A's Manufacturing, Agricultural, Energy, Construction, Engineering, Technology, Retail, Logistics, and Media Syndicates. There are various ways representatives of the LEC may be elected. To qualify, LEC representatives must be former or active members of an enterprise and must have served as Syndicate representatives at least once. Retired workers or workers who have sustained disabilities leaving them unable to work, who have also served as a Syndicate representative may be elected to the chamber. Qualified applicants are added to the ballot that the Industry Syndicates provide to their enterprises. The problem comes when we consider that different Syndicates may have different policies for electing their own representatives. For instance, in our earlier example of City A's Construction Syndicate, enterprises were allowed additional representatives per 10 workers. It's possible and likely that enterprises of the same industry in different cities, states, and nationally, will have vastly different amounts of workers in their industry. For example, if City A has 90 construction workers, City B may have 1000 construction workers. Outside of the same industry, different rules for electing Syndicate representatives could give one Syndicate more representatives than another, for instance, City A's 3 enterprise Construction Syndicate has 90 workers and 12 representatives because they provide 1 additional representative per 10 workers, but City A's 3 enterprise Media Syndicate has 45 workers and 12 representatives because their policies state they can elect 1 additional representative per 5 workers. This issue could be hammered out if a universal standard for electing Syndicate representatives was set, but again, due to varying population sizes between cities and states, this could be hard to do.

The seemingly best approach would then be to simply consider the number of workers per industry because this number cannot be fiddled with by Syndicate rules. Let's scale the numbers up. City A has 3 Syndicates that represent 60,000 workers. Syndicate A represents 30,000 workers, Syndicate B represents 20,000 workers, and Syndicate C represents 10,000 workers. We could then apply a similar formula from the Syndicate election process but apply it to the city as a whole. As City A's workforce is

60,000 workers, we can set the representative selection process to 1 LEC representative per Syndicate and 1 additional LEC representative per 10,000 workers in an industry. So, City A's LEC would have 4 representatives from Syndicate A, 3 from Syndicate B, and 2 from Syndicate C, for a total of 9 representatives on the LEC. This formula could then of course slide according to city population. For example, a city with 1,000 workers would allow an additional LEC representative per 100 workers in an industry, and a city with 1,000,000 workers would allow an additional LEC representative per 100,000 workers. This formula allows all industries to have representation on their LEC while allowing industries with more workers to have proportionally more voting power. Going off active workforce population also allows for easier scaling to State and National Economic Chambers, because the issue of varying Syndicate representatives is taken off the table. Depending on one's view there is one more issue to consider. That is the societal importance of specific industries. While media and entertainment are important industries, a society could function without them, however, without energy and agriculture the economy shuts down and people starve to death. It can be argued that while we have democratized the economy into the hands of the workers, the workers of higher priority fields should have a heavier-weighted voice in economic decisions. This would particularly be of use in Economic Chambers where there are more Media representatives than Agriculture representatives for instance. If one wants to account for priority industries, they can apply the following formula.

Representation = (Number of Workers) x (Societal Importance Coefficient). Just as an example we have taken our earlier industries and applied a societal importance coefficient to them.

- Agriculture: 1.0
- Energy: 1.0
- Manufacturing: 0.9
- Construction: 0.8

- Engineering: 0.7
- Technology: 0.6
- Retail: 0.5
- Hospitality: 0.4
- Media: 0.3
- Entertainment: 0.2

Of course, societal importance is subjective and up for debate. The coefficients would have to be decided on by the National Economic Chamber and National Assembly if society wishes for the process to be completely democratic. No societal priority coefficient needs to be applied, it is simply something to consider.

Once the representatives from each industry are chosen the LEC is formed. The term chamber is used in place of council because it is a chamber of the assembly, the political sphere. While the chamber and the assembly are connected to ensure societal cohesion, their powers for the most part are kept separate, they provide oversight and advice to one another more than anything. The representatives of the LEC leave their individual enterprises and enter the chamber full-time. As representatives of their industry on the local level, they will be in consistent contact with the Syndicate representatives, receiving reports on their industry's status, productivity, efficiency, etc. Major issues threatening specific industries can then be brought before the chamber as a collective to come up with solutions. Alongside the representatives, the respective assembly, in this case, the Local Assembly, will allocate technicians to the chamber to perform advisory roles. A technician, in this sense, is an expert in the economic and business fields, and people with technical knowledge or academics. These technicians hold no voting power in the chamber, their role is to provide their technical knowledge so that the representatives may make well-informed decisions.

Besides collectively overseeing and representing the local economy, the LEC takes the place of the central banks in reinvesting in the local economy. Instead of enterprises seeking loans from boards of bankers, they will receive funding from their Syndicates. But how do the Syndicates get the funds to reinvest in their respective enterprises? The LEC! Following a system that we will go further into detail on later, the corporate tax on the profit of all enterprises goes to the National Assembly.[7] Once the National Assembly allocates the money required to maintain society's Social Service Agencies, the entirety of the remaining funding is sent to the National Economic Chamber (NEC). The NEC made up of representatives from the State Economic Chambers (SEC) will divide the total budget and distribute it fully to the SECs. The SECs made up of representatives from the LECs will then divide and distribute the funds to the Local Economic Chambers. It's trickle-down economics in its fullest form. A true monetary water cycle. The LEC with the funding allocated to it by its State Economic Chamber will then collectively decide how to allocate their funds to best suit the local economy. This is where the social priority of industries may come back into the fold. The representatives will meet, debate, and discuss said allocation of funds, or in the future, resources. Once they agree on a budget, the funds will be distributed to the Industry Syndicates they represent. If the representatives make bad decisions or fail their industries, they can be recalled by the workers they represent at any time. The representative role is structured in a way that is made to be rotated over time. As good representatives continue to rise through the chambers, new representatives take their place, and bad ones are weeded out by their own electorate. If society was just one city, our model could stop here. The enterprises would pay taxes to the assembly to maintain social services, then the economic chamber would distribute the surplus back to the syndicates for industry reinvestment. However, society is much larger than just a singular city. Under a federal system, there are several layers to society, and so the model continues.

---

[7] We didn't really detail this later. The Corporate Tax is simply a tax on the profit of an enterprise, and the Capital Assets Tax would serve as a fee or a lease for using the means of production and or the enterprise. Today, that fee would be paid to the landlord of the property from which the owner is leasing. Under Phase One, that fee/lease would be paid to the State/Local Assemblies as the land is not 'owned' by any one person, but controlled by the local collective for the benefit of said local collective.

State Economic Chambers (SECs):

The next level above the local economy is the state economy. The economy of a state is made up of the numerous local economies that operate within its borders. For every city that organizes its industries into an Economic Chamber, its state must do the same. Besides their differing levels on the federalized system, the key difference between the State and Local Economic Chambers is that the SECs divide and distribute their funds into its LECs, whereas the LECs distribute their funds into the Industry Syndicates. It is another step in the chain of ensuring the wealth created by the labor of society is put back into and reinvested in society itself. The role of the State Economic Chamber is to oversee the state economy, hear and discuss issues of the representative local economies, communicate in advisement with the State Assembly, and allocate funding to all their respective Local Economic Chambers. All Economic Chambers functionally work the same way and perform the same tasks, the difference is only their level on the federalized system, and the body they distribute or allocate funding. Representatives to the state chamber are elected from the local chambers based on worker representation per local economy. LECs that represent more workers get proportionally more representation in the SEC. For example, following a formula of 1 representative per LEC and 1 additional representative per 100,000 workers, City A with a workforce of 1,000,000 would have 11 SEC representatives, City B with a workforce of 500,000 would have 6 SEC representatives, and City C with a workforce of 100,000 would have 2 SEC representatives, for a total SEC of 19 members representing State A's workforce of 1,600,000. To qualify for the SEC, a candidate must have served at least once on an LEC, including retirees and disabled workers. Qualified applicants are added to the Industry Syndicates ballot provided to their enterprises. Like the representatives of the LEC, the representatives of the SEC will be in consistent contact with the local economies to ensure the issues of all cities of the state are both heard and addressed. They will also work in tandem with technicians provided by the State Assembly to make the most informed decisions possible.

National Economic Chamber (NEC):

The last level of the economic portion of the federalized system is the National Economic Chamber. The NEC is the national representative body of the economy for the working-class proletariat. Making our way up the chain, the National Economic Chamber is made up of representatives from every State Economic Chamber within the nation. Like the other Economic Chambers, the NEC provides oversight to the chambers below it, listens to their concerns, and responds accordingly. The difference is that at the highest stage of the federalized system, the reception and allocation of resources are slightly different. Instead of their budget being handed to them by a chamber above them, the National Economic Chamber receives its allocated budget from the National Assembly itself - the highest political body in the federalized system. These funds as described earlier are derived from the corporation tax levied against the profit of all enterprises. The revenue of the corporation tax goes 100% to the National Assembly. With that revenue, the National Assembly will allocate the necessary funds to upkeep and maintain the National Social Services Association (N.S.S.A) which we will describe later; all remaining funding is to be directly transferred to the National Economic Chamber. Once the NEC receives these funds, the representatives will then discuss and debate its allocation. When the allocation is agreed upon, the funds will be distributed to the respective SECs for allocation to their LECs and so on. NEC representatives are elected following the same formula as the others, 1 representative per SEC and an additional representative per a set number of workforce population. For example, following a formula set at 1 additional representative per 500,000 workers we see the following. State A has a workforce of 1,600,000 and therefore elects 4 NEC representatives, State B has a workforce of 3,000,000 so it elects 7 NEC representatives, State C has a workforce of 5,000,000 so it elects 11 representatives, for a NEC of 22 members representing 9,600,000 workers. The numbers in these examples are of course only for demonstration, if society wishes to have more representatives, they may lower the number of workers represented to earn additional representatives and vice versa. The key is to find the sweet spot where there is as much representation, and therefore democratization as possible without heavily sacrificing efficiency. Efficiency will likely begin to stagnate or degrade at around 500 representatives per chamber. Qualified applicants are added to the Industry Syndicates ballot provided to their enterprises.

Economic Summary:

This federalization of the economy creates a direct chain from the individual enterprises to their industry, to the local economy, to the state economy, and finally to the national economy. This chain centralizes the workforce, it collectivizes the workers by industry, city, and state, bringing them together to provide for society at large. While still operating under a capitalist, profit-driven mode of production, society will begin to develop a deeper nature of comradery, solidarity, and cohesion. The workers themselves, through performing both labor and managerial roles, will no longer be treated like cogs in a machine. Their minds will be exercised just like their bodies, creating a stronger, smarter, and more skilled workforce and population. The dilution of capital accumulation by the removal of private property ownership and the democratization of the enterprise leads to an overall leveling of the balance of economic power and in turn, political power. We have ended private monopolization and massively limited the scale of possible cross-state monopolization, ensured a transparent vertical movement of funds directed by the workers themselves, structured a system where the vast majority of taxes benefit both the population and economy at large, and strategically decentralized the power of the economy into the hands of the working class. While this is a great reformation of the capitalist system and would mark a serious improvement from today's world, the battle is not finished. We cannot stop here because we haven't yet addressed all of capitalism's contradictions, and if these contradictions are left unsolved then, like a cancer, the great reforms will become infected and die leaving in its wake a system far worse than the one it evolved out of.

We can either march on and continue the transition to socialism by solving capitalism's contradictions, or we can stop and pat ourselves on the back, and within a century, our great reforms will have done nothing but lay the groundwork for a new era of fascism.

POLITICS:

Political Introduction:

While the fundamental building block for the economy is the individual enterprises, the fundamental building block for the political sphere is the individual proletarian. In theory, our proposed system of political governance doesn't differ that drastically from the federal system we see in the U.S. today. There will be Local and State Assemblies, and a National Assembly that represents the entirety of society. Our differences come in the role and purpose of the political system, the powers given to it, and its control over society. In our critique of Capitalism, as it pertains to the U.S., we argued that the economy controlled the government and therefore the state. Our issue with that power structure is not that the economy controls the government, it is that a small class of bourgeois capitalists directs the economy that controls the government. We seek to establish an economy that controls the government that is run and directed by the working class themselves. The phrase *"Of the people, By the people, For the people,"* coined by Abraham Lincoln, is the basis for the structure of both our economic and political systems. Still, unlike the false promises of freedom, justice, and equality that have echoed across capitalist societies, we will create an economic and political structure that not only promotes, but ensures these promises. That structure can be viewed by the statement: of the workers, by the workers, for the people. We do not seek an oligarch-led economy controlling the state nor do we seek a state or government controlling the economy. This does not mean a complete rejection of the theory of the Vanguard Party, it simply means that the working class cannot be dragged across the coals to a socialist revolution; they must lead and transform themselves as a class, or their societal transition will fail. The proletariat and the structures they build both politically and economically will evolve over time including throughout these phases. The questions we must answer first and foremost are the role of the party, the starting structure of the political apparatus, the question of democracy versus authoritarianism, and the relation between the political and economic spheres of society in the first phase.

The Role of the Party:

There is heated debate over the role of the party. Some argue, like Lenin and Bordiga, that a communist party must be the 'Vanguard' of the proletarian masses, leading them to revolution and victory over the bourgeois capitalist class. Anarchists and the more libertarian communists like Pannekoek argue that the party is akin to a false prophet, an organization that preaches to the masses a path to liberation but merely uses them as a tool in establishing the party as the new ruling class. Let us take a closer look at their viewpoints.

Lenin:

Lenin's definition of the party can be seen in a news report on his *Speech on the Agrarian Question, "A party is the vanguard of a class, and its duty is to lead the masses and not merely to reflect the average political level of the masses."*[8] The party is the vanguard of the class, whose duty is to lead, not just represent, the wishes of the class it represents - in this case, the proletariat. His definition makes two things clear, to Lenin, the party is the head of the proletariat, its director, and its leader; and because its role is to lead, not merely represent the class's perceived interests, democracy is not a heavily weighed factor. Lenin explains the dichotomy of democracy further in his text *State and Revolution,*

"And the dictatorship of the proletariat, i.e., the organization of the

---

[8] Lenin 1927

vanguard of the oppressed as the ruling class for the purpose of suppressing the oppressors, cannot result merely in an expansion of democracy. Simultaneously with an immense expansion of democracy, which for the first time becomes democracy for the poor, democracy for the people, and not democracy for the money-bags, the dictatorship of the proletariat imposes a series of restrictions on the freedom of the oppressors, the exploiters, the capitalists. We must suppress them in order to free humanity from wage slavery, their resistance must be crushed by force; it is clear that there is no freedom and no democracy where there is suppression and where there is violence... and so in capitalist society we have a democracy that is curtailed, wretched, false, a democracy only for the rich, for the minority. The dictatorship of the proletariat, the period of transition to communism, will for the first time create democracy for the people, for the majority, along with the necessary suppression of the exploiters, of the minority. Communism alone is capable of providing really complete democracy, and the more complete it is, the sooner it will become unnecessary and wither away of its own accord."[9]

Lenin's point on capitalist society is apt as are the vast majority of his theoretical contributions. It is a fact that bourgeois democracy is nothing more than the dictatorship of the capitalist class over the proletariat, and that true democracy can only be found through the proletarian revolution and eventual abolition of classes, but that is not what we take issue with. Our issue is with his opening sentence, *"the dictatorship of the proletariat, i.e., the organization of the vanguard of the oppressed as the ruling class...,"* to Lenin, the dictatorship of the proletariat is reached through the vanguard party becoming the new ruling class, we find this completely antithetical to proletarian liberation. History shows us the vital importance of the vanguard party to a successful revolution (though it is very questionable whether said revolution is proletarian), but in turn, it also shows us that once the bourgeoisie is overthrown, the vanguard party tends to take direct control over the political and economic direction of the country. The power

[9] Lenin 1917, Ch. 5

lies in the hands of the party, not the workers. The party holds the keys to the workers' freedom and in turn, establishes itself as their new ruling class. Let's take a look at Anton Pannekoek's analysis of the Russian Revolution in *Workers' Councils*,

"...all the capable elements among the workers and intellectuals, supplemented as such by the former officials and officers as were willing to co-operate, had to combine into the Bolshevist Party as the leading body. It formed the new government. The soviets [councils] gradually were eliminated as organs of the government apparatus. The name of Soviet-Republic, however, was preserved as a camouflage, and the ruling party retained the name of Communist Party. The system of production developed in Russia is state socialism. It is organized production with the state as universal employer, master of the entire production apparatus. The workers are master of the means of production no more than under Western capitalism. They receive their wages and are exploited by the state as the only mammoth capitalist. So, the name state capitalism can be applied with precisely the same meaning. The entirety of the ruling and leading bureaucracy of officials is the actual owner of the factories, the possessing class. Not separately, everyone for a part, but together, collectively they are the possessors of the whole... They had to change Russia from a primitive barbarous country of peasants into a modern, civilized country of great industry. And before long, in often cruelly waged class war between the peasants and the rulers, State-controlled big agrarian enterprises replaced the backwards small farms." *He concludes,* "The revolution, therefore, has not, as deceptive propaganda pretends, made Russia a land where the workers are master and communism reigns. Yet it meant progress of enormous significance."[10]

We believe Pannekoek's conclusion to be the most important takeaway when viewing the Russian Revolution. Russia was far from a developed nation, its proletarian class while numerous due to the country's population, was not nearly as solidified as the rest of Europe. The Russian proletariat

---

[10] Pannekoek 1947, Pt. 2 Ch. 5

still lived with a large population of peasants and serfs, not under the rule of a bourgeois democracy, but under the last remaining absolute monarchy in Europe. The collaboration of the Russian proletariat and peasantry can be seen in the revolutionary symbol of the hammer and sickle itself, the hammer of the laborer, and the sickle of the peasant. These conditions alone show us that while Russia was ready for revolution, it was not at the level of development demanded for that of a proletarian revolution, and that brings us to the crux of our issue with Lenin. When analyzing socialist revolution, Karl Marx predicted that said revolutions would come out of the developed industrial nations. History showed us first through Lenin, and then others, that the nations most ripe for revolution were those that were most backward and maldeveloped. While it is a historical fact that the 'socialist' revolutions occurred in underdeveloped nations, it is also a historical fact that none of these revolutions succeeded in reaching socialism. Should we then consider these revolutions failures because they alone could not usher in the next era of humanity? No, that would be silly. The conditions the country faced both at home and from foreign interference demanded the country rapidly transform from a backward agrarian society into a developed industrial nation. It just so happens the system best known for its rapid industrial development is capitalism, and so it was. Should we whine because the country adapted to its conditions, or that it didn't replace an absolute monarchy with a true and perfect direct democracy and worker-controlled society? Again, no, we must study why the revolution started, the type of revolution it was, the threats it faced once successful, and how it adapted to those threats. When Pannekoek says *"The revolution... has not... made Russia a land where the workers are master and communism reigns. Yet it meant progress of enormous significance."* We must understand that this revolution, just like that of China was necessary for the development of their nations. Through these revolutions, the proletarian working class will grow and expand as the serfs and peasantry are absorbed into it. The development of the proletariat and the development of capitalism in these countries will, as the historical struggle between classes demands, further bring the capitalist and proletarian classes into stronger contradiction. The raising of the living standard of the people, the development of industry and the means of production, the toppling of the monarchy by capitalism, and the rise of the proletariat are all immensely significant events of these revolutions. That is not a failure, it's a fact.

With that being said, Lenin's belief that Marx's analysis of revolutionary potential was wrong is incorrect. The maldeveloped nations are not ripe for socialist revolution, they grow on another tree entirely; these nations are ripe for national liberation movements or in other words, national bourgeois revolutions. These include Cuba, North Korea, China, Vietnam, and every other struggle of the Cold War era. The defense of Siege Socialism is ridiculous for the simple fact that it subordinates the proletariat to the party that controls the political and economic power of society. This party, which historically is led by members of the intelligentsia instead of proletarians, uses unnecessary authoritarian means to cement itself as the leader of the proletariat - and in the name of protecting the revolution from the bourgeois and counterrevolutionaries, turns its back on the masses which enabled it to seize state power in the first place. The fact of the matter is socialist revolutions can only come out of the developed nations because they are the only nations properly developed enough to abolish private property, wage labor, and generalized commodity production. These revolutions can only come when the era of uneven development levels out and the gap between developed and undeveloped nations is significantly diminished. And when that time comes, the proletarians of the developed nations will not require siege socialism, because the structures for reaching socialism will have already been developed under the rule of the bourgeois! There will be no need for the vanguard party to be the leader of the proletariat, much less be cemented as the ruling class as Lenin envisioned. The dictatorship of the proletariat is the proletariat seizing control of the political and economic levers of power, switching the societal relationship from the rule of the minority over the majority to the rule of the majority over the minority. To make the vanguard party the new ruling class is to make no change to that relation at all other than which group the minority encompasses.

Bordiga:

Amadeo Bordiga defines the party in his work *Party and Class, "A party is a school of political thought and consequently an organization of struggle. The first characteristic is a fact of consciousness, the second is a fact of will, or more precisely of a striving towards a final end."*[11] Although there is much more to Bordiga's conception of the party, we find this basic definition acceptable and workable in our own blueprint. The role of the party, particularly in the phase of the revolution, is to defend the revolution's ideological line from bourgeois influence and internal revisionism, while also helping to organize the proletariat into revolutionary organs. We believe these organs of revolution to be the workers' councils as first prescribed by Pannekoek, but unlike Pannekoek, we believe that a party is a requirement to build and unite these councils into a body with revolutionary potential, so long as the councils do not subordinate themselves to said party. Bordiga writes further,

"... only an advanced minority can have the clear vision of a collective action which is directed towards general ends that concern the whole class and which has at its core the project of changing the whole social regime. Those groups, those minorities, are nothing other than the party... Although the party includes only a part of the class, only it can give the class its unity of action and movement, for it amalgamates those elements, beyond the limits of categories and localities, which are sensitive to the class and represent it. This casts a light on the meaning of this basic fact: the party is only a part of the class. He who considers a static and abstract image of society, and sees the class as a zone with a small nucleus, the party, within it, might easily be led to the following conclusion: since the whole section of the class remaining outside the party is almost always the majority, it might have a greater weight and a greater right. However if it is only remembered that the individuals in that great remaining mass have neither class consciousness nor class will yet and live for their own selfish ends, or for their trade, their

[11] Bordiga 1921

village, their nation, then it will be realised that in order to secure the action of the class as a whole in the historical movement, it is necessary to have an organ which inspires, unites and heads it – in short which officers it; it will then be realised that the party actually is the nucleus without which there would be no reason to consider the whole remaining mass as a mobilisation of forces. The class presupposes the party, because to exist and to act in history it must possess a critical doctrine of history and an aim to attain in it."[12]

We shall break this down piece by piece. First, it is agreeable that the party cannot be led by the entirety of the proletariat, because that would be completely ineffective for one main reason besides size alone; that being the developed consciousness of the class. Prior to the revolution and even after, there will remain large chunks of reactionaries within the proletariat, which can only be excised through their further development and participation in a proletarian-led society. If these reactionary (or even revisionist) elements are allowed to influence the party, the party will lose its revolutionary edge and devolve into nothing more than a social democratic, liberal bourgeois party! Therefore, an "advanced minority," or in other words "class conscious proletarians" would be required to form, organize, and lead the party. Second, as stated previously, we agree that the party is a requirement for the masses to be organized into revolutionary organs, which are in our opinion the workers' councils. Third, with the understanding that the party requires an "advanced minority" to encompass it, it is acceptable to argue that the party is then the "nucleus" or brain of the proletariat, although we will slightly push back on this in our conclusion. Finally, Bordiga argues the party should then officer the class. We feel as though there is a difference between Lenin's theory of the vanguard directing the party and Bordiga's theory of officering the party, though if there is not, our critique of Lenin's theory would still apply to Bordiga. As Pannekoek will argue next, the party as a matter of historical record tends to supplant the old ruling class with itself instead of the proletariat. Defenders of the vanguard party will argue

[12] Bordiga 1921

the party is not distinct from the class, however, we would counter with this: if an organization controls both spheres of power, political and economic, then that organization is in power. Our theory of the role of the party can be best summed up with Bordiga's closing remarks,

"Revolution requires an organisation of active and positive forces united by a doctrine and a final aim. Important strata and innumerable individuals will remain outside this organisation even though they materially belong to the class in whose interest the revolution will triumph... But in order to assume this great task, the class must have its own thought, its own critical method, its own will bent on the precise ends defined by research and criticism, and its own organisation of struggle channelling and utilising with the utmost efficiency its collective efforts and sacrifices. All this constitutes the Party."[13]

To us, the party is the instrument of preserving and delivering revolutionary theory to radicalize the masses into a revolutionary proletariat. It should be involved both theoretically and physically with the movement and be made up of a majority extent of proletarians. It sees past the petty immediate aims of the unions and political movements, its eyes solely focused on the end goal of abolishing capitalism and reaching the era of socialism. It must not rule the proletariat, but work alongside it, pumping it with the knowledge and expertise required for the proletariat itself to unite, organize, and fight for its own liberation!

Pannekoek:

Anton Pannekoek, known most for his theoretical contributions to councilism through his theses on workers' councils, is unsurprisingly a strong opponent of parties in general. In his essay *The Party and Class,* he described a party as *"an organization that aims to lead and control the working class."*[14] A mainstay in his writings is the idea that the proletariat can only rise to

[13] Bordiga 1921

[14] Pannekoek 1941

the task of achieving its own liberation by seizing power for the class and taking its fate into its own hands. He writes further,

"...the present workers' parties have an entirely different character, for they have a different objective: they want to seize power for themselves. They aim not at being an aid to the working class in its struggle for emancipation but to rule it themselves and proclaim this constitutes the emancipation of the proletariat." *And* "We claim that there is an internal contradiction in the term: 'revolutionary party.' Such a party cannot be revolutionary... The 'revolutionary party' is based on the idea that the working class needs a new group of leaders who vanquish the bourgeoisie for the workers and construct a new government... Against this, we raise the question: what force can such a party raise for revolution? How is it able to defeat the capitalist class? Only if the masses stand behind it. Only if the masses rise and through mass attacks, mass struggle, and mass strikes, overthrow the old regime. Without the action of the masses, there can be no revolution... the party is an obstacle to the revolution because it wants to be more than a means of propaganda and enlightenment; because it feels itself called upon to lead and rule as a party." *He goes further to state that those who advocate for revolutionary parties* "... think they are the revolutionary vanguard because they see the masses indifferent and inactive. But the masses are inactive only because they cannot yet comprehend the course of the struggle and the unity of class interests, although they instinctively sense the great power of the enemy and the immenseness of their task. Once conditions force them into action they will attack the task of self-organization and the conquest of the economic power of capital."[15]

Much of this critique can be seen within his earlier quoted analysis of the Russian Revolution, but here he gives a deeper critique of the party. For the most part, we agree with Pannekoek's analysis, the vanguard party has proven historically to be after the seizure of power for the party, not the class, however, we do not go as far as Pannekoek to advocate for the absence of the party entirely. To Pannekoek, the proletariat can only win

[15] Pannekoek 1941

their revolution by organizing themselves as a unified class built out of workers' councils. We take issue with two of the quoted statements. First, *"the party is an obstacle to the revolution because it wants to be more than a means of propaganda and enlightenment; because it feels itself called upon to lead and rule as a party."* Our issue here is not with his general sentiment, but rather that this critique should not be universal. A party built to lead and rule like that theorized by Lenin, will, of course, pursue the seizure of economic power, however, a party built to preserve theory and enlighten the masses to organize said workers' councils, is of service to the revolution and the defense of said revolution once successful. Secondly, *"But the masses are inactive only because they cannot yet comprehend the course of the struggle and the unity of class interests..."* This is why the proletariat requires a party! The proletariat at large is unconscious and divided by the control of bourgeois society, it is true class consciousness can be gained through worsening conditions forced upon the proletariat via the contradictions of capitalism, but as conditions worsen, reactionary elements of the proletariat will continue to grow. An organized group of communist theoreticians and activists, a party, must stand as a counterbalance to this rise of radical reactionism amongst the proletariat. Through the struggle of the party and the developing consciousness of the proletariat, the workers' councils can grow to have revolutionary potential. Once the councils have seized control of economic power, the party must continue to battle reactionary elements within the proletariat and take up the mantle of political power to preserve the revolutionary theory and policy that led to the revolution in the first place.

Conclusion:

All three of these theoreticians have different conceptions of the role of the party. Lenin and Bordiga's main difference was not mentioned here but will be discussed later; that being Lenin's democratic centralism versus Bordiga's organic centralism. However, both Lenin and Bordiga advocated for a party whereas Pannekoek vehemently disagreed with the party, instead advocating for the workers' councils to lead themselves. We believe all of their ideas to hold extremely useful components for structuring the role of the party while also having their faults which we have critiqued. The role of the party, therefore, demands a synthesis of their ideas. From Lenin, we derive the necessity of a vanguard party, from Bordiga, the party's purpose of preserving, defending, and distributing revolutionary theory to the proletariat like the brain to the body; and from Pannekoek, the demand that the proletariat not subordinate itself to the party, by retaining economic control of society through the organization of workers' councils.

While the party may be the brain of the proletariat, a brain stuck in a jar, separated from its limbs and the rest of the nervous system is useless; it is dead. The party in isolation, without its proletarians and workers' councils is therefore useless, and with its uselessness comes the slow death of a revolutionary future! Like the brain and the body, the party and the workers' councils must work in tandem as one unit sending and receiving signals and performing the tasks demanded for the liberation of the proletariat. If one dominates the other, the nervous system of liberation is damaged. The operation slows and the brain and body begin to fight each other. When the brain and body, or the party and councils, enter conflict with one another, they betray their ends, they betray the goal of proletarian liberation for that of their own petty interests. This internal conflict will inevitably leave the winner be it brain or body, party or councils, isolated and functionally dead! It may, therefore, be better to look at the party and councils as one brain. The left and right brain. The left brain, the councils, controlling the economic power of society, and the right brain, the party, controlling the political power of society and preserving the revolutionary nature of the class at large. They both uphold each other and together finally lead the proletariat to its liberation!

On Democracy:

In our analysis of democracy, we do not debate whether or not our current society should become more authoritarian, for we deny the very existence of a democratic society today! Just as the bourgeois revolutionaries of the past age revolted against the authoritarian rule of the divine monarch, the socialist revolutionary revolts against the authoritarian rule of bourgeois 'democracy.'

I

Democracy means many things to many people, but broken down, 'Demo' derives from the Greek word 'demos' meaning people, and 'Cracy' the Greek word for rule. Combined, the term democracy means the rule of the people. Simple at a glance, but under the lens, not so much. In its earliest theorized form, democracy was supposed to be direct. Every person in society was to meet and voice their opinion in governance, the issue with this in practice is scalability. While in the context of a family, clan, community, or small population, this approach of direct democracy may work. However, on the scale of the large populations of the modern age, the idea becomes impractical. Some defend modern direct democracy with the belief that technology can connect these large populations together and disseminate political debate and decision-making abilities to them instantaneously. There may be truth to this practice and it will probably have its uses as society and technology advance, but the idea of life-altering societal decisions being decided by the equivalent of a push notification is absurd! Many people would ignore the vote entirely and others would make blind or uneducated decisions. It is precisely because of this lack of education, or for a better word lack of class consciousness, that direct democracy for the time being is an outdated practice for the large-scale dealings of society.

During the era of Feudalism, the right to rule was bestowed upon individuals and consequently families or bloodlines from a divine source. This source, whether it be God, gods, spirits, etc., is anti-materialist and entirely metaphysical. The divine rule of the minority, the individual or family, over the majority, the entire society, was absolute. In response to this oppression, alongside the developing Age of Enlightenment and the emerging middle class, this divine right to rule was challenged. Therefore, it is clear that bourgeois democracy developed in direct antagonism to divine monarchy. The rule of the minority was challenged by the majority, and after a long conflict, the majority won ushering in the ideas of the Enlightenment and the bourgeois. The right to rule was stripped from the hands of the royals and bestowed to all, but the question arises, who bestowed this right to man? We are told all humans are born not only equal but also with a set of unalienable human rights like the right to vote, but again, from where do these rights come from? You may answer the constitution or from governments, and to that we say fair enough. It is the governments of the world and their constitutions that grant these civil liberties to their citizens. They cannot grant them to the citizens of other nations as, they don't have the jurisdiction or authority to do so, and furthermore, they can only guarantee these rights to their citizens so long as said government retains its authority to rule. This is a step from the metaphysical to the material lens. Human rights and the ability to participate in bourgeois democracy is granted by the bourgeois state, therefore these human rights, including the right to vote are completely revocable; they are protected by nothing more than the actions of the bourgeois state. If however, you believe these rights to be truly inalienable by right of birth or from God, you have left the realm of materialism. This outlook has no functional difference than that of the feudal monarch. Both scenarios subscribe to the belief that a divine or spiritual force has bestowed these rights upon humanity. The only difference is what class these spirits serve. As Amadeo Bordiga put it in The Democratic Principle, the bourgeois have made reason their new divinity![16]

The question of democracy is therefore not where it comes from, but for what class does the 'people' encompass! The bourgeois democracy of the present means the rule of the people OF the bourgeois. The ruling class has so thanklessly given the common man the right to choose, to vote, for whichever member of the bourgeois class he wishes to rule over him. It is an

[16] Bordiga 1922, Pt. 2

endless cycle of self-preservation for capitalism and the bourgeois class. The workers, divided over the cultural issues propagated by bourgeois media and academics (two of the strongest stabilizers of bourgeois democracy), become too distracted by their work, life, and cultural divides to focus on the economic systems propagated by the people they vote for. Herein lies the problem, time! A person must allocate about eight hours of their day to sleep, eight hours of their day to work, and say one hour of their day to eating. That is seventeen hours dedicated to achieving sustenance so that they can wake up and do it all over again. That leaves seven hours free to them. Try to convince a person with only seven free hours to study economics, I dare you! The vast majority of people do not have the time nor the will to subtract from their leisure, from their escape, to do the necessary amount of studying to break free from the indoctrinatory grasp capitalist society and education has on them. It is because of this lack of time that politics to the average worker is just a higher-stakes version of team sports. Yet, they fail to realize that although their favorite players may be bitter rivals, the owners of the teams do not care who wins so long as the league continues to make money. And if a player enters the league who threatens that bottom line, well, they will not be playing there long! Bourgeois democracy is therefore propagated by the will of the people because they have bought into this system. All the wrongs of society are the fault of the other team, and when their team does not go on the offensive they blame it on the other team's defense or even worse accuse the referees of interference. They become so ingrained in the game of politics they cannot see that the teams or the parties are owned by the same people, the same class, the bourgeois!

The socialist, on the other hand, wishes to revolt against bourgeois democracy in favor of establishing proletarian democracy. The rule of the people OF the bourgeois must be replaced by the rule of the people OF the proletariat; the working class. This is the same sentiment behind the replacement of the dictatorship of the bourgeois by the dictatorship of the proletariat, yet the word dictatorship strikes fear in people unreasonably. This fear of course stems from the fact that people believe their current society to be democratic, that is because they have only ever heard of the dictatorship of a person, not the dictatorship of a class. So, to the question of democracy for whom? The socialist stands and answers unequivocally, "for the proletariat!" The socialist does not proclaim democracy for all because that would be a farce. After all, the nature of class society is that the classes cannot be equal! The socialist with the goal of a classless society in mind, advocates for the first step in that development. They continue the class struggle that has been raging for all of human history. They advocate for the shift from the minority to the majority, for control of the state from the bourgeois to the proletariat and only the proletariat, and for the domination of the bourgeois by the proletariat. In other words, they advocate for proletarian democracy or interchangeably, the dictatorship of the proletariat!

II

With the understanding that socialists seek proletarian democracy - the rule of the people OF the proletariat - we can tighten the lens and further examine what this entails by analyzing what it means to rule.

As we established, the authority to rule is not given by a divine being, but by the controller of power. In the case of ruling, might makes right to a certain extent. The controller of power does not have to be open. Like in the case of bourgeois democracy, politicians are projected to the commons as the ruling class while being beholden to the capital of capitalists to hold onto their seats of 'power.' The question then arises, what is power? In the case of ruling society, the answer is simple. There are two major spheres of power by which all other spheres are influenced (although they still influence one another). These spheres are political power and economic power. Political power encompasses governments from the local to national level, the ability to dictate policy both domestic and foreign, and the ability to influence and organize the masses. Economic power is simply control of the economy, this can range from control of capital and the means of production to a vast amount of liquid assets. Every new era of humanity brings along new classes that relate to these spheres of power differently. For example, under feudalism, the monarch, mercantile middle class, and peasantry all competed for these spheres of influence (the church could also be lumped in with these classes). Capitalism has simplified class antagonism to a one-front war, the bourgeois versus the proletariat. Under the capitalist system, the bourgeois has a monopoly on both political and economic power, this is the relation the socialist seeks to flip on its head!

It is therefore rational to presume that under socialism the proletariat will hold a monopoly on both political and economic power, which it will use to oppress the bourgeois on its way to building a classless society. Once it succeeds in this aim, the world will have entered the new era of communism which we cannot possibly make predictions about in our current state. Until that stage is reached, the next question which must be answered is how control of political and economic power should be distributed to the proletariat. This is what the debate about the role of the party and workers' councils post-revolution is about; we proposed a synthesis of the two. What concerns us now is the distribution of this power to the individual proletarians. This debate falls on a sliding scale of authoritarianism versus libertarianism. As a general rule - the fewer hands controlling power, the more authoritarian society is. The more hands controlling power, the more libertarian society is. The goal is to find the sweet spot on the scale that allows society to be as libertarian as possible while retaining the authority that allowed the proletariat to lead a successful revolution in the first place. The first rule to set is straightforward, only the proletariat shall control political and economic power. In our proposal, the economic sphere would be in the hands of the vast majority of the proletarians through a federalized system of workers' councils, which would work in coordination with the political sphere controlled by the party of the proletariat. By the act of working in the economy through the workers' councils, each proletarian will hold as equal an amount of economic power as ever before in modern human history. But then, the question remains of how political power is distributed. The rule of proletarian control necessitates that only members of the proletariat (working class) be given the right to vote. This rule breaks through all barriers of race, sex, identity, and most notably, nationality. If an immigrant works in a socialist nation they are a member of said nation's proletariat, making them eligible to vote regardless of citizenship status. Unemployed people seeking work and those disabled to the point of being unable to work would still be considered members of the proletariat and be eligible to vote.

While only members of the proletariat would be eligible to receive the right to vote, that does not necessarily mean that all members of the proletariat should be granted said right. You might ask, "Who gets to decide who gets to vote and who doesn't?" The party of course! This will no doubt come off as authoritarian to some, and they would be correct, but that does not make it any less of a necessity, specifically in the early stages following a successful revolution. The rule of the proletariat, like all ruling classes before, it must retain elements of authoritarianism. However, through selective use and the colossal distribution of economic power, this authority is checked, not solely by 'branches of government' like today, but by the entirety of the proletariat. Unfortunately, to ensure the proletariat does not immediately devolve into revisionism, opportunism, nonsensical division, or be poisoned by bourgeois thinkers, the right to vote on the election of political positions must be gatekept to a certain extent. This is not a new phenomenon. It is a mark of the old society that must be adapted as the new world order is in its infancy. The right to vote (again, this right is referencing strictly the political sphere, the councils operate separately), and therefore the right to join the party, should be open to all members of the proletariat, but they need not be accepted solely for being a proletarian. In our current world, the right to vote is granted to all citizens of a bourgeois democracy, however, this right can be deprived from the people for several reasons. Most notably, in the U.S. children do not 'earn' the right to vote until they reach adulthood at eighteen. The reasoning for this deprivation is logical, the children are young and uneducated, and their brains are not yet fully developed. Rationally then, their reason for depriving them of the right to vote is so that in their youthful ignorance they do not alter the character of the bourgeois nation. To indoctrinate the youth to support the bourgeois nations' national character, the youth are taught in a system designed to instill national values and belief in one political and economic system. Better yet, these children are raised by parents who went through the same process before them, with each successive generation further solidifying the indoctrination of the last (although the internet and social media are throwing a wrench in this cycle, but don't worry, the bourgeois will be sure to tame this new frontier). This same logic applies to proletarian democracy and the right to vote. Above all else, the ideology that organized society into a strong enough force to seize the means of production and therefore the societal spheres of power, must not be allowed to be compromised by a sudden flood of millions of members at varying stages of class consciousness, theoretical understanding, and many still being reactionaries! The party as an instrument of theory, guidance, organization, and a dealer or developer of class consciousness; as some describe it 'the brain of the proletariat' cannot become infected or the 'brain' will lose its consciousness. In other words, it will die.

Just as the proletariat will deprive the bourgeois and the freeloaders of their right to vote, so must the unconscious and underdeveloped elements of the proletariat be temporarily deprived of theirs. Again, this deprivation is based solely on the individual proletarian's developed level of class consciousness. A large portion of the proletariat will develop class consciousness to an acceptable extent through the process of revolution, this development will be furthered by working and participating in the workers' councils. In tandem, this should provide the vast majority of the proletariat with enough knowledge to participate in the political sphere. For those that are still underdeveloped and those that come after the revolution, outside of the workers' councils, education can be developed through schooling, classes, personal study, organizing with local groups, and most importantly working alongside party members of which there should be numerous opportunities open to the general public. The threshold to attaining voting rights is variable. It could be to where one requires an invitation from a party member, or perhaps a recommendation from a party member to take an entry test. The entry test would operate like a citizenship test for immigrants today. For the immigrant, their test requires they take classes, study, and understand the nation and its character to achieve citizenship and the rights that come with it. For the proletarian, their test would require they take classes, study, participate, and understand the class and its character to join the party and receive all the rights (like voting) that come with it. This is all of course completely speculative. However, this process will allow the party to be both large and efficient, and as libertarian as possible without compromising its character.

We can therefore conclude that bourgeois democracy is nothing more than the dictatorship of the bourgeois, which must through the revolution of the proletariat be replaced by proletarian democracy - the much-feared dictatorship of the proletariat! This proletarian democracy should be participated in by the proletariat alone, and this participation should be locked behind a testable set standard level of class consciousness and/or education to ensure the proletarian character remains the ruling class of society. Over time the amount of participants involved will increase following the dying off of the old ideologies of the bourgeois just as the ideologies of feudalism died off under the development of capitalism.

III

We would like to add a brief note on voting as used in the above section. The deprivation and gatekeeping of the right to vote pertains to the election of party positions and inter-party policy. It is our belief that the party should have no executive head like a president, general secretary, or prime minister, other than the proletariat. And to put the 'proletariat' in the highest executive body of society, the proletariat themselves must decide on what becomes law and what does not. Therefore, on issues like the passing of new laws, instating a draft, declaring war, etc., the proletariat must ratify the decision of the party via a voting process naturally scaling by federal level.

Structure of the Political Apparatus:

Following the idea that the individual proletarian is the base unit of the political sphere, we will work in reverse showing the blueprint for the political apparatus from the top down. First, we will discuss the organization of the party, as it will be involved at every level of the political sphere. Second, as we detailed the economic chambers in the economy section of this work, we will detail the federalized political assemblies at the local, state, and national levels. Third and finally, we will discuss the role of the individual proletarian and how they interact with the political apparatus of society.

Organization of the Party:

Make no mistake, while we critiqued Lenin and Bordiga's conceptions of the party, we still acknowledge the necessity of a communist party for guiding the proletariat to their ultimate liberation. As this is a war between classes, the proletariat as a class can only have one true party, so one should not shake their head at the term 'single-party state.' Regarding the organization of the party, there are a few questions that must be answered. First, who shall encompass it? Second, what is to be done about inter-party factionalism? Third, how the party should be structured? And fourth and finally, how does the party serve its previously stated role? We will be answering these questions from the point of a successful revolution, the revolutionary tactics of the party can be found elsewhere.

On the question of who shall encompass the party, we appeal back to Bordiga's statement of an advanced minority of the proletariat. As stated, the main role of the party is to preserve, defend, and distribute revolutionary theory to the proletariat. To do this, the party must then be made up of revolutionary communists. This demands a certain level of rigidness and purity testing regarding recruitment. It should not be overly rigid to the point that the party is nothing more than an echo chamber or hive mind, but not so flexible that the party devolves into a reformist or petty bourgeois party. The basic tenets one should uphold to join the party is the militant belief in the revolutionary overthrow of the bourgeois for the establishment of the dictatorship of the proletariat to abolish private property, wage labor/generalized commodity production, and value-form economics. This should be an easy bar to clear for a communist and yet it would probably eliminate the vast majority of 'communists' when their beliefs are put to the test. For example, reforms can be used as a tactic alongside revolutionary means, but a movement solely based on reformism, that completely abandons revolutionary tactics, is a movement striving for peace, not liberation. Peace is comfortable. The reformist on the path to peace argues with the warden to give the prisoners memory foam pillows, more time on the rec yard, and rib-eye steaks on Tuesdays. The revolutionary organizes the prisoners and leads them out of the prison, to their liberation. If the memory foam pillows or rib-eye steaks help expedite the process, the revolutionary will advocate for them, but they will never lose sight of the true goal - liberation. The party, therefore, must purge itself of reformists. That is not to say those that advocate for reforms, but those that only advocate for reforms, completely neglecting revolutionary activity. Most communists meet the low bar of demanding the abolition of private property[17], but it seems many require a pole to vault over the bar of abolishing generalized commodity production. As established, generalized commodity production is one of the strongest pillars of capitalism, and the states that these 'communists' uncritically support have never cleared this bar and yet they proclaim them to be socialist anyway. These 'communists' have fallen to the same revisionism as the market socialists that they so often ridicule, and so they too must be purged from the party. It's impossible to predict how, when, and who will initially form the party, but by the time it is able to guide the proletariat to a successful revolution, it will surely be large in number and have chapters in all provinces or states of its nation. In our analysis of democracy, we stated all proletarians should be eligible to join the party, but that not all proletarians need to be admitted to the party. The proletariat will still hold large masses of uneducated, unconscious, and reactionary people that would threaten both the revolutionary and socialist character of the new society. Therefore, the right to vote on inter-

[17] Though many still support the private property of the class.

party policy and elections should remain within the party. This right to inter-party voting can be earned upon admittance to the party which as a blueprint could be earned in a variety of ways. One, the party may accept new members solely by invitation from current members. Two, party members may recommend people to take a party entrance exam further detailed in our analysis of democracy. Three, there may be a test open to all proletarians, operating like a modern-day citizenship test that upon passing admits the proletarian to the party, giving them the right to participate in inter-party voting. These are just blueprints, there is an uncountable number of possibilities for party admittance.

From the idea that the party should not be a hivemind past the point of being revolutionary and militantly supporting the abolition of private property, wage labor, and generalized commodity production, it follows that inter-party factions will inevitably form. This is not something that should be fought against but instead recognized as a natural form of internal democracy. This brings us to the debate between democratic centralism and organic centralism. Bordiga writes in *The Lyons Theses*, *"The communist parties must achieve an organic centralism which, whilst including maximum possible consultation with the base, ensures a spontaneous elimination of any grouping which aims to differentiate itself. This cannot be achieved with, as Lenin put it, the formal and mechanical prescriptions of a hierarchy, but through correct revolutionary politics."*[18] This distinction is further summarized in the ICP (International Communist Party) article (*The Communist Party in the Tradition of the Left*), *"democratic centralism implies a less complete centralism, because it is invalidated by the need for periodic consultation of the rank-and-file; organic centralism implies 'absolute centralism' insofar as no longer is anyone consulted and all decisions are referred to the leading centre whose power is absolute and whose decision is final. In short: democratic centralism, minus democratic processes, equals organic centralism."*[19]

While the argument for organic centralism holds merit, we do not see

---

[18] Bordiga 1926, Pt. 2

[19] ICP 1974, Pt. 4 Ch. 4

a strong enough reason to abandon the model of democratic centralism. The ICP argues that to prevent factionalism, the party's leading center must hold absolute authority, this is further supported by their belief in the abandonment of the principle of democracy (of which we agree to a certain extent). We contest this belief on the basis that an authoritarian center, while preventing instead of repressing factionalism, will inevitably create a hive-minded party. In our view, the strictness and rigidness of the party should be found in the admittance process, with the idea that so long as all party members meet the basic requirements of being a revolutionary communist, their ideas and insights will be valuable to the party and therefore the proletariat. Again, inter-party factions should not be feared, prevented, or repressed because the principle of democratic centralism unites the factions after the period of debate. Joseph Stalin's commissioned book, *HISTORY OF THE COMMUNIST PARTY OF THE SOVIET UNION (BOLSHEVIKS)* sets the 'rules' of democratic centralism as follows...

"1) That all directing bodies of the Party, from top to bottom, shall be elected;

2) That Party bodies shall give periodical accounts of their activities to their respective Party organizations;

3) That there shall be strict Party discipline and the subordination of the minority to the majority;

4) That all decisions of higher bodies shall be absolutely binding on lower bodies and on all Party members."[20]

Regarding our model, we believe these rules and therefore democratic centralism, to be the most effective policy regarding the organization of the party. First, through the federal political system that we will detail later, inter-party elections to leadership positions at the local, state, and national levels, and in other offices (to be detailed later) is the best way to ensure the party remains both united and full of diverse radical thought. Second, the party should be in constant communication between members, factions, and federated levels. Third, as admittance to the party is strict, those same

[20] Stalin 1939

standards should be applied to all members of the party, as well as members being held to the highest moral and ethical standards because of the nature of their position. The subordination of the minority to the majority is the main benefit of democratic centralism, and is the reason it's so effective in keeping factionalism from being a bane to the party and society. The party and its internal factions may ferociously debate decisions, but at the end of said debate they shall vote, and the passing resolution will then become the official party policy to be followed by all members. This policy can be later challenged and debated once more, but until the resolution is repealed, all party members must stand behind it as a united front as a law of the party. This prevents the internal factions from splitting into a civil war. Fourth and finally, following the federalized system, some policies pertain to the local and state levels only. These policies may be decided by the members of the local or state assembly so long as they do not break or revise the party line like reinstating capitalist policies. However, on national policies that affect all levels of society, the national decision must be strictly followed by the local and state levels. This last point is no different than how the U.S. operates today.

Party Structure:

We will keep this section brief, as the role of the party at each level of the political apparatus will be further detailed later. The party itself will consist of the vast majority being general members, those elected to party leadership positions, and others elected or assigned to offices. For example, the party may elect or assign members to positions that directly interact with the workers councils' or other local, state, or national projects. The distinguishing feature of our party structure is that there is no executive leadership position at any federated level. There are no mayors, governors, or presidents. Party leadership positions are simply elected officials who hold equal status to one another, like members of Congress or parliament for example. As stated previously, executive leadership is given to the proletariat at large by the act of voting; this right to vote is given to all proletarians, regardless of status within the party.

Role Execution:

The main role of the party is to preserve, defend, and distribute revolutionary theory to the proletariat, as well as help guide them to their liberation. On top of this, the party will serve a few other roles as well. First, besides the preservation of theory, the party adapting to the changing conditions of society around them will be tasked with developing and putting into practice theory of their own. For obvious reasons, we cannot predict what that theory is, but if the party cannot develop the theory of the next era of human development, then society will stagnate politically and a status quo will be formed. Second, the party will be charged with providing the people with their needs. We will delve into this topic further but for now, it can be understood as the party overseeing sectors like healthcare, housing, parts of agriculture, infrastructure, transportation, water and power management, etc. as society develops out of capitalism. The councils of these sectors will be lumped into the N.S.S.A (National Social Service Agencies), which will be directed and overseen by the party. The party, after collecting taxes, will fund the maintenance of these sectors and then deliver the excess to the workers' councils for reallocation. Once we have entered the era of socialism and the party and state wither away, the councils will assume full control of these sectors. Third, when conditions are right for society to completely break from the market for a planned system, the party can experiment with this system within their sectors and if successful, prepare its application for society at large. Once a planning system is fully established, the party can assign skilled engineers/technicians to the workers' councils to operate the planning systems alongside council discussion and oversight. Fourth, the party on the local and state levels must be actively involved with their communities, organizing projects, listening to the concerns of the proletariat, and staying in contact with and listening to the concerns of their respective economic chambers. Fifth, the party will have the task either nationally or on the state level of handling the education policy for the masses; this would likely be done with the input from experts in education. Sixth, the party will handle diplomatic affairs with other nations, but war must be approved by the proletariat through a national vote. The list of roles of the party could drone on forever, but this covers its main tasks. Remember, these roles are following the revolution. Leading up to and during the revolution, the party serves a much different task as it is on the offense of the class war instead of the defense.

Political Structure:

The political structure of our model follows the federal model seen in the present-day U.S. with deviations made to better fit with our economic and political lines of thought. The federal system allows for the political apparatus to operate collectively across all levels of society from the city to the state to the entirety of society! With our conception of the party in control of said political apparatus, society will progress through the scourge of bourgeois democracy into a better future. From the bottom up, the apparatus is structured as follows: Proletarian, Local Assembly, State Assembly, National Assembly. Each assembly will also be responsible for overseeing Social Service Agencies labeled for each federated level: Local Social Service Agencies (LSSA), State Social Service Agencies (SSSA), and National Social Service Agencies (NSSA). All of these levels and agencies will be further detailed below. We will exclude the proletarian as their relation to the party has already been expressed.

Local Assembly: (LA)

The Local Assembly is the building block of the political apparatus. In every city or town large enough to require political governance, a Local Assembly will be found. These LAs are not some new phenomena invented following the revolution, they can be found through the combination of two separate items: the old political apparatus and the party. Regarding the old political apparatus, it is understood socialism will be built out of the foundations of capitalist society, and with that comes the organization of the state. The seizure of the state will also grant us a blueprint with already established organization and links that can be transformed to liberate the proletariat by the party. Any successful revolution would require a large and organized party with chapters in most, if not all provinces or states; and these state chapters are likely to have many local chapters of their own. It is these state chapters that make up the State Assemblies and their local chapters that make up the Local Assemblies. The LA will be controlled by the local party chapter, but not all members of the chapter will serve on the assembly. There are a few ways assembly members could be chosen. For instance, the local chapter could elect members to the assembly, the assembly seats could rotate between members, the members could be chosen by draft, or the party could nominate members to the assembly and allow the local proletariat to confirm them through a vote. The decision is not that important and could either be mandated nationally or left to the local and state chapters to decide. If a member of the assembly is not performing at a satisfactory level, the party may recall them at any time. Or, the local proletariat may petition their removal. The role of the local assembly is to act as a cohesive branch connecting the party to the local proletariat and the Local Economic Chamber. Besides the standard role of the party, the assembly acts as the local governing body and as such has important local responsibilities. First, the assembly (when in session) must always be open to the people to view and there must be designated time to hear community input. Second, with the collected taxes and funds distributed to the LA by its State Assembly, it must fund and maintain its Local Social Service Agencies. This entails overseeing and up-keeping the programs that provide the local population with their needs, like housing, healthcare, power, transportation, etc. Third, it may act legislatively to pass new local policies, but said policies must be ratified by the local proletariat through a vote. Fourth and finally, the assembly will, by their chosen means, provide an envoy and experts/technicians to their LEC. This is so the chamber may have a transparent line of communication to the assembly and so they can make better-informed decisions economically. These are the basic roles of the Local Assembly.

State Assembly: (SA)

The State Assembly will be created from the collective efforts of the state's Local Assemblies. Like the local chapters of the party become the LAs, the state chapter of the party will become the SA. The seats in the assembly will therefore be filled by members of the LAs. Every LA must be represented in the SA, but there may be weighted representation to account for population differences represented by each LA. Like the LA, delegates for the SA could be chosen in a variety of ways. Delegates could be directly chosen by their LA, nominated by the party and confirmed by their local proletariat, or some other method developed. The LAs and their proletariats may recall or petition the removal of SA delegates at any time. The role of the SA is identical to that of the LA, except that it is responsible for the governance of the larger land area and population. It must address the concerns of all the LAs and their populations, as well as be cohesive with their surrounding SAs. With their collected taxes and allocated funds from the National Assembly, the SA will be tasked with distributing funds to its LAs to fund the Local Social Service Agencies. The SA will also provide its SEC with an envoy and experts/technicians to provide direct communication and the knowledge required for better economic decision-making. On top of this, like the U.S. system of federalism, there are items the National Assembly may delegate to the states to decide on, whether this be social policies or setting educational standards. In that scenario, the SA will set the policy for the state, which is then binding to all the encompassing LAs.

National Assembly: (NA)

Following suit, the National Assembly will be created from the collective of State Assemblies. At the end of the revolution, however, there may already be a formed assembly; in that case, going forward, delegations from the lower assemblies would begin to replace and/ or fill in seats on the NA. The NA would consist of delegates chosen or elected from every SA with weighted or proportional representation to ensure the proper representation of each state. The defining feature that truly separates the NA from the present-day federal system is that the legislative and executive branches are combined into one body - the assembly! As stated before, there is to be no 'leader' of the party. No general secretary, president, or prime minister. In this model, the executive head of the state is the proletariat, who will have the final say on the passing of laws and declarations of war. The functions of the NA are as follows...

Legislative Functions:

- Crafting, debating, amending, and passing laws.
- Representing the interests and concerns of the proletariat.
- Addressing societal issues through policy debate and discussion.
- Approving budgets and allocating funds to the NSSA and NEC.
- Overseeing the NSSA and its departments.

Executive Functions:

- Implementing laws and policies.
- Managing government operations and administration.
- Appointing and overseeing government officials.
- Handling foreign relations and diplomacy.
- Managing national security and defense.
- Leading disaster response and emergency management.

The National Assembly serves as both the legislative and executive authority of society. Through this consolidation of the branches, the system avoids concentrating undue power into the hands of a single head executive, thus promoting accountability of party members and collective decision-making. The 'checks and balances' of the present day are replaced by the assembly's and or party's internal mechanisms, and the absence of a head executive in favor of the rule of the proletariat reduces the risk of abuses of power. If wages are still in use, assembly members and party members for that matter should receive an income capped at no more than a 50% rise from the median income of the area they represent, though there may be adjustments for regional income disparities. This income cap should be applied to all assembly levels until wage labor is abolished, as party work is not for personal enrichment, but service to the proletariat.

Note on a Conflict of Interest:

There is a potential conflict of interest that could compromise the idea of the workers' councils and party being checks on each other's power. This conflict could arise if an active party member seeks a seat in a Syndicate or Economic Chamber, or vice versa. To ensure the purity of control on the levers of power, a few measures may be taken. First, Syndicate representatives seeking to join the party must step down from their representative role so long as they remain in the party. Additionally, a cool-down period could be established, requiring people to wait a set period of time after stepping down from an economic role of power to run for a political role of power. This dual approach should further ensure the repression of this conflict of interest, and therefore the sanctity of the model's separation of power.

Social Service Agencies (NSSA, SSSA, LSSA)

It is important to remember that this first phase acknowledges that it does not fully reach socialism. It is, after all, the first phase in the process of societal transformation. However, as society evolves out of capitalism, it moves to rein in the worst horrors of capitalism and further equity, collectivity, and cohesion across society. These are the positive side effects of a socialist revolution, but not the end goal, and we must remain focused on the end goal of the abolition of capitalism. But until the world has developed to the point of a successful international revolution, we can only go so far. For that reason, in this first phase, the party must not only preserve its revolutionary theory and character, but it must also preserve its authority to rule by securing the support of the proletariat. It shall secure this support by being hands-on in executing its role of providing the proletariat with its needs. To do that, Social Service Agencies must be established, these agencies are comparable to present-day executive departments. These agencies, overseen by the party and political assemblies, will be committed to providing the proletariat with access to sustainable healthcare, housing, infrastructure, water, power, etc. The agencies will follow a similar structure to that found in our economic model, building a series of federal councils linked at the local, state, and national levels. These councils will then be nationalized and or subordinated to the direction and oversight of the party and assemblies. We will analyze the role of a few of these agencies in the first phase. Note that there will obviously be more agencies than the ones listed below, these are to just be understood as an example.

Healthcare:

- Universal Coverage: Every citizen's right to access healthcare services regardless of financial barriers.
- No Private Insurance: Healthcare will be rationed by need, not by ability to pay.
- Vast Expansion of Rehabilitation Facilities: People need quality care, hospitality, and assistance in overcoming addiction and mental health crises, not jail time.
- Expansion of Community Health Centers.
- Provide Comprehensive Services.

Hybrid Agricultural System:

It may be wise to combine collective or farming councils/chambers with a series of nationalized farms to ensure food security and sustainability.

- Farming Collectives: Agricultural councils operating under the direct control of the proletariat through the workers' councils.
- Nationalized Farms: Controlled by the party and assemblies for strategic control of resources and planning in the case of shortages or disaster response.

Housing:

- Limited Property Allocation: Prohibiting a citizen from occupying more than two residential properties in their name.
- Rent-to-Own: If necessary, the rent-to-own model is preferable to standard rent during the period before the complete abolition of private property.
- Focus on Vertical Development: Building housing around communal areas and businesses to lower commuting time and build active communities.
- Affordable Housing: Focusing on building many cost-effective yet efficient homes versus a smaller amount of large more expensive houses.
- Housing First Homeless Programs.
- Sustainable Building Practices.

Infrastructure:

- Modernized Ports and Harbors
- Develop High-Speed Railways
- Renovate and Expand Highways
- Develop 'Smart' Transportation Systems
- Better Connect Rural and Urban Centers
- Provide Universal Accessibility to Public Transportation

Water Management:

- Adhere to Water Quality Standards

- Promote Conservation and Sustainability
- Develop Robust Plans to Reserve Water for Emergency Relief
- Nationalization of the Bottled Water Industry

Organization of the NSSA:

Most of these are rather straightforward. Through the control of these fields of necessity, the party can begin the process of decommodification. This process is called 'selective decommodification.' This acknowledges the fact that it is unlikely we would be able to abolish all commodity production in one fell swoop, but ensuring the decommodification of the proletarian's direct needs, a strong step has been taken! Now we shall look at structuring the organization of the NSSA to ensure minimal bureaucracy and maximum efficiency.

First, the NSSA should be divided into functional divisions or departments based on each agency's key responsibilities. Each functional division will focus on its specific policy area ensuring specialized expertise in each division. These divisions were briefly laid out above as healthcare, housing, infrastructure, etc. Second, above these divisions should be an advisory board or board of directors. This board will consist of one expert elected by each division to serve as a spokesperson for their division's concerns and needs. The board will act as the NSSA's main decision-making body. Third, within each division or department, there will be an executive or administrative team that oversees the day-to-day operations and policy implementation. These administrators can be chosen by the workers of the division, or they could be nominated by the workers and then subject to approval by the National Assembly. The administrative team manages the division, its resources, and its personnel included. Fourth, to ensure cohesion between federal levels of the agencies, the role of Regional Affiliate should be created. These Regional Affiliates would be assigned to an SSA and be responsible for tailoring policies to meet regional needs and help with coordination and communication between the state and national agencies. Fifth, there should be regular evaluations of agency performance regarding outcomes and community impact to ensure efficient policies, resource allocation, and coordination are in effect and constantly improving and adapting to changes. This structure should effectively minimize bureaucracy while allowing the agencies to efficiently achieve their goals of providing the proletariat with their needs.

Connection Between the NA and NSSA:

As the NSSA is under the direction and oversight of the NA, the two must remain closely connected, coordinated, and in contact with one another. Therefore, the NSSA must regularly provide the NA with reports on its activities, initiatives, and progress. These reports allow the NA to have a clear view of the status of each NSSA division, which will be important for budget allocation. Speaking of which, the NA as overseer sets the budget of the NSSA. The administrative teams will provide the NSSA board with budget proposals which are then discussed and presented to the NA, where the assembly will review, debate, and decide on the funding for each NSSA division. The process of nominations was discussed earlier, but to reiterate, the workers of the agencies elect one spokesperson to represent their agency on the board of directors and elect members to their administrative teams. It is up to the discretion of the party if they wish to allow the agency's autonomy in this regard or if they wish to incorporate an approval hearing. The NA may influence the NSSA through legislative action by passing laws or regulations that expand the agency's capabilities or address emerging challenges. To summarize, the relationship between the NA and NSSA is one of information exchange, budgetary oversight, and collaboration.

Political Conclusion:

We have now firmly established the blueprint for both the party and the construction of the new political apparatus of society. The party following the revolution will seize the existing political apparatus and transform it into an organ of liberating the proletariat. Democracy (while of extreme importance) as seen by the desire to adopt democratic centralism over organic centralism, must not be a higher priority than liberation, which can only be achieved through the abolition of capitalism. The party, with control of the political apparatus, will work cohesively alongside the workers' councils to provide the proletariat with their needs, along with the knowledge and expertise required of them to achieve their own liberation.

CONCLUSION:

Phase one is marked by the time period immediately following a successful revolution, in which the proletariat must begin to radically transform the society they live in. To do this, the proletariat must seize control of power which we have defined as relating to two spheres: political and economic. Politically, we have defined the role of the party and outlined a general blueprint for its organization and the structure of the political apparatus through the assembly system. Economically, we have laid out the blueprint for the collectivization of the economy into a federalized system of workers' councils to empower the masses of the proletariat to control the economic sphere of society themselves. Here we will now provide a few diagrams to provide a visual aid to these blueprints of ours.

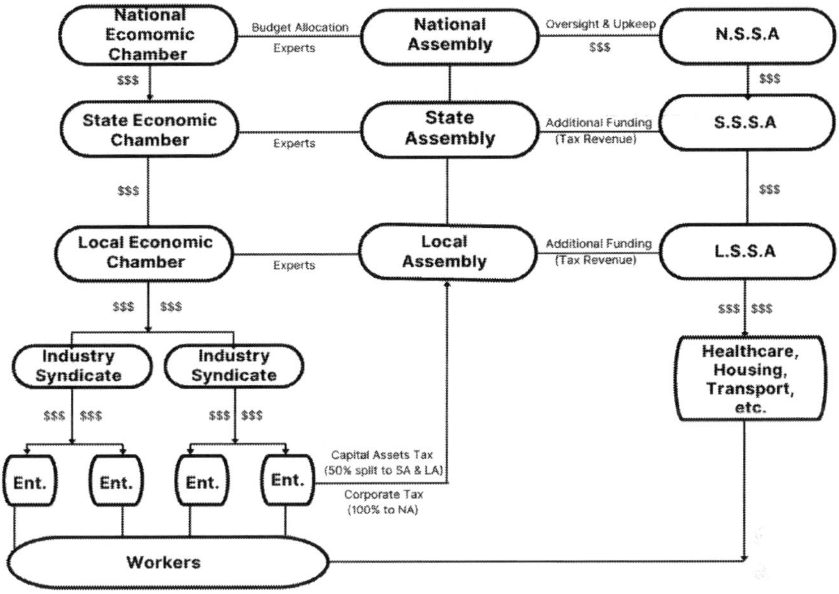

1.1: this model provides a more macro-level visual of the model

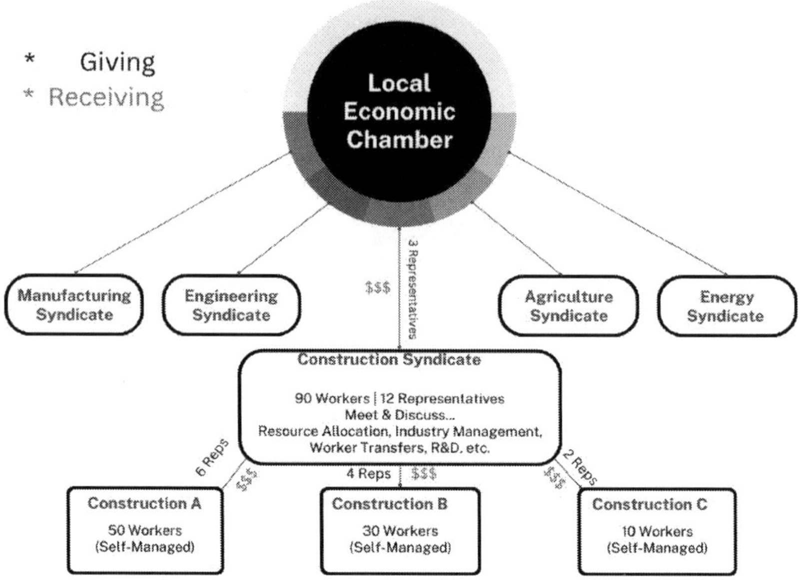

1.2: This diagram zooms in on the relationship between the LECs and the Industry Syndicates and their encompassing enterprises.

Finally, we must remember that though a lot will have been accomplished in the first phase, socialism has not yet been reached as society has not yet completely abolished the contradictions of capitalism. When analyzing how the party-state conceptions of Marx's socialism were caricatures of Marxism, Paresh Chattopadhyay wrote in his book *Socialism and Commodity Production,*

"Through the play of immanent laws of capitalist production, the process of accumulation entails concentration of capital as well as centralisation of capital necessitating 'decapitalisation of smaller capitalists by bigger ones'. This ultimate form of expropriation within capitalism finally reaches the point where capital is negated as the property of individuals/households and is transformed into common capital of what Marx calls 'associated capitalists'... [Marx] observes that 'capital which in itself is based on the social mode of production and presupposes social concentration of the means of production and labour, directly assumes here the form of social capital in opposition to private capital'. 'This is the abolition of capital as private property within the limits of capitalist production itself'."[21]

We contend that this analysis coincides with our model of the first phase of societal transition. Acknowledging the fact stated by Engels over a century ago, that a socialist revolution cannot occur in one country since it requires an international movement of the proletariat, it can be understood that there must be a limit to what one proletarian nation can achieve. That limit we argue, is phase one. The organization of the proletariat over the political and economic spheres of power of society can deliver the abolition of private property within the limits of capitalist production that it cannot yet abolish without international support. Therefore, it can be argued that phase one marks the final stage of capitalism! If that argument rings true and our model sits at the precipice of reaching the next era of human evolution, then only two choices remain, socialism or barbarism!

[21] Chattopadhyay 2018, p. 17

2

Phase Two

Introduction:

While the first phase marked the creation of a blueprint for the construction of a socialist society, it did not solve the contradictions of capitalism and therefore it did not achieve socialism. The best term to describe society at the end of the first phase is Democratized Monopoly Capitalism, or as earlier coined, Cooperative Federocracy. This term reflects the highest point capitalist society can reach before it must successfully transition to socialism. Under Democratized Monopoly Capitalism, we solved the problem of private property by ending the private ownership of the means of production. However, three contradictions of capitalism remain, and until solved, render claiming socialist victory an impossibility. They are as stated before - generalized commodity production, wage labor, and the value form. Once these three are abolished as we will describe in this second phase, society will have at last reached socialism. Before we delve into the abolition of these, there is another problem we must answer. Is socialism in one country possible? The answer, as Engels put it over a century ago, remains unchanged - no! We covered this question more in depth in our essay on revolution, so we shall simply provide a brief summary of our prediction of what steps must be achieved for a socialist revolution to succeed. First, following that a lone socialist country would not be able to sustain itself for very long, other socialist revolutions must succeed alongside it. It is extremely unlikely that every nation on earth will experience a socialist revolution at the same time, therefore the most likely form that an international socialist revolution will take is that of neighboring countries forming 'socialist' blocs to both sustain and protect themselves from the capitalist menace. These blocs, if stable, would expand by bringing their neighbors into the bloc; not by invasion or annexation, but by act of the outsider nations proletarians rising up and voluntarily joining the bloc or union for another word. Following the economic model of phase one, the National Chamber of each nation would form a Regional or Bloc Chamber connecting the economies and proletariat of all neighboring nations into one system. As these blocs form on all continents of the world, they can then form international bonds and unite the international proletariat. This unification would take the form of the Bloc Chambers combining into a singular International Chamber, thus uniting the world proletariat into one system! For phase two to commence, there must be enough nations developed to the point of forming a socialist bloc! With that understood, we can take a look at how to abolish generalized commodity production, wage labor, and the value form. First, we will need a lesson on Socialism 101!

Capital 101:

Before we begin, we must preface that even if this section were one hundred pages long, it would still be a brief introduction to Marxian socialism. The purpose of this section is to provide the reader with a base understanding of the problems diagnosed by Marx over a century ago so that you may understand why we propose the changes we do. Again, you should not take our explanation as an authority, nor any other interpretive authors' for that matter. If you wish to understand the ideas of Karl Marx and Frederick Engels, you must read their works and come to your own conclusions or you will become an ideologue of an ideology you do not understand!

Marx explains in his first volume of *Capital* that the mode of production of modern societies, capitalism, "presents itself as an immense accumulation of commodities, its [base] unit being a single commodity."[22] That is where he begins his investigation and critique of capitalism and political economy. So, according to Marx the base unit of capitalist production is the individual commodity, a commodity being a product produced purely for its exchange value. In other words, a good or service that is produced not for its direct use but to be exchanged or sold for profit. For example, when you go to the store and buy a new couch, a toaster, or even a bag of chips, you are purchasing commodities. However, if you grow a tomato in your backyard to use in a stew you are making for dinner, that tomato is not a commodity because you produced it directly for consumption; you therefore produced a use value. On the other hand, if you took your tomatoes and set up a tomato stand at the end of your driveway and sold each tomato for $1, you have converted the tomatoes into commodities because you produced them to be sold; you therefore produced an exchange value - a commodity. Although through selling your tomatoes you are utilizing their exchange value, their use value does not vanish into thin air. Commodities hold both a use value and an exchange value. The commodities use value is its direct usefulness. The use value of the tomato is consumption, the user of a tomato consumes it. A commodity must have a use value because if a product has no use, it cannot have an exchange value. The commodities exchange value is the ratio in which it can be exchanged for another commodity. In the case of the tomato, the formula would be 1 Tomato = x Commodity A, or as our earlier example showed, 1 Tomato = $1 (although money will be further discussed in the next section). To cover it briefly here, instead of comparing the exchange value of a singular tomato to Commodity A, B, and C, a universal equivalent of exchange or a currency is established that all other commodities are then compared to. Currency is therefore the mediator of commodities. Ideally, the price of a commodity or its exchange value is constantly fluctuating towards equilibrium as it is affected by the laws of supply and demand. At market equilibrium, the price of a commodity stands outside of the forces of supply and demand. This equilibrium price can be raised or decreased

[22] Marx 1867, Ch. 1

in concurrence with increases and decreases in the cost of production. However, a commodity sold at equilibrium is still profitable to the capitalist. This is because profit is only realized via market exchange, it is created in the circulation of production. Here again, Marx's differentiation of value and exchange value becomes important. Value being the socially necessary amount of labor time required to produce a product. Socially necessary labor time (SNLT) was Marx's adaptation of the Labor Theory of Value (LTV) used by Smith and Ricardo. SNLT accounts for normal working conditions, average skill, and labor across the entire productive apparatus. Therefore, if you go to work producing widgets and you decide that you work better with your hands than with machinery and it takes you twice as long as everyone else to produce a single widget, your widget does not magically have double the value of the other widgets because 'more' labor was applied to it; because that labor was not socially necessary. Nor can you grab a comically small spoon and start digging a hole to China in your backyard, then proclaim the hole to be valuable because it took you days to dig because again, that labor was not socially necessary. So as opposed to the use and exchange value of a tomato, its true value or value is the SNLT it takes to produce one tomato. Under a market system, the price of a commodity then fluctuates away from its true value, according to the law of supply and demand. This is something we do not need to concern ourselves with at this point in time.

As technology advances, so do the forces of production. New technology and machinery lead to increased automation, and increased automation speeds up the production process, correspondingly lowering the average SNLT to produce a product. The use value of the product would remain the same, however, more productive labor expresses itself in an increase in commodities produced. The lower the SNLT needed to produce a product, the lower its true value becomes, which correspondingly lowers the product's exchange value or price (at market equilibrium).[23] The faster my tomato processor works, the more tomatoes I produce an hour. This

[23] Marx 1867, Ch. 1

increase in supply, if not matched by an increase in demand, will lower the price at which my tomatoes are worth on the market. The capitalist, Mr. Tomatohed, can now sell his tomatoes at the adjusted market price. Or, with the new influx of tomatoes, he can lower the price below the market rate in an attempt to secure more of the tomato market by underselling his competition! If less SNLT leads to a lower value, then the inverse, more SNLT leads to an increased value, must be true. More SNLT required in production will express itself in fewer commodities, in which accounting for demand, their exchange values or price would increase. The capitalist's goal here would be to drive down the cost of production, which if done through innovation, would lead to a decrease in SNLT required for production - leading to the creation of more commodities which thus brings the exchange value or price back down closer to market equilibrium. The use of this innovation under the capitalist system serves to increase the amount of surplus value possible for the capitalist to extract because, again, they are not paying for labor performed, but for the ability of the worker to labor!

Within the frame of the class war, the capitalists are members of the bourgeois (petty or otherwise) because their relation to capital is that of owner. The capitalists derive their profit from the extraction of surplus value from the workers and production in general. In regards to the worker, this is done through the process of wage labor. Wage labor is the process through which a worker sells their ability to labor (their labor power) to a capitalist for an hourly wage or salary through a work contract (employment). The distinction between labor and labor power may seem entirely insignificant to you, but it is integral to the extraction of surplus value and the capitalist system itself! Labor itself is the concrete amount of labor given by the worker, for example, Mr. Tomatohed's worker produced exactly fifty tomatoes. Labor power is the worker's capacity or ability to perform labor. This capacity to labor is what the worker sells to the capitalist, not the concrete labor itself. Therefore, you can understand labor power as the commodity of the worker that is then rented or purchased by the capitalist from the labor market. The price of labor power is the wage or salary - although the value of labor is still subject to SNLT, this gets into the difference between skilled and unskilled labor. The difference is self-explanatory, it takes more time and training to produce a brain surgeon than it does to produce a cashier, therefore the labor of a brain surgeon is more valuable than the cashiers. Those who take offense to the term unskilled labor (or even worse, proclaim unskilled labor to be a capitalist myth) are either theoretically infantile or anarchist, but those terms are quite redundant.[24] Back to the topic at hand, the worker sells their labor power to the capitalist in return for a wage, and it is through this process that the capitalist extracts surplus value. Because the worker is paid by time instead of productivity, the worker produces more value than they receive in the form of their wage. In life, the socially necessary labor a worker needs to provide is that which is required to provide for their immediate sustenance. In other words, enough to provide for the worker's basic needs.[25] If the worker was paid the full value of their labor, they would meet this basic need rather quickly, but instead their labor power is rented! This means that for the x amount of hours the worker's ability to labor is rented, the value created by the worker belongs to the capitalist. The worker's wage covers the replacement of their basic needs, but the equivalent value of that wage is provided back to the capitalist through the worker's production of commodities. On top of that, because the worker works per hour, they must continue to produce past the point of meeting their basic needs. The value created by the worker in production past the point of their own social necessity (means of sustenance), is the surplus value extracted by the capitalist! In the past, the capitalist would keep the work day as long as possible to capitalize on this process. In the developed nations today

---

[24] We jest! There are many great anarchists and from experience, anarchists are some of the most passionate and proactive practitioners you'll find out on the streets. Their critiques of authority hold some validity, particularly regarding horizontal structures over vertical structures, though their innate fear of hierarchy will make it impossible for them to ever seize the power required to abolish the contradictions of capital. The best cure for an anarchist is to cook them up a fresh batch of Pannekoek literature!

[25] The price of labor power is influenced as well by the supply and demand of the labor market and wage laws like minimum wages.

with better workers' rights, the capitalist capitalizes on this process by increasing the speed of production to produce more commodities in the allotted time or by using cheaper materials to lower the cost of production. Wage labor is the expression of the domination and exploitation of the worker under the capitalist mode of production because it details clear for all to see that the worker is divorced from the means of production and the fruits of their labor! Instead, the control of the means of production and the disposal of its products is in the hands of the capitalist. The workers are dependent on capital and are therefore its subjects. This system of wage labor relies on the practical law that the capitalist knows the worker will produce more value than that for which they are being paid![26] To abolish it then means the reunification of the workers to have control over the means of production and the disposal of its products. However, we cannot seek to hand this control over to the workers as individuals, as that would be a highly regressive procedure. Industrial capitalism has developed production into a highly socialized mode that removes the distinctions between individual workers in favor of treating them as one class of workers - the proletariat!

---

[26] Marx 1849, Wage Labor & Capital

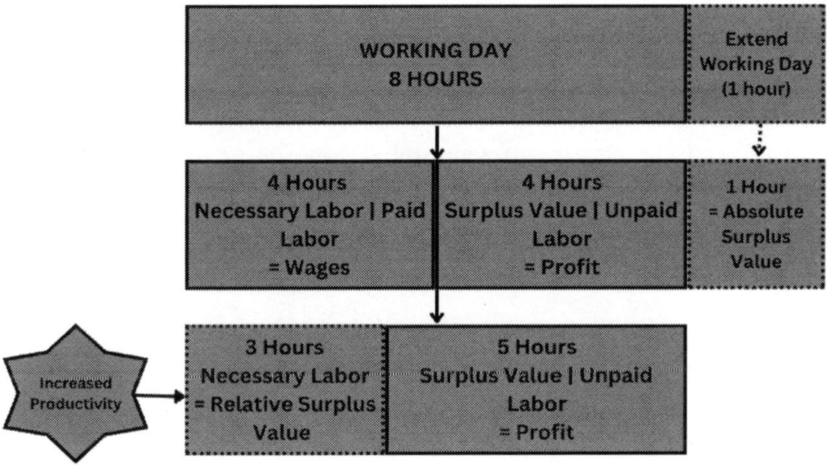

This brings us to the process of simple circulation. Marx explains the economic process the capitalist uses, M-C-M' (Money-Commodity-Money'). This process is where money is transformed into commodities and those commodities are then exchanged for money. This works in tandem with the inverse process, C-M-C' (Commodity-Money-Commodity'), in which the commodity is transformed into money, and then the money is exchanged for more commodities. This process can be easier understood through the lens of a workplace. The business owner, following the process M-C-M', uses their money to purchase resources that are then transformed into commodities by the labor of workers. Those commodities are then sold on the market in exchange for more money, the owner's profit. Inversely, the worker provides their commodity - labor - to the owner's resources, creating a new commodity - the product - in return for money - their wage - which they then take to said market and buy or exchange for the commodities they desire - food, clothes, entertainment, etc. Following this process, you can hopefully better see the problem. The worker sells their labor power in order to buy commodities that maintain their ability to work, whereas the capitalist buys the labor of the worker to sell commodities for a profit. The profit is not gained simply through the process of circulation but through the extraction of surplus value during production. Circulation is the means by which that surplus value is realized.[27]

To summarize the process, the capitalist uses their money to purchase two types of commodities, the labor power of workers and ownership of the means of production. This is the first half of the formula M-C. Through the process of production, the workers use the means of production to create a new commodity, a good or service. Because the value of labor is bound to SNLT, before the capitalist may extract their surplus value they must pay the workers' wages and for the maintenance of the means of production. Therefore, the surplus value realized by the capitalist is the excess exchange value above all the inputs of production, not just wage labor, though it is a major factor! Once this surplus exchange value is realized on the market and the capitalist receives their profit, the end process C-M' is completed. From this process of simple circulation, you can visualize the unending cycle of capital accumulation required by the capitalist mode of production. The process of circulation does not end, it simply loops back to the start, M-C-M'-∞.[28]

This analysis allows us to see a basic overview of the capitalist mode of production. Hopefully, you can see how wage labor and surplus value are intertwined with one another. However, they are also integrally tied to the third process of which we object - generalized commodity production! Simple commodity production existed long before the development of capitalism, it refers to a mode of production of private individual laborers producing commodities. Generalized commodity production is the evolution of simple commodity production under capitalism, as under generalized commodity production there is a higher socialization of production to the point that the laborers or labor itself becomes

---

[27] Marx 1867, Ch. 1

[28] Marx 1867, Ch. 1

commodified. As expressed earlier, these commodities are then bought or rented by capitalists for a wage (wage labor). Generalized commodity production is therefore a more progressive mode of production compared to simple commodity production, and it cannot exist without wage labor, and without wage labor, there is no surplus value for the capitalist to extract! The answer to the abolition of capitalism is then clearly the abolition of generalized commodity production, but that is a broad term because as Marx explained in the opening of *Capital,* the base unit of capitalism is the singular commodity. Therefore we should say capitalism will be abolished through the abolition of the commodity! That is true, but how do you abolish the commodity? You abolish the commodity by abolishing its exchange value! And to do that you must abolish the value form. So, the final target standing in our way is not generalized commodity production, wage labor, or surplus value. Those are all just Jenga blocks teetering atop the singular block holding the entire tower together - the value form. And the first step in knocking that tower down is the abolition of the universal equivalent, the abolition of money!

The Abolition of Money:

Once the new political and economic structures of society following a revolution are stabilized, and the threats of foreign intervention and domestic counterrevolution are tamed, society can move on to the next phase in transition; the abolition of money! The abolition of money is a direct attack on the commodity form or value form. Once complete alongside the structures set in place after the revolution, we will have finally reached a transition to a socialist society, albeit in a lower phase of development.

However, before we proceed we must respond to the claim that commodity production can exist under socialism. Many defenders of the so-called 'Already Existing Socialist' (AES) states (China, North Korea, Cuba, Laos, Vietnam, etc.) claim that these nations, by virtue of establishing a 'proletarian' dictatorship, have already reached socialism and are now on the road to building communism. It would be wonderful if this were true, but it simply is not. This belief comes from those who have tried to read the 'disciples' of Marx and Engels before grasping a rudimentary understanding of the latter two. They find that the world they once knew was a facade and in their rush to find the truth, they skip over foundational theory and choose instead to read the works of the *great evils* painted by the West, Stalin and Mao. This is a mistake and a common one at that. The USSR and the PRC[29], while indeed forces of historical progression, at no point achieved a socialist mode of production, for that can only be achieved through the abolition of the value form. If we were to sum up our reasoning in a single sentence, it would be that the root cause of all the contradictions of capitalism can be boiled down to the value form, which expresses itself through money.

Money is capital just as commodities are capital. In fact, money itself can be a commodity. It is unique however; it stands outside the realm of normal commodities, because as a currency, it acts as the universal equivalent of exchange for all other commodities. As Marx writes in *Capital Vol. 1*

"The general form of relative value, embracing the whole world of commodities, converts the single commodity that is excluded from the rest, and made to play the part of equivalent – here the linen – into the universal equivalent."[30]

Money is a specific commodity chosen to be the universal equivalent of exchange for all other commodities, however, the specific commodity can technically be anything. Historically, the universal equivalent was gold. The Yap Islands today even use stone disks called Rai, and following 1971 we left the gold standard in favor of fiat money. No matter if the currency is an ounce of gold, a stone disk, a piece of paper, or magic money, it serves as the medium through which one exchanges one commodity for another.

[29] Prior to the failure of the other proletarian revolutions, the USSR was actively transforming the relations of production from capitalist to socialist. It lost its proletarian character due to the failure of the international revolution, leading it into a stage of siege socialism or state capitalism under the NEP. (Which Lenin admitted was a defeat on the economic front.)

[30] Marx 1867, Ch. 1 p. 44

There are, of course, differences between money backed by gold and fiat money that is backed by essentially trust - mainly, money under the gold standard was directly convertible into an equivalent amount of gold, and it derived its value from that connection. Whereas due to the need to have more currency in circulation, fiat money backed by the trust and stability of a government is inconvertible, it cannot be directly converted into another commodity. Instead, it is more representative of the value of the economy at large. The issues of loans, debt, and interest rates are irrelevant to the basic argument being made, whether backed by gold or created in thin air, money is a commodity because it has both a use value and exchange value. It has use as a currency in that it serves as a measure of value, but it has further use as it can be stored to accumulate, and it can be transferred to others. Hell, it even has a use value as a piece of toilet paper if you are willing! Money has an exchange value as the universal equivalent of exchange for all commodities represented by its dollar value. For example, if you take $30,000 worth of carrots to a car dealership and try to exchange them for a car, you'll be laughed out of the parking lot. It also serves as a measure of exchange against other currencies, like converting USD to Yen.

The accumulation of capital is only possible because of the dual purpose money serves in its current form. First, as the universal equivalent of exchange, and second, as a tool of capital. Simple circulation, described through the processes of C-M-C' and M-C-M', allows money to be a self-valorizing asset that the owner of money can further accumulate through continuing the unending cycle of circulation. The facade of trickle-down economics can be seen by looking at the growing wealth inequality around the world. The capitalists as a class get richer by reinvesting their money into expanding their capital and by storing their money in stocks and high-interest savings accounts to accumulate further. As their money and capital continue to grow, so does their control over the political and economic levers of power over society. This form of money must be abolished, and until it is, no society may rightfully claim they have reached socialism, not even one of a lower stage. Now, let's look at value further, Marx opens his *Critique of the Gotha Program* by stating,

"Labor is not the source of all wealth. Nature is just as much the source of use values as labor, which itself is only the manifestation of a force of nature, human labor power. The above phrase is to be found in all children's primers and is correct insofar as it is implied that labor is performed with the appurtenant subjects and instruments. But a socialist program cannot allow such bourgeois phrases to pass over in silence the conditions that lone give them meaning. And insofar as man from the beginning behaves toward nature, the primary source of all instruments and subjects of labor, as an owner, treats her as belonging to him, his labor becomes the source of use values, therefore also of wealth. The bourgeois have very good grounds for falsely ascribing supernatural creative power to labor; since precisely from the fact that labor depends on nature it follows that the man who possesses no other property than his labor power must, in all conditions of society and culture, be the slave of other men who have made themselves the owners of the material conditions of labor. He can only work with their permission, hence live only with their permission."[31]

Labor cannot be performed without the resources provided by nature, and natural resources cannot be extracted and transformed into use values without labor. The relationship between labor and nature is an inseparable part of human life and struggle, and is therefore part of what defines human nature. We learn that the factors of production are land, labor, and capital. Land is the buildings and natural resources, labor is the human workers, and capital is the money and tools (mental and physical) required for production. The capitalist mode of production adds a fourth factor, the entrepreneur, or capitalist. It's said because this entrepreneur takes on the risk of consolidating the land, labor, and capital, that they are entitled to all the wealth of production. This is an abstraction from reality. Capital is not simply money and tools, it is a social relation of ownership and or possession of the means of production. Making not only the Econ 101 definition of capital irrelevant, but also the additional fourth factor of the 'entrepreneur' because it is already embodied in the capital relation.

---

[31] Marx 1891

Under this mode of production, the worker is treated as nothing more than a tool. They are no different to the capitalist than a hammer or machine, to be used until their usefulness dwindles threatening the bottom line in which case they are discarded and replaced. As shown earlier, the worker is paid a wage not based on their productivity or contribution but as another tool. The capitalist will seek to pay the worker the least amount possible while maintaining a profitable efficiency by cutting the workforce, increasing automation, purchasing cheaper materials, or lengthening the work day. This relationship of owner and worker across not just society, but the world, develops a human nature of greed and selfishness even while actively fought against by the human desire for community and companionship. As Marx writes, the worker is slave to the whims of the owner. He cannot work without the owner's permission and therefore he cannot obtain the means of sustaining his life without the owner's permission. While worker cooperatives seek to address the issue of ownership by democratizing the workplace and the economy, they do not change the overall mode of production from one of profit (producing goods or services to exchange), to one of social production (producing goods or services directly for the use of society). In order to produce for direct use, money in its current state must be abolished. Now the question arises that with the abolition of money, how are these goods and services distributed to the population? It's a great question, an important one, and one that has been raging among leftists for centuries. Our school of thought will no doubt cause some socialists to scoff and proclaim us another capitalist reformer, our proposal? A modernized system of labor vouchers!

A labor voucher, certificate, credit, or however you slice it, is simply a measure of labor performed. When following the idea of recording the socially necessary labor time to produce a good or service, or the industry average time to produce a good or service, the voucher can be viewed as follows. One hour of average labor is equivalent to one labor voucher, above-average labor is equivalent to two labor vouchers, and below-average labor is equivalent to half a labor voucher or possibly one labor voucher and inter-enterprise penalties. This system will obviously have to accommodate workers with disabilities because their disability hinders their ability to perform their share of the socially necessary labor. Also, people disabled to the point of an inability to work will have to be accommodated by society as a whole, whether it be through upholding social services, establishing a minimum allocation of labor vouchers to said disabled persons or their caretakers, whether that be family, friends, or local institutions. All of this of course sounds the same as the current monetary system, especially similar to a model where profit allocation is distributed by productivity, however, there is a stark difference between money and the labor voucher. This difference as we will argue is that the labor voucher breaks from the value form. Our argument hinges on that belief. The question then arises, what is value? Let's ask Marx! He writes in *Capital Vol. 1,*

"...exchange value appears to be something accidental and purely relative, and consequently an intrinsic value, i.e., an exchange value that is inseparably connected with the commodity, inherent in it, seems a contradiction in terms. Let us consider the matter more closely."[32]

In *Value, Price, and Profit,* he writes,

"As the exchangeable values of commodities are only social functions of those things, and have nothing at all to do with the natural qualities, we must first ask: What is the common social substance of all commodities? It is labour. To produce a commodity a certain amount of labour must be bestowed upon it, or worked up in it. And I say not only labour, but social labour. A man who produces an article for his own immediate use, to consume it himself, creates a product, but not a commodity. As a self-sustaining producer he has nothing to do with society. But to produce a commodity, a man must not only produce an article satisfying some social want, but his labour itself must form part and parcel of the total sum of labour expended by society. It must be subordinate to the division of labour within society."[33]

Again in *Capital Vol. 1,*

---

[32] Marx 1867, Ch. 1 p. 27

[33] Marx 1898, p. 15

"Magnitude of value expresses a relation of social production, it expresses the connexion that necessarily exists between a certain article and the portion of the total labour-time of society required to produce it. As soon as magnitude of value is converted into price, the above necessary relation takes the shape of a more or less accidental exchange-ratio between a single commodity and another, the money-commodity. But this exchange-ratio may express either the real magnitude of that commodity's value, or the quantity of gold deviating from that value, for which, according to circumstances, it may be parted with. The possibility, therefore, of quantitative incongruity between price and magnitude of value, or the deviation of the former from the latter, is inherent in the price-form itself. This is no defect, but, on the contrary, admirably adapts the price-form to a mode of production whose inherent laws impose themselves only as the mean of apparently lawless irregularities that compensate one another."[34]

Marx's pen pal, Fredrick Engels wrote in the preface to Marx's *The Poverty of Philosophy*,

"First, continual deviations of the prices of commodities from their values are the necessary condition in and through which the value of the commodities as such can come into existence. Only through the fluctuations of competition, and consequently of commodity prices, does the law of value of commodity production assert itself and the determination of the value of the commodity by the socially necessary labour time become a reality. That thereby the form of manifestation of value, the price, as a rule looks somewhat different from the value which it manifests, is a fate which value shares with most social relations... Secondly, competition, by bringing into operation the law of value of commodity production in a society of producers who exchange their commodities, precisely thereby brings about the only organisation and arrangement of social production which is possible in the circumstances. Only through the undervaluation or overvaluation of products is it forcibly brought home to the individual commodity producers what society requires or does not require and in what

[34] Marx 1867, Ch. 3 p. 70

amounts."[35]

And lastly, in his text *Anti-Duhring*, Engels writes,

"Political economy, in the widest sense, is the science of the laws governing the production and exchange of the material means of subsistence in human society. Production and exchange are two different functions. Production may occur without exchange, but exchange — being necessarily an exchange of products—cannot occur without production."[36]

In critiquing political economy, the capitalist mode of production, and the value form, we could spend the rest of our lives studying the present, analyzing the past, and producing texts thicker than the bible, but that is not what we're seeking to do here. Instead of spending the rest of this essay dissecting each quote, we will attempt to quickly synthesize the conclusions of Marx and Engels into an operational definition. The variable that doesn't change no matter how much of Marx or Engels we read is that the basis for the capitalist system is the exchange of commodities. A commodity, being a good or service produced not for its use value, but for its exchange value. And as Marx writes, labor is the "common social substance" of all commodities. He then applies this individual action of labor to society through social labor, "...to produce a commodity, a man must not only produce an article satisfying some social want, but his labour itself must form part and parcel of the total sum of labour expended by society. It must be subordinate to the division of labour within society." Following up on his statement in his *Critique of the Gotha Program*, the value of a good is that of the socially necessary labor applied to the natural resources required to produce it. It can then be understood that even under capitalism, the true value of a product is its production cost because that cost factors in the land, labor, and capital required to produce said product. The issue of course is that the capitalist, the owner of the land, labor, and capital, now takes this newly produced product and artificially inflates its value through the anarchy of the market, which changes its price. Price is subject to the law of

[35] Engels 1847, Preface p. 7

[36] Engels 1877, pt. 2 ch. 1

supply and demand, value is not. This is explained further by Marx in *Value, Price, and Profit,*

"Supply and demand regulate nothing but the temporary fluctuations of market prices. They will explain to you why the market price of a commodity rises above or sinks below its value, but they can never account for the value itself. Suppose supply and demand to equilibrate, or, as the economists call it, to cover each other. Why, the very moment these opposite forces become equal they paralyze each other, and cease to work in the one or other direction. At the moment when supply and demand equilibrate each other, and therefore cease to act, the market price of a commodity coincides with its real value, with the standard price round which its market prices oscillate. In inquiring into the nature of that VALUE, we have therefore nothing at all to do with the temporary effects on market prices of supply and demand. The same holds true of wages and of the prices of all other commodities."[37]

From the understanding that the value of a product and its price are two separate entities, we can further see the truth in Engels' statement, *"Production and exchange are two different functions. Production may occur without exchange, but exchange — being necessarily an exchange of products— cannot occur without production."* Production exists in every economic system, but generalized commodity production is unique to the capitalist system. Commodities, products produced to be exchanged, have existed long before capitalism, however, it is only under capitalist production that the vast majority of production is used to produce commodities. For example, under feudal production, serfs would produce crops on their lord's land. Most of their harvest would be directly consumed by them and their community, however, a portion of the harvest would be taken by the lord to sell on the market; that portion taken to the market to be sold has become commodified. Under capitalism, the production of commodities becomes generalized, meaning that commodity production is widespread. It becomes the predominant purpose of production, reaching a point that labor itself

[37] Marx 1898, p. 13

becomes a commodity to be bought and sold on a labor market.

Commodities as the base unit of exchange moved away from the bartering system of an exchange of equivalent products, like trading a pig for a barrel of wheat, to a system based on a universal equivalent of exchange for all commodities, money. It's here again we see it doesn't matter if said money is backed by gold or a genie in a bottle. The money form is the axis that commodity exchange circulates on, and therefore is also what capitalism itself rests upon. That is why a socialist society cannot exist until the value form or money form is abolished. Now, we must explain why the labor voucher is not just different than money, but also how it separates itself from the value form.

Money, as we use it today, has several purposes. At its most basic, it serves the role of a currency as the universal equivalent of exchange for commodities, a measure of value. However, it's also a self-valorizing asset that can be stored in savings accounts to collect interest, or be invested into the direct ownership of the means of production and/or partial ownership of the means of production through shares. It can be transferred at- will to whomever or whatever the money holder wants, whether it be an innocent $50 birthday gift, or a multi-million-dollar bribe to a government official to repeal environmental regulations so the money holder's company can save on production costs in order to - you guessed it - accumulate more money! The famous phrase, "You need to spend money to make money", applies to the capitalist system as a whole. The more money you accumulate, the more decision-making power you acquire and the less risk making said decisions takes. The issues of monopolization, bribes or lobbying, lowering working standards, shipping exploitation abroad, etc., all boil down to the capitalists' need to constantly expand in order to 'win' the real-life game of 'Monopoly,' and the base unit that expansion is built on is exchange value, which is expressed through money itself. It's an endless cycle. Monopolies rise and fall, giving way to new monopolies that rise and fall, but what they leave behind is an ever-increasing gap in wealth inequality, further exploitation of workers and underdeveloped nations, and further damage to the environment and the natural resources humanity needs to sustain itself. This cycle can only be broken by a socialist economy, and that can only come through the abolition of money. How does the labor voucher solve these problems? We will again defer to Marx. He writes in *Critique of the Gotha Programme,* (It's a long quote, you'll survive!)

"What we have to deal with here is a communist society, not as it has developed on its own foundations, but, on the contrary, just as it emerges from capitalist society; which is thus in every respect, economically, morally, and intellectually, still stamped with the birthmarks of the old society from whose womb it emerges. Accordingly, the individual producer receives back from society – after the deductions have been made – exactly what he gives to it. What he has given to it is his individual quantum of labor. For example, the social working day consists of the sum of the individual hours of work; the individual labor time of the individual producer is the part of the social working day contributed by him, his share in it. He receives a certificate from society that he has furnished such-and-such an amount of labor (after deducting his labor for the common funds); and with this certificate, he draws from the social stock of means of consumption as much as the same amount of labor cost. The same amount of labor which he has given to society in one form, he receives back in another. Hence, equal right here is still in principle – bourgeois right, although principle and practice are no longer at loggerheads, while the exchange of equivalents in commodity exchange exists only on the average and not in the individual case. In spite of this advance, this equal right is still constantly stigmatized by a bourgeois limitation. The right of the producers is proportional to the labor they supply; the equality consists in the fact that measurement is made with an equal standard, labor. But one man is superior to another physically, or mentally, and supplies more labor in the same time, or can labor for a longer time; and labor, to serve as a measure, must be defined by its duration or intensity, otherwise it ceases to be a standard of measurement. This equal right is an unequal right for unequal labor. It recognizes no class differences, because everyone is only a worker like everyone else; but it tacitly recognizes unequal individual endowment, and thus productive capacity, as a natural privilege. It is, therefore, a right of inequality, in its content, like every right. Right, by its very nature, can consist only in the application of an equal standard; but unequal individuals (and they would not be different individuals if they were not unequal) are measurable only by an equal standard insofar as they are brought under an equal point of view, are taken from one definite side only – for instance, in the present case, are regarded only as workers and nothing more is seen in them, everything else being ignored. Further, one worker is married, another is not; one has more children than another, and so on and so forth. Thus, with an equal performance of labor, and hence an equal in the social consumption fund, one will in fact receive more than another, one will be richer than another, and so on. To avoid all these defects, right, instead of being equal, would have to be unequal. But these defects are inevitable in the first phase of communist society as it is when it has just emerged after prolonged birth pangs from capitalist society. Right can never be higher than the economic structure of society and its cultural development conditioned thereby. In a higher phase of communist society, after the enslaving subordination of the individual to the division of labor, and therewith also the antithesis between mental and physical labor, has vanished; after labor has become not only a means of life but life's prime want; after the productive forces have also increased with the all-around development of the individual, and all the springs of co-operative wealth flow more abundantly – only then can the narrow horizon of bourgeois right be crossed in its entirety and society inscribe on its banners: From each according to his ability, to each according to his needs!"[38]

This passage by Marx lays the groundwork for how distribution within a socialist society can operate, and in our opinion, is one of the most useful of Marx's arguments. The labor voucher operating in a socialist society, the lower phase of communism, a world still dealing with scarcity, is the main distinction that denotes a society's successful transition from capitalism to socialism. How? The labor voucher buries the value form. Again, you ask how? Allow us to explain. Firstly, it serves the role of currency, as it still

[38] Marx 1891

acts as the universal equivalent of exchange. However, it measures value based on the socially necessary labor time needed to produce a good or service. The labor voucher is a measure of value in the strictest sense, as it is directly representative of the industry average time required to produce a good or service. The labor voucher cannot be stored in a savings account to further accumulate because it is not an asset that can accumulate value. The voucher, whether a token, slip of paper, or digital, is representative of labor performed by that specific laborer. Labor, once completed, cannot collect interest nor depreciate, at least not in the same sense as money does today. Again, the vouchers represent the labor performed by a specific laborer; they cannot be transferred, not as a birthday gift or a bribe. The voucher is in the name of the person who earned it. That person could use their voucher in exchange for a good and then gift it to someone, but they cannot gift the voucher itself to someone else. An expiration date will likely be applied to the vouchers, whether it be a year or a lifetime, the vouchers will not be kept in reserve or inherited by one's next of kin. As the vouchers serve as a representation of all the labor done across society and therefore the economy at large, any voucher that is not used by its expiration date will be destroyed under the assumption the holder didn't need any more from society's stocks. And lastly, when exchanged for a good or service, the voucher does not enter circulation, but is rather destroyed. A digital voucher can be 'burned' and a paper voucher, much like a coupon or movie ticket, is a one-time use item, once it's used or expired it cannot be used again. The differences between money and labor vouchers are clear, the voucher can only be earned through providing labor to society - working - and it can only be exchanged for goods or services. With the abolition of private property, one cannot use their vouchers to own any means of production whether it be an office building, factory, farm, or rental home.

To summarize, the labor voucher is a form of currency measured through labor time performed, and can only be exchanged for other goods and services. Said voucher is a single-use, non-storable, non-transferable, and non-circulatory currency that expires at a predetermined date. Amadeo Bordiga discusses the relation of labor vouchers to the value form in his text, *Dialogue with Stalin,*

"Lower stage of communism, or if you want, socialism: society disposes already generally of products, which are allocated to members of society by quotas. This function doesn't require commodity exchange or money anymore – one cannot let Stalin's statement pass, according to which the simple exchange without money, but still based on the law of value, should bring us closer to communism: rather it is about a kind of regression to bartering. The allocation of products on the contrary follows from the center, without return of an equivalent. Example: If a malaria epidemic breaks out, in the affected region quinine is distributed for free, but solely one tubule per person. In this phase, not only compulsory work is necessary, but also the recording of the performed labour time and its certificate – the famous 'labour voucher,' so much discussed in the last century. The peculiarity of this certificate is, that it cannot be kept in reserve, so that any try to accumulate it leads to the loss of the performed labour quantum without compensation. The law of value is buried."[39]

The law of value is buried and thus alongside the structures set following a revolution, socialism will have at last been reached! Congratulations team, we did it, the era of socialism has arrived! There is just one small problem. We have here abolished the contradictions of capitalism all stemming from the root of the issue, the value form, however, we have replaced it with nothing. Now that the contradictions have been settled, we must apply 'socialism' to the existing structures we prepared in the first phase. To do this, we must detail the methods of socialist accounting, production, and distribution!

Basic Formulas:

Under socialism, production is no longer run for the creation of exchange values. Instead, production is increasingly socialized for the express purpose of producing use values, products made directly for use by the population.

---

[39] Bordiga 1952

Following that, the abolition of capitalism will also abolish the general formula of capital:

M-C(MoP + LP)-C'-M'-∞

Money and circulation in this new system are gone, so adjustments must be made. To start, at an elementary level, there are a couple of basic formulas of socialism:

SNLT= (Total Labor Time/Total Output)

Value (Cost of Production) = (MoP + SNL)
MoP = Means of Production | SNL = Socially Necessary Labor

Simplified Production Process = I-(MoP + SNL)-O-D or I-SNLT-O-D
I = Input | O = Output | D = Distribution

The third formula, or the general formula of socialist production, is a non-circulative process as it ends directly with distribution. There is no extraction of surplus value, as there is no wage labor or commodity created during production, and it applies to both intermediate and final goods. For final goods or consumption goods, the finished product is distributed directly to the population, however that process is done (likely through distribution centers). While for intermediate goods, or goods used in the production of other goods, the distribution is to the next chain in production and therefore the output is converted into an input, beginning a new process of production.

Total Output Value = (MoP + SNL) - Labor Time Procurement - Labor Time Maintenance - Overhead Costs

This formula provides us with the total value of outputs produced by the economy at large. (MoP + SNL), or the cost/value of production, represents the total labor hours expended during production before accounting for reproduction. Labor Time Procurement accounts for labor time spent acquiring raw materials, and Labor Time Maintenance accounts for labor time spent covering the depreciation of machinery during production. Lastly, Overhead Costs represent costs required for production that are outside of the production process itself; this includes things like administration and accounting. The purpose of this formula is to provide us with an estimate of the total output value generated by the economy in terms of socially necessary labor time.

Accounting:

Setting everything else aside, we must first recognize that production and distribution are a social process; and not only that, labor itself is a social process. The development of simple commodity production to generalized commodity production under the development of capitalism solidified this socialization to the highest known degree. We simply seek to take this socialization and use it as a force, producing for the common need instead of one following the profit motive. As argued previously, this switch from production for exchange to production for use will require the abolition of the market, and with it, money and prices. Therefore, before we can begin production, we must prepare the productive apparatus to work without its price signals, or in other words, without the market. As we argued, money shall be replaced with a form of labor voucher that measures socially necessary labor time. Emphasis must be put on 'socially necessary'. The act of simply performing labor is not a relevant measurement, as it has no connection to society's needs. Hence, it has no connection to production! Pannekoek writes in *Workers' Councils,*

"In a society where the goods are produced directly for consumption there is no market to exchange them; and no value, as expression of the labor contained in them established itself automatically out of the process of buying and selling. Here the labor spent must be expressed in a direct way by the number of hours."[40]

The economy of time is agreed on by most socialists, as Marx succinctly wrote in *Grundrisse*, *"Economy of time, to this all economy ultimately reduces itself."*[41] For Marx and any true socialist, the fight for the liberation of the proletariat is also the fight for the liberation of humanity. To free the people from their chains is to make them 'the master of their fate and the captain of their soul.'[42] This liberation from the exploitation of capitalism, and more so wage labor, is the fight for the worker's access to more leisure time. From this standpoint, the goal is to form a society where the populace provides society with their socially necessary work and is then free to enjoy their free time. That is true wealth, as Marx explains again, *"For real wealth is the developed productive power of all individuals. The measure of wealth is then not any longer, in any way, labour time, but rather disposable time."*[43] Our goal then is clear. We are not attempting to maximize productive power or drain the population for every hour of labor they have to offer, no - in actuality we chase the contrary. Our goal is to provide the workers with as much disposable or free time as possible while maintaining a functioning society! That is why the distinction between socially necessary labor time and labor time is of the utmost importance! Paresh Chattopadhyay discusses labor time in depth in his excellent collection of essays titled *Socialism and Commodity Production.* In particular, he claims that socialists often neglect three 'vital aspects' when considering measuring labor time. We are concerned with two for the time being. The first, we just covered - the neglect of leisure time; and the second, he argues, is the neglect of 'materialised or past labor time'[44] These are important things to consider when accounting for the total amount of SNLT available to society.

Two tasks lie in front of us regarding accounting, finding the total amount

[40] Pannekoek 1947, p. 25

[41] Marx 1857

[42] Henley 1888, Invictus Poem

[43] Marx 1857

[44] Chattopadhyay 2018, p. 148

of available SNLT, and collecting knowledge on the needs of the populace. We will work through these tasks in coordination with the economic apparatus laid out in phase one. To start, at the base level, the enterprise, a new position must be created. That position is the Enterprise Accountant or EA. The EA could be chosen from the current workers, or an entirely outside worker could be brought in to fill the role. In past models, this enterprise administrator would be tasked with bookkeeping and/ or recording the productivity of the workers by keeping records of the hours worked by each worker and the amount of labor time objectified in each completed product. They would then average these numbers and find that specific enterprise's SNLT.[45] With modern technology, this method of record-keeping has become tremendously easier and correspondingly will take less skill to perform. This allows for a larger pool of available EAs, which will be necessary as one will be required for every enterprise. There are tons of ways this record-keeping can be done, and as time goes on, the process can be further automated. For example, a simple punch card a worker uses to clock in could populate directly on the EAs spreadsheet. However the process is done, the first job of the EA is to measure both the hours worked per employee and the labor time objectified in the products, and then average those numbers to find their enterprise's SNLT. Another function of keeping a record of the hours worked by each worker is so they can be allocated their proper amount of labor vouchers. If the ABC grading system is in effect of above-average, average, and below-average labor affecting the allocation of labor vouchers, then the EAs would track those numbers as well.

The second job of the EA is to collect knowledge on the needs of the workers. This would be completed through a standard inter-enterprise survey that should be distributed to all members of the enterprise at regular intervals whether that be weekly, bi-weekly, or monthly. A good format for this survey would be a one to ten satisfaction scale with the ability to leave comments. Some of the items on this survey might include the

[45] Pannekoek 1947, p. 25

following: condition of work, housing, food & water, healthcare, access to transportation, clothing, entertainment, etc. The survey should obviously be kept as short and concise as possible because otherwise, the worker will just breeze through it to get back to work. As well, it should be anonymous. The survey could be given out completely electronically where the answers, again, automatically populate and sort themselves into the EAs spreadsheet. With both these tasks completed, the EA would compile their data and submit it up the chain to the Syndicate, where another new position will be created - the Syndicate Accountant, or SA.

The SAs should keep and store the records of each enterprise for discussion amongst the Syndicate, including things like the most or least productive branch, which could be used to move workers around to promote better efficiency. From there, their role is very straightforward. They will compile the data from all the enterprises comprising their syndicate and combine the data into one. This data will now reflect the SNLT and the knowledge of the needs of an entire local industry. Following the chain, the Local Economic Chamber will also have an accountant who compiles the SNLT and survey responses of every local industry into one location. With that, we now have the SNLT and knowledge of the needs of an entire local population! At this point regarding the survey questions, there should be a large enough sample size to recognize trends that could be affecting the local community. Analyzing the results, any category below an average score of five must be addressed. For example, if access to transportation has an average of one, the comments should be combed through to find the common issues facing the community, and then those issues should be addressed. A copy of the local community's survey responses should be relayed to the Local Assembly so a cooperative solution can be found. Every LEC accountant will send their data to their State Economic Chamber accountant who will complete the same process just with larger data sets. Following this, the National Economic Chamber will receive a data set representing the SNLT of the entire national economy and the overall satisfactory scores of the entire nation (with socialist blocs and internationalism, this chain can be continued to the bloc and international levels; the data sets just continue to grow). This bottom-up, more decentralized method of accounting allows for more accurate data of both labor time, and knowledge of workers needs to be collected as compared to a completely centralized system of planning. From here, the NEC will know its projected total amount of available SNLT. This projected total could also be estimated by taking the average hours worked per worker a year and multiplying it by the total work force. This number is then theoretically equal to the nation's total amount of allocatable labor vouchers, however, that theory is quickly busted because it is impossible to give the workers the full value of their labor.

That is because before these vouchers can be allocated, certain deductions must be made. These deductions start at the enterprise level in the reproduction/repair and reinvestment in the means of production. Then there are emergency/reserve deductions. And finally, deductions must be made to maintain social services like healthcare, housing, transportation, education, child and elderly care, etc. All of these deductions are made prior to distribution and can be regarded as non-consumer expenses, or the expenses for the maintenance of society.[46] After these deductions are completed, the NEC will be left with the total amount of allocatable labor vouchers. It should be noted that SNLT is not a static number. For one, if a large number of workers perform above-average or below-average labor, the time to reach the socially necessary amount of labor will decrease or increase accordingly, thus altering an industry's SNLT. Also, as technology and innovation advance, more goods can be created in the same amount of labor time before said innovation, thus again lowering the SNLT. Another thing that must be accounted for is skilled versus unskilled labor. Skilled labor requiring technical training often requires specific field studies, therefore as a part of the deductions from the common fund of society, one will be allocated labor vouchers for seeking higher-level education. With this general understanding of the socialist accounting process, the planning of production can begin!

---

[46] Marx 1875

Basics of Production Planning:

In a socialist system, the basic enterprises are all equal cogs in the machine of society's economy, that is they individually produce the goods and services that are needed to maintain the production process of the other enterprises and that of the workers that encompass them. The exchange or transfer of goods here differs from that of the capitalist system, because under capitalism this exchange is based on the private ownership of property, whereas under socialism that relationship has been abolished in favor of exchange based on common or social ownership. What we must then plan is the transfer or exchange of these socially owned products and services to the maintenance of society's production process starting as the basic enterprise, and the distribution of final goods to the consumers - the population. As stated before, following the abolition of the value form or money form, goods and services are now measured by the socially necessary labor objectified in their production. The universal equivalent of which all goods are compared is now an object's socially necessary labor measured in time or SNLT which is measured by the working hour. That number is the product's value! As mentioned in the brief on socialist accounting, each enterprise must keep account of the SNLT objectified in production, and their internal surveys but we can put that aside for now. The simple formula for measuring value or the cost of production is:

(MoP + SNL)

This formula can be further broken down. The means of production, while already split between constant and 'variable' capital, can be further broken down as follows: The 'variable' capital- SNL, can be represented as just labor, and the constant capital- MoP, can be broken down into fixed assets (factory and machinery) and raw materials. Remember to note each is still measured by the socially necessary hour. Fully simplified the formula reads:

(Land & Machinery) + (Raw Materials) + (Labor) = Good or Service

At the micro level, we can examine a factory producing chairs. To keep it simple, this factory only produces one type of chair made with the same materials. After accounting for a year, the factory expends 10,000 hours on land and machinery, 50,000 hours acquiring and processing raw materials, and 200,000 hours on human labor; that equates to 260,000 hours expended on production. If the factory produced 130,000 chairs at the end of the year, that would leave us with an average of two hours per chair. Assuming this factory is not closing down, it will have to begin the production process once more. To do that is to reproduce everything expended during production. Assuming all variables remain the same from resource availability, technology, skill, and production methods, then the reproduction process takes the same amount of labor hours as the initial production process. "Each company reproduces itself. And thus, the entire social-economic life is reproduced."[47] The Total Output Value (TOV) formula shows us the total amount of labor hours directly spent in production. It negates the hours spent procuring raw materials and maintaining machinery for production.

TOV = (MoP + SNL) - Labor Time Procurement - Labor Time Maintenance - Overhead Costs

Using the same chair example we see the following equation:

TOV = 260,000 - 50,000 - 10,000 - 1000 = 199,000 labor hours

Therefore, if we needed 130,000 chairs produced, of the 261,000 hours allocated to its production, 199,000 hours of that would be direct labor. The simple formula (MoP + SNL), or the TOV, can then be scaled from the individual enterprise to the local industry, local, state and national economies, and finally to the international or global economy (if such a state has been reached). Logically, the number of hours will grow substantially

---

[47] G.I.C 1930, p. 113

larger as you raise the scale, which is why accurate accounting and a measure of SNLT are such fundamental requirements for a socialist planned economy. We can now apply this basic concept of planning to our model of an economic apparatus.

The base units or individual enterprises produce their goods, and the Enterprise Accountant keeps a digital log of the value of production. Let us analyze three different local furniture manufacturing enterprises, and their product of choice... chairs!

Factory A: (Efficient)

- Machinery: 6,000 hours
- Raw materials: 50,000 hours
- Labor: 300,000 hours
- Total hours = 6,000 hours + 50,000 hours + 300,000 hours = 356,000 hours
- Total Chairs Produced: 250,000
- Average Hours Per Chair: (356,000/250,000) = 1.424 hours per chair

Factory B: (Average)

- Machinery: 5,000 hours
- Raw materials: 40,000 hours
- Labor: 260,000 hours
- Total Hours = 5,000 hours + 40,000 hours + 260,000 hours = 305,000 hours
- Total Chairs Produced: 200,000
- Average Hours Per Chair: (305,000/200,000) = 1.525 hours per chair

Factory C: (Inefficient)

- Machinery: 4,000 hours
- Raw materials: 30,000 hours

- Labor: 300,000 hours
- Total hours = 4,000 hours + 30,000 hours + 300,000 hours = 334,000 hours
- Total Chairs Produced: 180,000
- Average Hours Per Chair: (334,000/180,000) = 1.855 hours per chair

It would be impossible for every enterprise, even those in the same industry, to operate at the exact same efficiency, because the factors of production fluctuate across society and within the individual enterprises. For example, one enterprise may have more efficient workers or more innovative technology than another, and in some cases, a tree may fall on an enterprise and temporarily inhibit its productive efficiency. To attempt to create equality of production across all enterprises would be a fool's errand. It is impossible! Instead, we unify these enterprises by industry into their Industry Syndicate so that while their individual efficiencies are unequal, they unite together to form a balance - the social average hour of production across the industry.

1.424 + 1.525 + 1.855 = 4.804 total chairs per hour

(4.804/3) $\approx$ 1.601 hours per chair (Industry Average)

The Industry Syndicate and its accountants gather this information along with the worker surveys and send it up the chain to the Local Economic Chamber. The LEC then has the industry average labor hours per output (good or service) for every industry that makes up the local economy. It should be noted that although services do not create goods, they are still integral to society, production, and distribution. The same formulas and accounting used for the production of goods can be used to measure services. For example, the logistics needed to transfer intermediate goods from enterprise to enterprise or final goods from producer to distributor/co nsumer, will require some form of transportation whether that be trucking, rail, or cargo ship. In the case of trucking, the (MoP + SNL) formula is easy to see. The machinery is the truck itself, the raw materials are the cargo to be transported, and the gasoline needed to run the truck; the SNL is provided by the trucker who operates the truck. The output of this 'production process' is not a product, but the service of transporting the cargo to where it needs to go. Just like with the furniture manufacturers, the trucking enterprise will also have an accountant who collects the necessary data and submits it to the Logistics or Trucking Syndicate until it eventually reaches the LEC and so on.

Basics of Distribution Planning:

The basic ideas around planning seen above provide a rough sketch of what the production process may look like. The main takeaways should not be the equations or the specifics of how the enterprises are linked together, those have important relations regarding our model, but our model is just that, a model. It is a blueprint of a blueprint, as it would be impossible to predict the exact method society will structure its economy by. However, some factors are more law than theory when it comes to socialist planning and it is these requirements that must carry over regardless of structure. The main requirement, being of course, the measure of value through socially necessary labor (measured in working hours). Through the basics of production, you can see the general process by which an enterprise or an industry produces goods for consumption. You can replace the chair example for any enterprise in the productive sector; the same formula and process holds true for every productive enterprise. The question now comes, how do the workers retrieve the fruits of society's labor? We have already declared the use of labor vouchers where one voucher equals one hour of SNLT, but here we come to an issue. You have probably heard before that socialists or communists want workers to receive the full value of their labor, and we would not judge you for believing in that slogan, but it is simply not true. It would be wonderful if every worker could receive the full value for their labor, but that could only be possible in a society where all labor is productive labor, and that is the impossibility! It was noted throughout this essay, including quotes from Karl Marx himself, that there must be deductions made from the 'common fund' - for the replacement of the means of production expended during production, and for the maintenance of social services like healthcare, education, and elderly care. These industries are Non-Productive in that they do not produce a good, instead they provide a necessary service. It would be asinine to even consider withholding medical services, access to education, and care for the elderly in exchange for the labor vouchers of the workers. These are industries whose services must be free at the point of use for everyone, and in order to ensure that is possible, every working member of society must pitch in to maintain the social services. Thus a Labor Tax of sorts must be implemented, though it will apply equally or flatly to all workers.

In the first phase, we already separated the Non-Productive sector, or the social services, into a separate branch of society, the National Social Service Agencies. In that section, we separated the N.S.S.A. from the National Economic Chamber by putting it under the oversight of the Party, although it was structured nearly identically to the councils of the Economic Chambers. For now, we can ignore the Party in regards to this basic planning, although it is quite possible at this stage society may be stable enough to wither the party out of economic control entirely by tying the N.S.S.A. to the NEC as one national chamber; or two separate but equal chambers representing the Non Productive and Productive sectors of the economy. Regardless, the individual agencies in the N.S.S.A work the same as the productive enterprises in their method of accounting, meaning they keep account of the MoP, raw materials, and human labor expended in production; and send that information up the chain respectively. For now, we will ignore the individual agency's total expended labor hours and look at the Non Productive sector's expended labor hours in their entirety. In *Fundamental Principles of Communist Production and Distribution,* the Group of International Communists (GIC) uses the following example:

Non Productive Sector:

"8 million + 50 million + 50 million = 108 million working hours"[48]

Productive Sector:

"100 million + 600 million + 600 million = 1,300 million working hours"[49]

It should be noted that both of these equations were used with entirely fictitious numbers and both represent the economy at large. Reading the equations from left to right, the numbers represent hours expended by the MoP, raw materials, and living labor. The group correctly argues that "...'social costs' can be borne solely by living labor power" because the productive sector must renew its time expended on the MoP and raw materials to continue production, leaving only the living labor remaining. We will let them explain the relationship between their stated equations,

"According to this budget, public operational units [non-productive enterprise] need 58 million working hours to renew their means of production and raw materials. These are therefore deducted from the remaining 600 million, leaving 542 million working hours on products. These 542 million correspond to the individual consumption of all workers... All workers work together work 650 million hours... but there are only 542 million working hours left for consumption. So, everyone gets only the 542/650 = 0.83 part... which means that a worker who has worked 40 hours receives only 0.83 x 40 = 33.2 working hours of compensation for consumption."[50]

Therefore, you must throw the old slogan of 'to the worker the full value of their labor!' to the side and face the reality of its impossibility. The worker will receive the full value of their labor after the necessary deductions for the maintenance of society and its social services/non-productive sector. No worker shall face the brunt of this deduction, as it will be flatly extracted from all workers at the same rate. After these deductions are calculated

48 G.I.C. 1930, p. 174

49 G.I.C. 1930, p. 175

50 G.I.C. 1930, p. 175

and made, the worker may receive their earned labor vouchers. As these vouchers are a measure of SNLT performed by the laborer, there is no central authority that can control their value or play with prices, as there are none to play with. They are a unit of measurement that entitles the worker to extract consumer goods from society's stocks equal to the SNLT measured in the vouchers. Therefore, the vouchers are not handed out at will by some higher power, party bureaucrat, or officer manager, they are distributed to the workers exactly as its measurement shows. This process of distributing labor vouchers will probably be entirely digital in this great modern age we live in. So, following the G.I.C example, a worker who was compensated 33.2 working hours for 40 hours of labor might receive 33.2 hours into their 'account.' This worker would then go to a distribution center and fill a shopping cart with items just as they do today, however, when they 'checkout', instead of looking at price tags and digging into their wallet for cash, they will look at the SNLT in hours of an item and swipe a digital card to confirm their exchange. If they took say, 20 working hours worth of goods from the distribution center, those digital labor vouchers would 'burn' as they do not circulate, leaving the worker's account with 13.2 working hours left to exchange for whatever consumer goods they desire. This scenario should look normal to you because it is not visually a radical change for the worker; the radical change is seen in the underlying relationship of the worker between the process of production and access to society's products of labor! It can therefore be understood that the oh-so-scary 'abolition of the market' does not mean the abolition of the distribution center or 'market stall,' because the abolition is not seen in the market's external relations, but in its internal relations. The external relation of the market being the transport of goods to a distribution center to be exchanged with the worker, and the internal relation of the market being the measure of value by labor time instead of prices.

The Economic Calculation Problem: (ECP)

The most prominent voice on the capitalist side of the economic calculation debate was Ludwig von Mises, a major voice representing the Austrian school of economic thought. Mises writes in his text *Economic Calculation in the Socialist Commonwealth,*

"It is an illusion to imagine that in a socialist state calculation in natura can take the place of monetary calculation. Calculation in natura, in an economy without exchange, can embrace consumption goods only; it completely fails when it comes to dealing with goods of a higher order. And as soon as one gives up the conception of a freely established monetary price for goods of a higher order, rational production becomes completely impossible. Every step that takes us away from private ownership of the means of production and from the use of money also takes us away from rational economics."[51]

However, Mises' main argument can be boiled down to this statement from the same text, "Where there is no free market, there is no pricing mechanism; without a pricing mechanism, there is no economic calculation."[52] He correctly surmises that under a socialist economy where the means and products of production are communal. Using money as a universal medium of exchange for economic calculation would be impossible; this is a lesson that market socialists still have not learned! The claim that only capitalism through its free markets and prices can calculate the economic value of goods is a bit preposterous considering that human societies for the vast majority of history existed before the dawn of capitalism. It is true markets have existed dating back to ancient civilizations, but these markets are not equivalent to the free market system of industrial capitalism, as well, many primitive indigenous societies operated on the basis of communal economies. Socialists at the time, like Oskar Lange, were able to 'debunk' Mises ECP by simply demonstrating a model based on trial and error production. The model did not have to be great, it just had to be possible. The debate cooled down for a bit and then heated up again with a much stronger argument in favor of the ECP, that being that capitalist economies are better suited to make economic calculations and therefore are more

---

[51] Mises 1920, Ch. 2 p. 17

[52] Mises 1920, Ch. 3 p. 25

efficient in allocating resources to production. Alright, this may very well be true, although what the truth is depends on what is meant by efficiency, and unfortunately for us, the proponents of the ECP never answer that question. The real problem here is that the capitalist and socialist economies are chasing two different goals, and so their definitions of efficiency will mean drastically different things! The G.I.C explains this further,

"For the bourgeois critics of communism, 'the abolition of the market' is the central point of their struggle and also their strongest weapon... In the struggle against communism, they can only oppose the hitherto prevailing conception of communism, which is nothing other than the replacement of the market by a statistical apparatus... The bourgeois critics all agree that the market, despite all its negative aspects, is in any case a measure of needs. The market 'playfully' solves the question of adapting the production apparatus to needs. The 'market mechanism' ensures that a change in requirements is immediately transferred to the production system without the use of statistics... From their point of view, the 'market mechanism' can very well do what the consumption statistics cannot do. Therefore they declare communism to be impossible as long as it cannot be specified what is to replace this 'mechanism'."[53]

As the G.I.C argues, Mises and later Hayek, both make critiques that may possibly be of validity towards rigid central planning or the oft quoted idea of the national economy representing that of one large post office. However, these critiques are not substantial when thrown against more multi-level or bottom up approaches to planning. There are, of course, proponents of centrally planned economies that will fight the ECP tooth and nail. For example, Scottish academic Paul Cockshott, who argues that the modern supercomputers posses enough computing power to simplify economic calculations to the point their model of central planning is sustainable; we will further discuss Cockshott's model later. As we stated under the basics of planning, the external nature of socialist production and distribution does not differ drastically from that of capitalism; it is the internal relations

[53] G.I.C. 1930, Ch. 12 p. 203-204

or social relations that mark the radical change of society. To this, the G.I.C. continues,

"Let capitalism... point to its market mechanism, which is supposed to be an indicator of need; in reality, it does not need to know needs... precisely because it does not produce for needs but profit... For the proletariat, the whole splendid market mechanism moves only within the narrow limits that the capitalist profit production leaves to the 'commodity' labor power."[54]

The socialist economy is not one of prices, but one of time! Both production and distribution are measured in time (socially necessary labor hours). The voucher, again, serves technically as a currency, but more so as the simple measurement of performed labor. As demonstrated in the basics of planning, this measurement of labor is not only found in consumer goods but in every aspect of the production process, from procuring the raw materials to the use and depreciation of machinery, to the living labor of the workers, to the finished product which may be an intermediate or final good, to its transportation, to another production process or distribution center where it finds the consumer. The 'price' of the good is not measured by the 'market mechanism' of supply and demand because its value has already been calculated through the production process! And there is no doubt with increasing technology and computing power, this calculation of value will only become quicker and easier to perform across society as a whole. As opposed to rigid central planning, we see here a society built from the bottom up, uniting all the individual workers and their enterprises into a cohesive system of federalized workers' councils. This system which unites the proletariat also provides the solution to Hayek's knowledge problem by allowing the workers of every industry to voice their concerns on the planning process at the individual, local, state, and national levels of the economy. This collection of knowledge is even better helped by the accountants' collection of workers' satisfaction of needs surveys and the assistance/advice of technical experts of the economic chambers. The G.I.C. continues its argument by answering the often-asked question of what will

---

[54] G.I.C. 1930, Ch. 12 p. 205

replace the market mechanism.

"We answer that capitalism has no measure of needs, and therefore we don't have to 'replace' anything at all. Communism can only achieve this by linking the distribution organizations directly to production so that the needs become the direct guideline of production." *They further claim that the capitalist production apparatus* "... is set up not according to the needs of millions, but according to purchasing power." [55]

This boils back to the start of the problem - capitalism and socialism operate on different premises, and so they see efficiency differently. Capitalism follows the profit motive. It seeks to constantly grow the economy, accumulate capital, and reinvest parts of that capital into the expansion of the means of production. It is not concerned with the needs of the people, its concern is growing the economy or as it is often measured, the nation's gross domestic product (GDP). The idea is that if the economy and GDP continue to grow, the needs of the population will be met as a result. There is, of course, truth to this method. The richer a country is, the better equipped it is to meet the needs of its population as opposed to an impoverished nation. However, the relation of GDP to quality of life (QoL) is not one-to-one, which is evidence of the fact that the driving force of capitalism is growth, not meeting needs. Social Democrats who are still proponents of the market system will make this same argument, although their solution is simply to focus on the inequality of income or more so wealth. The socialist economy abandons the profit motive in favor of producing for needs. It substitutes the market and its money and prices for the economy of time we have mentioned over and over again. It seizes the already developed means of production into the hands of the working class and produces what they as a class need. The socialist economy is therefore not concerned with growth, although it is also not chasing degrowth. If society needs to grow its productive apparatus it will do so, and if certain sectors are becoming unnecessary they will be shut down in accordance with the needs of the population. The socialist economy is therefore driven

---

[55] G.I.C. 1930, Ch. 12 p. 208-209

by the needs or demands of the people, not profit, and so it directly pursues raising the QoL of its population. Because these types of economies have two different goals and are driven by two different means, they have different needs. Because they have different needs, it would be silly to hold one to the efficiency standards of another whose production is for something entirely different; that relationship of course going both ways. Some needs are basic requirements of humanity and are therefore not subjective; these are items like food, water, housing, healthcare, etc. Capitalism divides these into wants and needs, whereas socialism considers any item produced as a need because otherwise, it would not be produced. This argument echoes back to every commodity having both an exchange and use value. However even in a society that does not differ between wants and needs, there would surely be priority needs, which makes the distinction quite irrelevant. The answer to the ECP therefore depends entirely on what drives the mode of production, because if your goal is to make profit, resources will be allocated toward that goal; and if your goal is to meet societal needs, resources will be allocated toward that goal.

We still have to answer the question of how we allocate the resources to reach the goal of meeting societal needs. To do that we must answer the following question: How do we know what to produce? That question can really be broken down into three parts: What are we producing? Why are we producing it? and How much of it are we producing? If we were starting our society from scratch, where all of its history was burnt in the raging flames of revolution, these questions would indeed be a problem. If that were the case, we would have to gather everybody up and start asking a lot of questions about their wants and needs, and by the time we got all the data we needed... well the people would probably be turning to cannibalism due to the onset of starvation. Thankfully, we are not starting on a blank canvas, we are dealing with a socialist society, as Marx put it, *"not as it has developed on its own foundations, but, on the contrary, just as it emerges from capitalist society; which is thus in every respect, economically, morally, and intellectually, still stamped with the birthmarks of the old society from whose womb it comes."*[56] This means the production and distribution apparatus' of society is already constructed and adequately developed to maintain society, and that all of the data of the old society is available to us immediately. One piece of important data will be items like the census, to provide us with accurate population records of both productive (workers) and non-productive (dependents /elderly) citizens. The other vital piece of information is economic data which will serve as the blueprint of planned production! While we stressed accounting was vital to socialist production, it is also enormously intertwined with capitalist production, and that data will show up-to-date records of what each enterprise has been producing and how much it has been producing. Other available data can give us a better picture of production costs under capitalism, for example, the production costs of machinery could be found through receipts on the purchase or lease of said equipment and depreciation and maintenance expenses. The production costs of raw materials could be found by finding how many unique materials there are, the total quantity of these unique materials, the cost per unit of each unique material, and the cost to process and transport said materials to the factory. Lastly, the cost of labor can be found by measuring salaries/wages and hours worked. We will also be able to see the individual enterprise's inputs and outputs of capital goods, and the fluctuation of the product's price over time! This data can be examined from different periods of time like the past week, month, year, and x amount of years, to provide us with different production trends. That is not even mentioning the knowledge of production already known by the workers themselves, it is not like we are entering some new pre-made society on Mars, we already live within it! Working backward, we can convert the production process from a monetary cycle to a labor hour cycle. The production of chairs requires the direct labor of workers and the indirect labor of the machinery and procurement of the raw materials like wood for instance. As we are not considering expansion at the moment, the machinery is already built, and the workers will only have to worry

[56] Marx 1891

about its maintenance and depreciation. The raw material, the wood, is a capital good that must be transferred to the chair factory from the factory or enterprise that harvests and processes the wood to be used in other facets of production. This transfer under capitalist production would take place through a monetary exchange; the chair factory would put in a purchase order for a set amount of wood. Therefore under socialist production, we only care about the quantity of the raw material required, not its price. This quantity may be measured by unit count or weight, and the amount required would correspond to how much of a product needs to be produced. The more chairs the factory needs to produce the more wood it will need to import from the wood processing plant. The wood processing plant finds its demand from the import orders of every industry that requires wood for production. These import orders will read as export orders to the processing plant. If only 10,000 units of wood can be harvested in a single production cycle, then the total export orders of that production cycle may not exceed 10,000 units of wood. If for instance, the processing plant receives a total export order of 12,000 units of wood, a system of budgeting or rationing must take place based upon societal importance. For example, imagine there are only two industries that require this wood for production; the construction sector requesting 6,000 units of wood to build housing, and the entertainment sector requesting 6,000 units of wood to build toys. Both orders cannot be fulfilled, so the production of either houses or toys must be lowered. Assuming both are equally in demand, the construction of housing would take precedence, as it is of greater societal importance than toys. If the budget or rationing debate centered around two vital industries, like supplying either housing or healthcare (meaning there are no fields of lesser need to be rationed from), the export orders should be filled evenly and the local economic chamber should immediately begin planning the expansion of the specific raw material processing industry. The value of the export order is calculated by SNLT to extract, process, and transport the order to the assigned import location. This value would be measured by both the processing plant and the transport enterprise. The G.I.C. theorizes how the inputs and outputs from enterprise to enterprise can be measured through general interbank recurring order (GIRO) transactions.

"... as soon as goods are brought into or out of the operational unit, it comes into contact with other operations... when one believes that goods can be transferred without charging, the receiving operational unit must 'charge' the incoming goods against the supplying operational unit... In capitalism, this is done either by direct payment in cash or... through a bank or giro office. In this case, it is merely a transfer or wiring. The payments are made without cash being put into circulation, it is a 'cashless' transfer... In the course of development, all settlements must be carried out by a central giro office... if all settlements are carried out via the giro, then we have here a complete record of the goods traffic through the entire society... We will see that the accounting terms - profit and loss, income and expenditure, assets, and liabilities - lose their validity under communism... The operational unit can speak of the quantity of goods which it has taken out of the company and which it transferred to society... if the operational unit purchases production means or raw materials from another operational unit. In this case, although it is established how many working hours were spent on this product by the society and although the general giro office transfers this amount to another account, it is by no means an 'expense', just as it is not an 'income' for the other operational unit. Again, this is merely a registration of the transport of goods... the terms should, therefore, be used:

Withdrawn from the Community: What comes into the operational unit as a means of production or as raw material, expressed in working hours. Also the consumption of consumption money [Labor Vouchers]

Transferred to the Community: The quantity of the delivered product."[57]

This registration of the transport of goods will be considerably easier today than it would have been in the 1930s because we can make these transfers electronically at the snap of a finger. Following the necessity of working

[57] G.I.C. 1930, Ch. 11 p. 185-189

backward to convert the capitalist production apparatus into the socialist production apparatus, we should begin these conversions from the bottom up - we should first calculate the labor hours required to produce capital goods, then the labor hours to transport those capital goods, then the labor hours to produce final goods, and finally, the labor hours to transport those final goods to the consumers. The capitalist mode of production may be temporarily maintained while these calculations are being made so that there is not a societal collapse due to a lack of production and distribution of goods.

Following past production trends, we will have a general idea of the amount of each product needed to produce. Drastic changes in population may require an estimated increase or decrease in production amount, respectively. This first production cycle will ultimately be the first trial and will have errors. Priority needs like food, water, and power should be given extra attention to ensure there are no shortages in vital sectors of the economy. The workers having now earned their respective labor vouchers will 'exchange' them for an equivalent amount of goods and services in objectified labor time. We can then measure the consumption rates of products to compare supply and demand, and recalibrate the production process by reallocating labor. For example, If Product A is in high demand with low supply, more labor be transferred to the production of Product A from Product B - a product with high supply and low demand, thus bringing both products closer to equilibrium - their cost of production. This would be best done at the level of the Industry Syndicates. Take the above example and substitute the products for chairs. If there is an industry dedicated to producing chairs, and it only produces two types: Chair A and Chair B, then following the example, the Industry Syndicates would inform the Enterprises that encompass them to allocate resources and labor away from the production of Chair B to the production of Chair A, helping to meet the demand of the consumers. As we look at the model further in the next section, prices need not be applied to the products themselves. Instead, the demand signal can simply be used to alter production while a form of rationing is used in the distribution of the products, ensuring their value remains true. Therefore, the trial and error method of Lange can be adopted without his reliance on the market, in a way that the errors will grow smaller and smaller as the system grows and works out its kinks.

Interestingly, the free market itself has shown that it can be incredibly inefficient in allocating resources to meet the needs of its population. The libertarian economists that follow the views of Mises and the Austrian school see the problem of modern capitalism - not with the free market, but with statism! They decry any influence of the government or state over the economy devolves capitalism into a 'crony' version of itself. They fail to understand that the state is just as natural a development of capitalism as the socialization of production and monopoly. The state is the being that uses its authority or violence to make property rights real! It is the tool that monopolies, the big bourgeois, use to secure and defend their positions over the market and their competition. We have seen the failure of the free market to meet needs on several occasions, most notably in the case of agriculture. Most developed nations, including the U.S., have subsidized their farming industries. Why do they do this? To better control the supply of food commodities. Food is not a plaything; it is a priority need that, if unavailable, leads to famine, starvation, and death. By subsidizing the farming industry, farmers are able to overproduce food without suffering the loss that would usually entail. The overproduction or surplus of food allows the price for food commodities to be both lower and stable. Putting aside how this can be used as a bludgeon against the third world, the state intervention in the agriculture market shows why Neo-liberal economics will always be more progressive than libertarian economics. No economic system has perfect knowledge and not everything will go according to plan. Accidents happen. Disasters strike. However, because the capitalist system chases after profit instead of fulfilling needs, it will send resources and human labor to build Funko Pops instead of building more houses for the homeless. Socialism chasing after the needs of its people may not be able to provide everyone a Funko Pop, nor will it try to until the priority needs of its population are met. Efficiency, here again, is shown to mean different things for both systems. Now, let us examine a more modern model of economic planning.

Towards a New Socialism:

In 1993, Paul Cockshott, an economist and computer scientist, alongside his friend and fellow economist Allin Cottrell, wrote a revolutionary book tackling the concept of modernized economic planning, titled *Towards a New Socialism*. Building off the theories and attempts of planned economies in the past, they proposed a bold vision for a new era of planning. A future that harnesses the power of the ever-innovating modern technology, specifically found in the capacity of the computing power of supercomputers to develop society into a post-capitalist era. The roots of this bright future they offer trace back to Marxian economics as they anchor their model in Marx's theory of value. The authors rightfully lambaste market socialists on the idea that their models do not go far enough to break from the capitalist mode of production. However, while Cockshott and Cottrell reject the traditional markets of the past and present, they advocate for a pseudo or artificial market. They do this in response to criticisms levied at old planned economies pertaining to a lack of responsiveness to consumer demand.[58] Their model makes a few distinctions between the artificial market and the traditional markets under capitalism. First and foremost, the artificial market relies on labor-time accounting as the basis for economic valuation instead of relying on the subjective valuations caused by market participation. Like most socialist models including our own, Cockshott and Cottrell advocate for products or goods and services to be valued at their cost of production or more specifically, the socially necessary labor time objectified in their production, therefore removing the profit motive from the equation. Secondly, the artificial market, while being subordinated to labor-time accounting, is also only in effect for consumer goods! The process of production, the inputs and outputs leading to the creation of final consumer goods, is completely controlled through the model's planning

[58] Cockshott and Cottrell 1993, p. 118

process. The prices in the artificial market are not that of a cash value or even necessarily change in price, they serve as a quick demand signal that allows for planners to rapidly alter production. The process of artificial pricing works as follows: Consumer goods are initially priced at their true value (market equilibrium) which is equivalent to the SNLT required to produce them. In regards to pricing they then write,

"...the actual prices (in labour tokens) of consumer goods will be set, as far as possible, at market-clearing levels. Suppose a particular item requires 10 hours of labour to produce. It will then be marked with a labour value of 10 hours, but if an excess demand for the item emerges when it is priced at 10 labour tokens, the price will be raised so as to (approximately) eliminate the excess demand. Suppose this price happens to be 12 labour tokens. This product then has a ratio of market-clearing price to labour-value of 12/10, or 1.20. The planners record this ratio for each consumer good. We would expect the ratio to vary from product to product, sometimes around 1.0, sometimes above (if the product is in strong demand), and sometimes below (if the product is relatively unpopular). The planners then follow this rule: Increase the target output of goods with a ratio in excess of 1.0, and reduce the target for goods with a ratio less than 1.0."[59]

The goal of the price system for consumer goods can therefore be understood as a possibly necessary method of discovery for the planning board to quickly learn of changes to demand in the interest of altering supply. These prices will easily allow planners to shift production to produce more of Product A, whose price is above its true value, from Product B, whose price is below its true value, thus bringing both closer to their true labor value or market equilibrium. Suppose one cannot budge on having these artificial prices in a socialist economy. In that case, they advocate that instead of raising the prices, they can solely be used as a demand signal while alternatively rationing the actual products to consumers.[60] Ultimately if we use an artificial market, price changes or rationing, measuring consumption

---

[59] Cockshott and Cottrell 1993, p. 118

[60] Cockshott and Cottrell 1993, 119-121

rates, and trial and error will always be the basis of measuring supply and demand under socialism. Following consumption rates instead of price signals would lead to essentially the same result, although there may be differences in efficiency in switching production from low-demand to high-demand products. Another factor to consider when planning is knowing the labor content of a good, which is both the direct and indirect labor objectified in a product. To discover a product's labor content, they write, *"to know the labor content of each good we need to know the labor content of several more."*[61] While a simple input-output table could be used to find the labor content of a specific product, the complexity skyrockets with scale to an impossible level. However, the authors argue that the impossibility brought about by scale only holds true to manual calculation, and that by harnessing the computing power of modern supercomputers, we can make the impossible possible![62] Their approach to this is using 'successive approximation,'

"...as a first approximation we ignore all inputs to the production process apart from directly expended labour. This gives us a first, approximate estimate of each product's labour value. It will be an underestimate because it ignores the non-labour inputs to the production process. To arrive at our second approximation we add in the non-labour inputs valued on the basis of the labour values computed in the first phase. This will get us one step closer to the true labour values. Repeated application of this process will give us the answer to the desired degree of accuracy. If about half the value of an average product is derived from direct labour inputs then each iteration round our approximation process will add one binary digit of significance to our answer. An answer correct to four significant decimal digits (which is better than the market can achieve) would require about 15 iterations round our approximation process. The time order complexity of this algorithm is proportional to the number of products times the average number of inputs per product, times the desired accuracy of the result in

[61] Cockshott and Cottrell 1993, p. 53

[62] Cockshott and Cottrell 1993, p. 55

digits. Assume 106 products each requiring on average 1000 inputs. This requires 109 steps per iteration. If each of these steps requires perhaps 10 arithmetic operations then each iteration would require some 10 billion arithmetic operations. Experience with the use of such algorithms teaches us that less than 20 iterations are required to achieve accurate results. On our previous assumptions about server performance in the year 2000 this could be computed on a fast machine in a couple of seconds"[63]

Furthermore, Cockshott and Cottrell's model advocates for a centralized planning committee that again utilizes the computing power of modern supercomputers to plan the economy. We briefly break from their model here, as we prefer a more multi-level or decentralized approach to planning through our system of federated councils. This multi-level approach is beneficial in a few ways. First, it allows for more people to have access to the economy's planning which will help avoid crucial errors and allow for a more democratic structure of the economy. Second, it allows for more accurate and concise planning at the local and state levels of the economy; and third, it allows planners better access to knowledge of the needs of the people at the local and state levels. Putting aside the debate over centralization, Cockshott and Cottrell's model also adds three different types of planning that can be done: Macroeconomic, Strategic, and Detailed planning.

Macroeconomic planning deals with the overall breakdown of total labor time. It answers general questions of where this total labor is distributed to whether it be maintaining social services or producing consumer goods, and how much of the total labor is necessary to use because again the goal of socialism is using only the labor that is socially necessary while leaving the workers with as much surplus of leisure time as possible.[64] Strategic planning deals with 'the changing industrial structure of the economy.' This includes deciding which industries or sectors to invest in further developing and which to phase out, considering environmental impact, and planning the

[63] Cockshott and Cottrell 1993, p. 57-58

[64] Cockshott and Cottrell 1993, p. 66

distribution of goods and services.[65] Detailed planning covers the 'precise allocation of resources' deciding what, where, and how goods are produced or the allocation of inputs.[66] We will be adapting portions of these great authors' model into our own, but for a more in-depth understanding of the types of planning, mathematical formulas, and Cockshott and Cottrell's model in general, we recommend you read *Towards a New Socialism* for yourself.

Detailed Planning:

The process of detailed planning deals with the precise allocation of resources. This process has been more thoroughly explained in the previous sections on the basics of planning. While all levels of the economy would obviously be involved with detailed planning, the levels where it will be most prominent are the individual enterprises, their syndicates, and the local economic chambers. The enterprises are the actual economic units that produce. They extract and process resources, use machinery, and produce and distribute all goods - intermediate or final. The syndicates and economic chambers are just the methods of organizing these individual enterprises and workers into one united whole. The first element of detailed planning is to estimate the total types and quantities of final goods that must be produced to meet societal needs. From there, the industries can work backward and account for the types and quantities of intermediate goods that will be needed to produce the desired number of final goods. If the necessary amount of intermediate goods can be produced then the production process can begin, however, if resources are scarce, then budgeting or rationing resources to lines of production of higher societal importance must be done. Detailed planning therefore includes how the local economies allocate their available means of production, raw materials, and human labor time. Cockshott and Cottrell offer ways that this planning can be made more

[65] Cockshott and Cottrell 1993, p. 69

[66] Cockshott and Cottrell 1993, p. 67

efficient through computerization, which the reader may want to read into further.

Strategic Planning:

Strategic planning deals with long-term economic planning. Whereas detailed planning focuses on the immediate allocation of resources for production, strategic planning deals with allocating resources to produce projects that will take several years to finish. Some types of these projects might include the construction of housing, ports (air and sea), railways, bridges, power plants, etc. Allocating resources to the construction of these products requires that the allocation of resources to the immediate/current production cycle be reduced. As those resources cannot be taken away from maintaining social services, the population must bare the bane of this deduction in resources by having less consumer goods be produced and the temporary lowering of the value of their labor vouchers while the project is under construction. There is not an inherent difference in the societal importance of building a new railway as opposed to a new seaport that could be compared to come to a decision. The choice between which project to pursue must be decided through debate and democratic decision-making by the State Economic Chambers. If the SEC agrees upon creating a new railroad across the state, it must then design the production plan for the railroad by accounting for the total labor hours required for production and the projected number of years construction will take to complete. There are not enough resources for every special project to be started at once, nor for every state to start these projects simultaneously. Therefore, the National Economic Chamber will collectively green-light certain special projects and reject or postpone others.

Macroeconomic Planning:

The macroeconomic planning of the economy will be handled by the National Economic Chamber (NEC). As it covers the broad view of the national economy and the distribution of total resources and labor, the NEC will make policy decisions that have broad sweeping effects on all levels of the economy. We briefly discussed how the NEC will hear special project plans from the SECs and approve or deny them, but there are other policy decisions and responsibilities the NEC will have to make and uphold. For example, it must maintain social services (N.S.S.A.) by allocating sufficient resources and labor away from the production of consumer goods, it must maintain the emergency fund to deal with pandemics or natural disasters by keeping a certain amount of resources and labor in reserve, and it must set the general rule for economic expansion. On top of these, it will have to balance policy decisions and their effects on the economy, like environmentalist policies for example. Switching from gas to electric cars alters production times and resource allocation, pursuing the mass expansion of railways will alter the speed of transporting raw materials and final goods, and pursuing a policy of vertical housing over horizontal housing will affect the layouts of cities which carries its own domino effects. It should be noted that although we have adapted these terms from Cockshott and Cottrell's model, our uses of these different types of planning have vast differences, and the reader should not assume to understand their model without reading it for themselves.

We mentioned the general rule of economic expansion, which can be better explained by the G.I.C.,

"An expanding operational unit not only needs to replenish its worn parts and raw materials but in addition, it needs to absorb more production resources and raw materials. However… the entire social product has already been consumed. Therefore, it is necessary to make additional efforts for expansion. For example, the working time would have to be extended by 5 hours per week, which would be used exclusively for the expansion of the operational unit. In other words, we cannot exploit the 'full yield of our work', but must 'save' part of it. The expansion… is… always at the expense of social consumption. The speed of expansion… determines how much product is left for consumption… The third rule to be added is a fixed rule for the extension of the operational unit… Operational Organizations…

should... have the right to expand their stocks... However, the expansion of the operational unit cannot take place arbitrarily... For example, congress can stipulate that the operational unit may not be expanded by more than 10% of the means of production and raw materials. This simple decision will then regulate the entire economic life as far as the expansion of the operational unit is concerned... It is clear, however, that not every operational organization will have to exercise its right to expand its activities, as several sectors will be able to meet all requests. On the other hand there are other industries that are still far from being able to meet their needs for the time being. Such industries require a far greater expansion than 10%... however, they cannot go beyond the general requirement, as this could lead to supply problems. However... several operational units [could] transfer their rights of expansion to such 'needy' industries, thus providing them with a larger expansion fund."[67]

The setting of the general rule for expansion, or as their example stated a 10% limit, would be the responsibility of the NEC, which is of course made up of worker representatives of every industry and state of the nation.

Railway Construction Problem:

Proponents of the ECP and knowledge problem often use the railway construction problem as an example of why socialism and specifically central planning will not work, or at least why they are inefficient as compared to capitalist free markets. The problem asks, how can society build a railroad between two cities with a mountain between them under socialist production? How can it decide between using steel or some other metal without market prices telling us their worth and measuring their demand? And finally, how can it decide to go through the mountain or around the mountain?

Under the free market, the prices of metals can be compared to one another. For example, while vibranium may be stronger and more durable

[67] G.I.C. 1930, Ch. 13 p. 217-222

than steel, the fact that it is incredibly rare and hard to process can be easily seen by construction planners by noting the drastic price difference between vibranium and steel, which is much more widely available. The argument at the time was that socialist planners having total control over prices would be unable to effectively discover these differences necessary to decide on a metal, because the prices would have no real meaning! Under our model, the socialist planners do not control the prices of the metals because there are no prices to control. The 'price' of a metal is its cost of production measured in social labor time, otherwise known as its value. The value of different metals can be compared just as prices would be under the market. If vibranium takes four times as many labor hours to produce an equivalent amount of steel, then the cost-effectiveness of steel should be self-evident for all to see! Building through the mountain and around the mountain raises a different concern, this one pertains to the allocation of skilled versus unskilled labor. To go through the mountain requires less steel for construction and thus less unskilled labor, but instead calls for more skilled labor from engineers who have the knowledge needed to safely tunnel through the mountain. Going around the mountain requires the inverse, as it will require more steel for construction and more unskilled labor to complete the project in the projected amount of time. Putting aside local concerns that may influence the decision - a community protest, environmental concerns, problems of cultural significance, etc. - which could be heard through community hearings, these decisions will still always be made on a case-by-case basis based on the general availability of skilled and unskilled labor. If the total allotment of unskilled labor is stressed entirely in producing and maintaining society's priority needs, then the goal would be to allocate the minimum amount of unskilled labor away from those needs as possible. On the other hand, if a good sum of the total allotment of unskilled labor is set to produce less prioritized goods (like entertainment or luxury cars) while the available skilled labor of engineers is relatively scarce due to prior allocation to other projects, then planners can comfortably allocate more unskilled labor to the railway project. If the availability of both skilled and unskilled labor is relatively equal, then planners should take into account future projections of both groups. For example, if there are many projects in the pipeline requiring skilled labor, planners may opt to go around the mountain. However, if a large group of engineers is about to be certified through graduation, the planners may opt to go through the mountain knowing more skilled labor will be able to be allocated to the project over time.

Following the method of multi-level planning, the SEC would craft the strategic plan for the railway project - executed by consulting with the LECs of the two cities the railway will run between, along with the state's engineering, construction, and manufacturing industries - thus collecting valuable information from all facets of the construction of the project. Once agreed upon by the SEC, the plan would be submitted to the NEC where the state's representatives would argue for its approval on behalf of the SEC. The NEC would review all the states' special projects and either approve, deny, or postpone them for later discussion. In this way, the general process of starting the construction of a railway under socialist production can be seen through the balancing of total labor hours away from consumer consumption to project construction, and the balancing of skilled and unskilled labor.

Planning Conclusion:

Once the basic measures of the planning system modeled above are implemented and the workers united through federated workers' councils directly and collectively control the economic power of their society, socialism will have at last been realized. For these workers' councils do not fall into the same pit trap as the syndicates and cooperatives who resign themselves to only make concessions to the capitalist system. No, the workers' councils represent the reunion or association of free and equal producers that Marxian socialism demands. Private property of both the individual and of the class has been abolished, alongside commodity production, wage labor, surplus extraction, and the value form that drove them all. Society no longer produces for profit, but to meet the needs of society along a common plan that is designed through cooperation at multiple levels. Through the use of detailed accounting, value measured through socially necessary labor time, digital labor vouchers, consumer satisfaction surveys, modern computation power, and the tracking of consumption rates to watch supply and demand and consumer trends, this multi-level approach makes a central decentralized planned economy possible. At this stage with the world still struggling with the scarcity of resources, society will operate from each according to their ability, to each according to their contribution after the necessary deductions for the maintenance of society and the public works.[68]

It's important to remember that as socialist society is born out of capitalist production, we do not lose the knowledge gained over its history. Already established businesses keep records of their production (especially their most recent production) as well as the sale or distribution of their goods and services. At the start of the socialist economy, these previous production runs can be used to predict supply and demand in the short run until more accurate consumption data and trends can be established. And while it is true that supply and demand influence the price of goods and weed out unwanted businesses, this isn't particularly unique to a free market system. For example, under a socialist economy, a business's product may be unwanted, leaving society two choices: continue production even though its output has been deemed socially unnecessary, or transform the 'business' to produce a new output. Under capitalism, this transformation is the shutting down of the business and the sale (or more often, rent) to a new prospecting capitalist who will continue the cycle. Under socialism, that transformation is overseen and agreed upon by a collective of people. The free market is a filter system, not a magical cure for inefficient production and so socialism will deal with inefficient production in externally similar yet internally different ways as is with most changes between the two.

---

[68] Marx 1891

II

On Revolution

3

Critique of American Bourgeois Democracy

As the constant culture wars continue to rage on, the thin rubber band of the United States political spectrum is being stretched to its limits. It's important to note that these culture wars are the fundamental weld that holds our current political duopoly together. In a sort of symbiotic show of controlled opposition, the Democrat and Republican parties can uphold the same economic system and foreign policy that suppresses the standard of living of their citizens and people all around the globe in exchange for an unending expansion of wealth and power for the class they truly serve, the bourgeois. As stated before, however, the two parties clash on cultural issues. Put simply, the Democrats are 'progressive' and Republicans are 'conservative,' and as with all groups there is overlap; there are Democrats who strongly believe in traditional or religious values, and there are Republicans who are for the most part 'socially liberal' yet vote Republican because they insist it is best for their pocketbook.

This cultural divide is by design. It allows for these two parties to appear as if they are on polar opposite ends of the political spectrum when in reality, they are both pushing further and further to the right. The purpose of this design is straightforward; if to the general public, two right-leaning parties appear as left versus right, the voters have the veil of democracy pulled over their eyes. They believe their vote carries the political power to bring about change, but it doesn't in any meaningful capacity. All their vote can do is affect the cultural policy of our country for the next four years, which in the world of politics is not often enough time to make any truly damaging changes. However, when over time that rubber band of the Overton window keeps pulling to the right, real damage to our society can be done. Why? Because these policy changes do not magically disappear at the end of presidential terms, no, the shift right has been a long game that has been played in our faces and behind the curtains of government and business. It brews under the surface while people argue not about economic issues, but rather if adding gay or minority characters to movies and television is 'woke.' The public narrative is purposely drawn away from economic issues, even when talked about on the news it is in simple terms like "minimum wage increase mean print more money, print more money mean inflation, inflation bad!" The news media distributes basic economic talking points to its audience and then spends the rest of the news cycle tackling cultural issues. And every election cycle when people raise honest concerns about the economy and social programs, the Democratic party and their mindless voters will echo the same statement, "We can get to that after we win this extremely important election, you have to vote for the lesser of two evils!

The Lesser of Two Evils:

To delve deeper into the issue of the lesser of two evils, we must examine both evils and how they work to indoctrinate the masses into wholeheartedly supporting a false duopoly. To analyze the indoctrination done by the Democratic Party, we must recognize in what form it is coming from and for what purpose it serves. If you ask a Republican their thoughts on the Democratic Party, they will tell you all about how they're a part of the establishment or in their words the 'swamp' that is Washington D.C. And in that regard, they are not wrong! However, in recognizing the faults of the Democratic Party, many Republican voters will ignore any faults on their side as long as their vote serves a role in "draining the swamp!" This blind faith in voting for "anti-establishment" politicians leads them headstrong further down the path of right-wing politics as we will get into later. Republican politicians and political commentators capitalize off of this misguided belief that they are somehow not a part of the same establishment and continuously push the narrative that their opposition, the Democratic Party, has been taken over and controlled by "radical left Marxists." This would be a great thing if it were true, but sadly it is not. The easiest way to tell this is a bald-faced lie is to look at the numbers. The group of politicians that Republicans decry as "radical Marxists" the most is The Squad, which consists of eight members; the four founders, Alexandria Ocasio-Cortez, Rashida Tlaib, Ilhan Omar, and Ayanna Pressley; and the four subsequent members, Jamal Bowman, Cori Bush, Greg Casar, and Summer Lee.[69] That is eight House Representatives! These eight are correctly labeled the left-wing of the Democratic Party, but that is only because they are in the United States. On a true political spectrum, these politicians fall closer to the center or slightly to the left, but they are by no means radical. And while they may agree on a lot socially with true leftists, that doesn't make them Marxists, nor Socialists for that matter. But, if for the sake of argument, we assume these eight politicians graduated from Karl Marx University and are advocating for Communism on the house floor; that would set the balance of power in the house to four hundred and twenty-seven capitalist politicians to eight communist politicians. And in the Senate, the numbers are even weaker with a balance of ninety-nine capitalists to one 'socialist,' that one being Bernie Sanders. This would leave us with a total of five hundred and twenty-six pro-capitalist politicians to nine anti-capitalist politicians. The power is not exactly in the hands of the left then, is it?

As stated in the opening critique, this is where the Democratic Party's indoctrination is held. They have convinced the public that they are the

[69] As of the publishing of the 2nd Edition, Jamal Bowman and Cori Bush have both been ousted from office.

representatives of the left in America when in reality they uphold the same economic systems as their arch-nemesis, the Republicans. In a political system where Bernie Sanders is considered a far-left socialist, or where healthcare for all is a radical idea, said system is centered on right-wing ideals. In reality, the Republican Party is sitting on the far right, centrists take up the middle of the right, and the Democratic Party follows right behind them. If our political spectrum was a seesaw, the right side would be firmly pressed into the dirt because there is no counterweight on the other side!

An America divided between a capitalist and anti-capitalist party would be cause for celebration, but that is not the reality we live in. We have to contend with the fact that the two biggest parties in America share the same right-wing economic ideals, and therefore form a pseudo-duopoly. As mentioned before, the tool the Democrats use to uphold their standing as the only oppositional force against the Republican Party is the culture war. The gist of it is this - every social victory progressives win emboldens the far-right elements in our country, doesn't address the economic issues caused by our capitalist system, and strengthens the Democratic Party's stance as the bastion and protector of left-wing ideals. That is not to say we need to stop fighting for social victories, quite the opposite actually. The battles we win embolden our side too, protecting people's rights, bodily autonomy, and identities, is of extreme importance in creating a better world, but when we see winning these social battles as winning culture wars, we are setting ourselves up to be unprepared when the real war inevitably comes; the war over the capitalist system. With every social victory, the Democratic Party gets to claim as its own, the more it solidifies itself as the only defense against the far right. But as we know, the current Democratic Party is incapable of standing up to far-right politics in the long run. For one, the party supports and is enriched by the current economic system, and without a solidified threat from the left like Donald Trump and his rock-solid base are to the Republicans, the Democrats are free to steadily keep trudging further and further right to appeal to centrist voters. Why? Because they know the 'progressive' left will never pick the Republicans over them because of the influence of the lesser of two evils argument. Their platform and politicians vocally support progressive and leftist ideas like decommodifying healthcare, solving the homeless crisis, police and prison reforms, and an expansion of rehabilitation facilities, because these ideas are popular with a lot of the general public. But when it comes time to vote and a progressive candidate is running like Bernie Sanders, we hear the same argument every time, "the Republicans are running the reincarnation of Hitler, these progressive policies are too radical to secure the centrist vote, so we need to vote for this politician who will uphold the status quo!" Progressive politicians and policies are pushed off every election cycle until the big bad is defeated. The lesser of two evils! It's two sides of the same coin, it doesn't matter which side lands face-up because the outcome is the same. It is a game with no stakes. Voting for the lesser evil accomplishes short-term cultural goals. Still, it does nothing to prevent the gradual pull to the right and that is the fundamental problem with our pseudo-duopoly![70]

Indoctrination:

---

[70] The reader should note that lesser evilism isn't a lie per se, if it were patently false then it wouldn't be the powerful tool that it is today. The Democrats are marginally better than the Republicans on many issues (although being better than the Republicans on an issue is a bar even an infant baby could clear), and the individual members of these parties are not a part of some shadowy cabal, rubbing their hands together as they scheme how to uphold the pseudo-duopoly. Again, the problem is systemic and institutionalized. Both parties uphold the same economic system that demands inequality and fosters division. Though the majority of the Democrats are tremendously better on social issues like LGBTQ+ rights, minority protections, and, in some cases, defending existing welfare programs, their ideology also demands they continue the policy of 'American Exceptionalism' and defend our role as the global superpower. It is this policy that is driving unequal development through trade around the world and demands that we keep large regions of the world destabilized to slow down and reverse economic and social development to prolong our reign as the top dog. So while yes, the Democrats are the lesser evil, the basis of their ideology and the pseudo-duopoly demands that they continue down a path that is constantly increasing radicalization domestically and internationally while continuing to propagate the system of imperialism abroad.

Many ideologues on the Republican side preach that "Leftist" Democrats have slithered their way into all branches of education from elementary schools to universities to instill "Marxist" values into the heads of children, or as they put it simply "indoctrinating the children with woke ideology." This is absolute nonsense for the sole reason that the Democratic party is neither leftist nor Marxist by any conceivable definition; one of, if not the furthest left member of their party is an old man whose main policy is free healthcare and education for all - basic policies in a lot of European nations! No, the Democrat's indoctrination has nothing to do with Marxism, it has everything to do with convincing their voters that they are left of center. As covered earlier, the basic foundation of the modern-day Democratic party is to serve as a counterbalance to the Republicans and yet they haven't balanced anything at all! All they have done is drag us along for the ride, and the ride will not end by "voting blue no matter who!" or voting for the lesser evil. Unless a wave of class consciousness crashes upon the majority of Americans, lifting the veil from their heads and leading to the establishment of a political party or class that opposes the monopoly on political and economic power held by the establishment parties - the only way this ride ends is by nosediving off a cliff! Either way, there will likely be bloodshed so don't shake your head at the word revolution like it is just a violent term found in history books. The indoctrination by the Democrats is no doubt bad and a dangerous hindrance to a better future, but it is typical and unevolving for the most part. It is what is going on with the Republican party and their ideologues that is such a drastic step in a relatively short amount of time that makes us think we are facing some of the final battlegrounds of the culture wars before these battles devolve from words to fists.

The war of words hasn't been overall competitive because 'progressives' metaphorically own the marketplace of ideas. After all, Republicans have been consistently losing every culture war they fight because most people in this country are indeed socially liberal. For example, as of 2021 over 70% of Americans support marriage equality, around 55% identify as pro-choice, and approximately 70% support the legalization of marijuana[71] - a small step for future prison reform. Battles still rage on across the country over issues like these along with a plethora of others, one of the most notable being gun control which is often used by the Republicans as a scare tactic to rile their base to the polls. To more 'moderate' politicians, these battles are based on their religious and traditional values, so they truly believe in their cause which is somewhat admirable; for most however, it is all about money. They collect checks from special interest groups to push agendas they do not know or care about, and for those on the far right, these cultural battles are nothing but a means to an end. They don't need to win the culture wars, they just need society to be socially progressive enough to strengthen their grip on their base, because as we can see from history you don't need a majority of the group to take it over; a strong-armed, militant, minority can oust a liberal bourgeois majority with ease. In the 1932 German Presidential Election Hitler didn't garner the majority support of the nation - he only received 37% of the national vote. Hindenburg won with 53% of the vote, but this didn't stop him from allying with Hitler and the Nazi party a year later to deal with the rising threat of the Communists. In January of 1933, Hindenburg appointed Adolf Hitler the Chancellor of Germany, handing him the keys to the kingdom! Voting for the lesser evil didn't stop the Nazi party because through strong-armed militancy, they enacted their policies without having to go through electoral means. The Nazis in Germany were not some extraterrestrial force. They were bred out of decaying liberal bourgeois societies in direct antagonism to the rise of socialist and or communist movements. They seized power in Italy, Germany, Spain, and the many puppet governments installed during the conquest of the Second World War. And this fascist movement did not die with Hitler's suicide or Mussolini's

---

[71] McCarthy, Saad, Gallup.com: 2021

While this data does suggest the majority of Americans are more 'socially liberal,' as the right wing of the conservative party falls further and further into reactionary politics, so will its base. It seems likely that within the next decade, this growth in reactionism will lead to a more radical conservatism amongst half the population.

execution. At the end of the war, some fascists were tried and executed, others were allowed to immediately resume governmental duties in East Germany, and some were even entered into witness protection programs of the highest order, serving liberal bourgeois governments. Because at the end of the day, liberalism and fascism are not truly opposing ideologies for they are made from the same class and serve near identical interests. The liberals just masquerade their oppression, imperialism, and genocide behind democracy and laws they themselves wrote. The oppression of liberalism will always lead to a rise of socialist movements amongst the masses, and with that comes the rise of reactionaries, the fascists. It is a cycle we as a species will be doomed to repeat until the socialist movement achieves total victory, which cannot be done at the ballot box but only through the armed revolutionary struggle of the international proletariat! A study out of Princeton University by Professors Martin Gilens and Benjamin Page claims that the U.S. is no longer a democracy, but rather an oligarchy![72] But the truth is even worse, that's what we've always been!

Our elected representatives do not uphold the preferred policies of their constituents because they do not need to! Their positions are secured by the funding of large donors and super PACs, not the petty donations made by those they represent, and so it is in the politician's best interest to adhere to the whims of their puppet master. Your vote will change nothing because it means nothing. You choose between two liars playing a game of deception with the stakes being the livelihood of an entire population! You get to fight tooth and nail with your coworkers and family at Thanksgiving over cultural issues while the real policy that defines the nation is handled swiftly behind closed doors - not by politicians, but once again by their masters, the owners of big capital! You elect the public representative of corporate interest and the Commander-in-Chief of the largest terrorist organization in the modern world! It does not matter if you elect the reincarnation of Jesus Christ the president of the U.S., the job entails being the mascot of the biggest empire this world has ever known, and with that comes the job of

[72] Gilens and Page, 2014

propping up corporate interests and embracing the role of a war criminal. There are no saints or sinners when it comes to bourgeois politics, only stooges, so ask yourself what that makes you for being so entangled in its web!

Conclusion:

You may conclude from our analysis of American bourgeois democracy that we claim the Republican and Democratic parties to be one and the same. Following our bashing of lesser evilism, you might also conclude that we take a hard line on electoralism. The truth, however, is much more complicated. The American political duopoly has functioned on a good cop bad cop basis for much of the countries history. The bad cop being hardline conservatism masked in star-spangled patriotism, the cop that kicks you in the nuts and tells you to get up on your own and thank him for it. When you make it back to your feet, the good cop will pat you on the shoulder and scold the bad cop under his breath, he will tell you they are not all like that, and then he will slap the cuffs on you and shove you into the back of his police car. Both cops are paid by the same institutions and uphold the same laws, but you prefer to deal with the good cop because at least he won't kick you in the nuts.

The problem we face now, however, is that this political foundation has radically shifted due to its own nature. Because the people prefer to deal with the good cop to escape the brutality of the bad cop, they never stop to question the system that is incarcerating them. This sense of invulnerability from actual consequences allows the bad cop to increase his brutality. To smack the people with his baton and believe himself to be above the law. And the more brutal the bad cop becomes, the less nice the good cop has to be for the people to still flock to him for protection from the bad cop. The answer again, is that the people must step back and question the system, its institutions, and its laws; but the sad truth is that they cannot do this because society has conditioned them not to see the duality of the problem. There are of course those who when confronted by the good and bad cops kick them both in the nuts. They see both cops for what they truly are - agents of oligarchy - and they run for their freedom, but they hit a wall. They get up and dust themselves off and run the other direction and hit another wall, and another, until finally they smack right into the iron bars of the cell door. Through the bars they see other people being arrested and they shake those iron bars, screaming to the people to run for their freedom. Some listen. Others do not. In the end they all end up in the same place, behind those cold iron bars.

The point of that long-winded analogy is to say the solution to destroying the American bourgeois democracy is not in answering the question of whether to participate in electoralism or not. Neither is it shouting into the void for a revolution where there are quite literally no conditions or foundations for one to take place. The key to escaping American bourgeois democracy is to recognize that it is a prison. It is not just a good cop, a bad cop, and a cell; but an army of cops and an endless row of cells, gates, and guns that keep you from reaching the road to freedom. Electoralism is just one of the many obstacles the working class will have to face.

The first point of order is to recognize that while the lesser evilism strategy is still in effect, the neoliberal status quo has lost containment. As the policy continued to further radicalize the Republican Party, it is only natural that we are now in the midst of a party collapse. This would have always been the natural conclusion of the lesser-evil policy, however, the process was expedited by the election of Barack Obama, the first black president. As we explained earlier, with every 'culture war' won by progressives, the conservatives become more militant and more radicalized. Following what was a relatively standard presidency of neoliberal capitalism, large deportations, and imperial foreign policy including terrorism in the Middle East via drone striking campaigns; conservatives had to punish the status quo. Did they have to punish it for any of the items we listed? Of course not, they had to make America great again! Back to the time where capitalism, imperialism, and law and order were directed by white men. The 2016 election of Donald Trump was a whitewashing of the country. However, we should note that neither the Democratic or Republican parties wanted

Trump to be the nominee let alone the president. He was and is a monkey wrench in the foundation of the pseudo-duopoly, although he himself is relatively unimportant. Donald Trump is a celebrity narcissist, headline chaser with the vocabulary of a grade school child. However, that vocabulary and his quite excellent comedic timing and charm somehow make him - a multi-billionaire real estate mogul from NYC - relatable to the blue-collar conservative voter. As a candidate, he comes off as brash and non-politically correct. His ideas and policies are not relevant because he is not campaigning on real issues, but instead running a spectacle that appeals to the emotion of the conservative voter. He is a modern-day Bonapartist, not a military officer, but most definitely an officer of the capitalist class seeking to restore the nation to its former glory through law, order, and nationalism.

The key to Trump securing control of the Republican Party was to, in 2016, slowly but surely paint his inter party and outer party opposition equally as the enemy of the people. And as he worked his way down the debate stage, correctly demonstrating to the public that these candidates did not represent their interests but the 'states' interests, his following began to grow, and so to did his cult of personality. While he is a part of the capitalist class he operates as an existential threat to the neoliberal order of capitalism, and so he is a threat to both the Democratic and Republican parties that represent the status quo. Trump and the MAGA movement represent a threat to the status quo from the position of the reactionary right, embodying the form of ill-defined political and economic ultranationalism/populism; making him and his movements automatically the enemy of the socialists and communists.

It should be remembered that if the scale was reversed and the socialists were an existential threat to the neoliberal order of capitalism, then the socialists would also be attacked like Trump and his movement; however, this by no means argues they should form a 'the enemy of my enemy is my friend' alliance. There is not a current leftist base strong enough to consider accelerationism, because if that were to happen today we would merely be signing our own death certificates. The Republican Party has been conquered from within its own ranks because the 'messiah' has returned and solidified that the voting base answers to him and not the man who swings the gavel. And so the establishment republicans are left with a choice, bend the knee or resign into obscurity. We see now that the pseudo-duopoly has in actual fact become a true duopoly.

While it is true both parties still represent the capitalist mode of production, the capitalist class itself is divided between neoliberalism and reactionary conservatism. Neoliberalism being the status quo and reactionary conservatism representing certain big capitalists and their strongest soldiers - the petty-bourgeois small business owners. The threshold or point of no return has long since been passed. When 'fascism' is on the ballot it is far too late to vote it out. So while the claim of our democracy being at stake is false from our understanding of democracy, it is true for current bourgeois democracy. We must deal with the fact that neoliberalism has strangled any semblance of a socialist movement or even the standard new deal democrat from holding power. We must deal with the fact that the victory of the Citizens United case in the Supreme Court has ensured the security of the American Oligarchy by allowing corporations or 'superPACs' to fund and influence political campaigns and policy, which is even more reason as to why our government works in the interest of corporations instead of the people! We must deal with the fact that the vast majority of Americans are indoctrinated or have been manufactured to consent to the rule of the oligarchs without even knowing they are doing it. And we must deal with the fact that there is currently seemingly no revolutionary potential in the United States.

4

On Fascism & Trumpism

Introduction:

Throughout these essays, we have used the term fascist in an analysis of both historical fascist movements and the contemporary rise of far-right political movements around the world. While it is necessary to make comparisons to the 'othering' or the dehumanization of marginalized groups to stir up radicalization amongst one's base, that in and of itself is not fascism. Too often, the term fascist is used as a method of scapegoating the negative effects wrought by the internal contradictions of liberal capitalism. People rightfully abhor the barbaric crimes against humanity perpetrated by Adolf Hitler and the Nazis - and Mussolini to a lesser extent - but then lay a blind eye to the horrific atrocities committed by the colonial empires across Asia and Africa throughout the Victorian Era. All of these events pack volumes of books with stories of rape, pillage, and genocide, but the former is looked back on as humanity's greatest evil and the latter as the ugly necessity of history. Although it is impossible to talk about WW2 without mentioning the Holocaust, it is also necessary to understand that the Second World War did not break out over the systematic and industrialized genocide of the Jewish people. Instead, like the First World War, WW2 was a war between imperial powers.

On Fascism:

Following the end of WW1, Germany ceded domestic territory to France, dispossessed of its colonies in Africa, Asia, and the Pacific, and faced an enormous recession following the Treaty of Versailles; and Italy, having agreed to the Pact of London in 1915, joined the war on the side of the Entente in return for large swathes of land, was subsequently denied much of that land at the peace conference. Germany's economic turmoil and Italy's political dissatisfaction laid the groundwork for the rise of Fascism in reaction to the increased unrest of the working class and the quickly organizing socialist movements. While Hitler had just established himself as the leader of the Nazi party in 1921, Mussolini would be preparing his March on Rome just one year later, ending with King Victor Emmanuel III naming him the Prime Minister of Italy. Amadeo Bordiga, a man who lived and organized socialist revolutionaries during the rise of the Fascists in Italy, stood before the Communist Party of Italy in 1922 and delivered a speech on his report of the Fascist movement in the country,

"Fascism based itself on the overall situation: the steadily growing discontent of all petty-bourgeois layers, the small merchants, the small landholders, the discharged soldiers, and the former officers, who, after the role they had played in the war, were disappointed by their current status. All these elements were utilised, organised, and formed up into contingents. And then this movement tackled the task of destroying the power of Red organisations in the Italian countryside...

Fascism cannot be described as an independent movement of any specific sector of the bourgeoisie... In reality fascism is a large and unified movement of the ruling class, capable of turning to its advantage and making use of every means and all particular and local interests of different groups of agricultural and industrial employers... All interests are welded together in a so-called national interest. We know well what such national unity means: the absolute and counter-revolutionary preservation of the bourgeois state and its institutions. The big capitalists of industry, the banks, commerce, and the big landowners, have a natural interest in the founding of an organisation of struggle that defends their offensive against working people. But the third factor also plays a very important role in constituting fascist power. In order to create an illegal reactionary organisation beside the state, forces must be recruited that are different from those that the high ruling class can find in its own social milieu. This is achieved by turning to the layers of the middle class that we have mentioned and advocating their interests, in order to ensnare them. That is what fascism set out to do, and it must be admitted that they succeeded. It recruited forces from the layers that are closest to the proletariat among those discontented because of the war, among petty bourgeois, middle-level bourgeois, merchants and traders, and above all among intellectual bourgeois youth. In joining up with fascism, they find again the energy to lift themselves morally and cloak themselves in the toga of combating the proletarian movement, achieving an exalted patriotism in the interests of Italian imperialism"

While Mussolini was struggling to subdue Ethiopia in hopes of catching up with the rest of the European colonists in snatching a piece of Africa, Hitler solidified his rule over the German state, suppressed the opposition, rearmed the military, and was ready to restore Germany to the height of its imperial power - or in other words, to establish the Third Reich.[73] However, the collapse of the Second Reich left the Germans handicapped regarding establishing new imperial outposts, as Africa had been carved up among the British, French, Portuguese, and Belgians, Japan had seized their Pacific islands, and the Middle East was under the dominion of the British and French. German nationalism had been stoked, 'Bolshevism' and the 'Jewry' had been demonized, the war machine was hungry, and their neighbors were unprepared and too busy dealing with the great depression and the uptick of nationalism in the colonies. The dispossessed were coming not for their lost territories or tiny parcels of uncolonized land; they were coming for the possessions of those who dismantled their empire, their Reich.

Ultranationalism, authoritarianism, militarism, economic centralization,

[73] The First Reich relates to the Holy Roman Empire, and the Second Reich relates to the German Empire

and the dehumanization of the 'other' are certainly traits of fascist regimes, but they are not particularly unique to them. It is often ideological liberals who classify these traits as fascist individually or collectively, completely ignoring the economic axis on which political philosophy rests. The reason for this is their lack of a deep class analysis, leading them to believe that we are at the end of history and that capitalism is the only 'true' or final mode of production. Because of this, excuses must be made to differentiate fascism from 'free market' capitalism and liberalism - Hitler must be crucified. Nailed to the cross to atone for the sins committed in the name of liberalism.

Ultranationalism, the exaltation of one nation above another, is just as applicable to 'American Exceptionalism' as it is to Nazi Germany. Is the United States unique? Not particularly. It is no doubt a powerhouse rich with natural resources and population, but it is still bound to class struggle, as is every other nation on Earth. Even its status as a powerhouse cannot be separated from its ultranationalistic foundations, as its borders were not preordained by nature. The conquering of the United States - Manifest Destiny - was only possible through the genocide, subjugation, and attempted assimilation of millions of natives. The settling of the original thirteen colonies and the construction of the nation's early economy were not possible without the enslavement of Africans stolen from their communities and cultures and subjugated to the whims of their white masters. The act of destroying the cultures of the enslaved created a new nationality, a Black nationality unique to America - a nation born out of oppression - it is one of the most literal examples of exalting one nation over another, but does that make it fascist?

Authoritarianism, the submission to the absolute authority of the state, and the question of dictatorship and democracy fundamentally changes once extrapolated out of the political superstructure. Anyone who has read the Communist Manifesto will understand that a dictatorship doesn't simply mean there is one mustache-twirling villain directing society, dictatorship can also be controlled by class. As we've covered throughout these essays, a class analysis points out that regardless of the orientation of the state - sole ruler, oligarchy, or representative democracy - class society dictates that the interests of one class will always rule over and suppress the interests of another. Indeed, that is the very purpose of the state. Namely, since the development of capitalism uprooted feudalism, so have the absolute monarchies been uprooted by the dictatorship of the bourgeoisie. The bourgeois class established as the new head of state assumes the role of dictator over the proletarian class. Elections, or the lack of elections, have no bearing on whether a society has a dictatorship, but if it does, does that make it fascist?

There is no shortage of militaristic liberal societies. In the past, Britannia ruled the waves because of its large and powerful navy, which allowed the gloomy rock to rule over its vast colonial empire. Once the sun set on the British Empire, the United States took up the mantle, using its astronomical military budget to police the world and its waves, toppling regimes, destabilizing entire regions of the world, and laundering money through military contractors in an unending cycle that all leads back to the belief in 'American Exceptionalism.' Is the utilization of a large and aggressive military to prop up hegemonic power fascist?

Economic centralization is simply how capitalism develops! The state can influence the rate at which its economy centralizes as it can also forcefully decentralize it if it wishes. Still, the free market trends towards monopolization, and monopolists will form a state apparatus to defend their positions. At best, the 'free market' is an extremely temporary economic phenomenon or an entirely theoretical/utopian outlook. Capitalism can exist with extreme petty bourgeois decentralization or highly regimented and centralized as seen under command/war economies. Does economic centralization, whether it be under the control of the bourgeois or the proletariat, dictate fascism?

The dehumanization or demonization of the 'other' or marginalized communities has been done throughout human history. The Nazis dehumanized all non-Aryans as inferior races, the colonizers have used racism as a tool to obfuscate genocide and assimilation with 'civilizing the savage,' Hutu militias massacred Tutsis in Rwanda seeing them as nothing more than 'cockroaches' in need of extermination, Arabs and Muslims have been internationally dehumanized in the wake of the 9/11 terrorist attacks, and LGBT+ people face constant dehumanization in the West even after securing legal protections. Is this unending process of dehumanization an inherent sign of a fascist society?

The answer to all of these questions is no! None of these traits are signifiers of a fascist society. All of these events from the founding of the United States to today are based upon the ideals and principles of liberalism. Fascism wasn't founded until the early 1900s, evolving within a liberal world. So ask yourself what is more likely - that all these events that happened centuries before[74] Mussolini coined the term "Fascism" should be labeled fascist, or that liberalism as an ideology just as capable of committing genocide, slavery, and apartheid, as the fascist regimes of the 20th century?

What you will find is that liberal bourgeois governments have always been dictatorial no matter how many different flavors of capitalist parties you can choose from. They have always put the nation above the people and have had no qualms about using race or a minority group to solidify their control over society. Economic and social regimentation is so ingrained into society that people don't realize they are the hamsters running on the wheel, and we have all seen what happens to those who truly show themselves to be oppositional to the capitalist global hegemony. In the United States, chattel slavery, native genocide, and racialized concentration camps were all done in the name of liberalism. The British Empire enslaved, colonized, and robbed the world for nearly three centuries in the name of liberalism. And Israel, an active settler colonial state, subjects the Palestinian people to apartheid, ethnic cleansing, and genocide once again in the name of liberalism. So again, we must ask - what is fascism? It seems it can be whatever you want it to be. If you ask one hundred people to define fascism you will receive one hundred different answers. Some will call it capitalism in decay. Some will call it reactionary. Some will call it the Republican Party, and some will call anything they don't like fascism. We derive our understanding of fascism from the works of a few great writers. The first is Anton Pannekoek, who describes the

[74] And will continue centuries after if things do not change.

phenomenon in *Workers' Councils* as such, *"Fascism is the political system of big capitalism in emergency,"*[75] and that *"Fascism was the response of the capitalist world to the challenge of socialism. Socialism proclaimed world revolution that was to free the workers from exploitation and suppression. Capitalism responds with a national revolution curbing them, powerless, under heavier exploitation."*[76] From this it can be surmised that fascism and liberalism, both finding their foundation in the capitalist mode of production, are in fact two sides of the same coin. Therefore, we can understand the natural development of society under capitalism will inevitably lead to the growth of radical reactionary movements - fascists - in the same way it leads to the growth of progressive movements - socialists. The capitalism in decay argument is valid, but let's dive slightly below the surface by examining what both liberalism and fascism always have in common, the capitalist mode of production.

Capitalism as a system is based on a commodity market that demands constant expansion, and therefore inevitable monopolization. Through competition, some firms win and some firms lose and die out or are absorbed by the winners. Through victory, firms grow stronger and accumulate a larger portion of their market share, and therefore also more capital to be further used in expansion. The drive to win means cutting out the competition by pushing them out of the market. This is done by lowering production costs which usually coincides with further exploitation of the worker, and by lobbying the power of the state to create higher barriers of entry to the market. Once solidified over the market, the firm can treat production however it pleases. The double-edged sword is that the worse working conditions get in a society, the more agitated the working class becomes; and the more agitated the working class, the closer the proletariat comes to revolution. A proletarian revolution would be the end of the bourgeois dictatorship and that cannot be allowed to happen, so jobs are outsourced and the firm's exploitation is exported to the proletariat of the maldeveloped nations of the global south. When a nation is unable to

[75] Pannekoek 2003, p. 139

[76] Pannekoek 2003, p. 138

export its exploitation abroad and the economy and working conditions deteriorate, the weight of said exploitation will bear down on the working class until it boils over into spontaneous riots. One could argue in this case that the violence and exploitation that capitalism exports abroad is turned inward onto the home front and onto its own citizens. This can be described as capitalism in decay. What happens next will decide whether a society will progress or regress. In this time of turmoil, the liberal establishment will end. In its place will rise one of two entities, socialism or fascism. The world most notably faced this when the liberal Weimar Republic of Germany failed. The social democrats (SPD), like they always do, betrayed the real movement for liberation by backstabbing Rosa Luxemburg and the KPD, and with them, any hope for socialism in Germany. What rose from the ashes? Adolf Hitler and the Nazi Party, a reactionary force evolving out of the failure of moderate liberalism in direct opposition to Marxism. In their defense of capitalism against Marxism, they can only be described as radical liberals or fascists if you wish.

Conclusion:

Here again, we see the utter uselessness that is the Anti-Fascist ideology. Dedicating one's entire being to fighting fascism is to ignore its direct relation to the liberal bourgeois state. Fascism springs to protect the bourgeois class from the threat of the proletariat and in doing so brings nothing ideologically new to the table except a reorganization of the state and a reactionary transformation of culture.

Society must progress from capitalism as history demands. The next evolutionary step is socialism, the lower phase of communism. The path to socialism is the collapse of capitalism under a liberal bourgeois government, or as we see more of today, social democracies. As we have discussed, there are two paths out of social democracy, socialism or fascism (socialism or barbarism). We can either keep flipping the coin in an endless cycle from liberalism to fascism or we can swipe the coin off the table and evolve as a species. There is no magical alternative. There is no secret third thing. There is no voting our way to a better future. There is no lesser evil. The choice is progress or regress, and no matter what promises a liberal makes they will lead us down the path of regression, the path of fascism! One must not be guided by charismatic characters and their catchy slogans, do not let pseudo-intellectuals or capitalist ideologues with fresh coats of red paint propagandize you from the truth. The problem we are facing is the capitalist mode of production and it will be protected not only by your starkest opposition but by your closest comrades. Anyone who proclaims to know the way to a better future without addressing commodity production and the value form is selling you snake oil. Only through the revolutionary overthrow of the capitalist mode of production, the abolition of the commodity and value form, can we toss both liberalism and its reactionary counterpart fascism into the dustbin of history forever!

On Trumpism:

It's important to remember the historical role of fascism. In the 1900s, it grew as a reaction to the growing threat of the socialist movement and actively fought against the oncoming proletarian revolutions across Europe. With only the Russian revolution succeeding, the international proletarian movement was doomed to failure. Following World War Two, the fascists were consolidated into the ranks of liberalism and put to the task of combating 'communism.' Before the end of the Cold War, the international socialist movement was defeated, but with its end, neoliberal capitalism solidified itself as the new world order. Socialism was crushed and forced to rebuild from scratch, while fascism was absorbed into liberalism and, while dormant, was allowed to fester and build itself behind the curtain into the very foundations of neoliberal society. The question we must come back to is if this resurgence of reactionary right-wing politics is traceable to the fascist movements of the 1900s or if it is another attempt to suppress the fact that without resolving the contradictions between the bourgeois and proletariat, the seeds of a new generation of reactionary politics are planted?

We would argue that today radical conservatism is not rising through reaction to an active socialist threat as did the fascists of old, but instead to the inevitable globalization of capitalism (that creates the conditions for international socialism). The debate between conservatives and liberals is the same as between nationalists and globalists. It is over the three-sector model of the economy![77] More specifically, the debate between conservatives and liberals, or nationalists and globalists, occurs over the expansion of the tertiary sector of the economy. The question concerns how much of the secondary sector should be outsourced. The nationalists are regressive as they attempt to prohibit growth, development, expansion, and socialization around the world, and the globalists, while correct, are so only in the interest of furthering the domination and exploitation of capital! The globalist position is to follow the natural evolution of capitalism as it continues to liberate, socialize, and develop the world into one cohesive economy. The nationalist takes the opposite stance because, as with all conservative ideologies, they seek to preserve the past. Though he is not the first, we see this today in the U.S. through Donald Trump and the growing MAGA and America First movement. This group rejects the natural evolution of capitalism because they cannot comprehend it. They are not driven by economics but by their emotional response or fear of progression. In the West at the very least, this conservatism is based on Whiteness. The natural change in demographics and social progression brought through the economic development of capitalism stirs fear in these people because they fear the retribution of equality. And so because of this fear, they would rather trade away their economic development and reverse progress than continue to be the strongest economy in the world but with racial equality! This is further evidence that although both the radical conservative and neoliberal support the capitalist system, the neoliberal is inherently the lesser evil. But so long as capitalism reigns as the global mode of production, these regressive movements will continue to populate and play on the fears of national groups, and that fear will not necessarily always be related to

---

[77] Detailed in the 'Three Sector Model' section.

Whiteness or even race for that matter.

The globalists/liberals want to continue to expand and grow the economy as the capitalist system demands (including its exploitation and domination). The nationalists/conservatives want to turn back the wheel of history by regressing into industrialization before it becomes historically necessary. They do not do this out of a humanitarian desire to not exploit the third world, but out of a fear of internationalism and multiculturalism. The liberal 'globalist' will always be more historically progressive than the conservative 'nationalist'. But as we have stated throughout these essays, this cycle can only be broken by the establishment of socialism at the international level.

The question remains: what does this have to do with Donald Trump and Trumpism? Truthfully, it has very little to do with Trump himself. The resurgence of the reactionary right is a global phenomenon that has developed directly from the failures of the first attempt at international proletarian revolution. However, as we have demonstrated, this resurgence is different from the fascism of the 1900s, although they may share similar characteristics, the strategies and end goals are very different. At the risk of being accused of Americentrism, we believe that although these reactionary movements carry different platforms, policies, and actions across nation-states, foundationally, they arise from the same fundamental premise of economic and political (ultra)nationalism and populism, mythologization of the past, and the dehumanization of an 'other,' all traits seen within 'Trumpism;' an ideology of absolute nothingness.

In the previous section, we defined Trump as "a celebrity narcissist... [whose] ideas and policies are not relevant because he is not campaigning on real issues, but instead running a spectacle that appeals to the emotion of the conservative voter. He is a modern-day Bonapartist, not a military officer, but most definitely an officer of the capitalist class seeking to restore the nation to its former glory through law, order, and nationalism." This is reflected in the instability of the MAGAmovement and his embodiment of the role of being the 'Great Man' that binds the many tribes together. He capitalized on the increasing disillusionment of the American population with the neoliberal status quo and appealed to the conservative base by promising to return the U.S. to greatness by fighting the globalists who were shipping their jobs to foreign lands and replacing their labor with that of Latin American immigrants. He doesn't speak about policy wonkery but rather brash appeals to might and right. We will solve the problem of asylum seekers by building an enormous wall and dehumanizing those fleeing dire political and economic conditions, not by addressing the actual conditions that lead to refugees in the first place. We will solve the country's growing wealth inequality and discontentment not by empowering the workers but by increasing tax cuts to the wealthy, leveraging tariffs to try and secure unnecessary trade surpluses to save face, and posturing about American excellence and reindustrialization while being viciously anti-welfare and anti-union. All of this verbose populist babble is a house of cards built atop a foundation of a nationalistic reaction to globalization and multiculturalism.

Making America Great Again and putting America First are not defined ideologies with comprehensive agreed-upon policies. It is an ideology rooted in its reactionary foundation. It unites based on fear and ignorance. This ignorance is ingrained in subsections of the population through how they are raised, conservative religious institutions, and media. Though they will deny it, there is just as large of a conservative echo chamber in America as there is a progressive one; one media station is just as 'powerful' as five media stations if their viewership is the same, not to mention the conservative monopoly on the radio and podcasting. It is through these tools of indoctrination that a population of reactionary conservatives is groomed and ready for a shepherd to herd them into one flock, all petty differences suppressed by his crook. Though it tries to portray an image as the last line of defense for freedom and liberty against authoritarianism, it is a collectivist ideology that subordinates the individual to the interest of the nation. Therein lies the issue of what is the 'American' nation. One's answer to that question is the precise reason why the ideology of MAGA, America First, or Trumpism cannot be defined! What constitutes the American nation? Is it the land of immigrants? Which immigrants? Is America a cultural melting pot, or is that a bumper sticker slogan that hides the oppression of nations within the multicultural project itself? Is it somewhere in between? Trumpism never seeks to define what constitutes the American nation because to do so would actively alienate subsections of its base. If it were to solidify specific positions on immigration, it would lose its facade of being pro-immigration but anti-illegal immigration. It would have to address whether it is okay to import high-skill, low-skill, or any workers at all. It would have to address whether mass deportations include all undocumented immigrants or just the ones who have committed additional crimes while in the U.S., and if the position is the latter, it must define what crimes demand deportation and what crimes can be swept under the rug.

Economically, it cannot educate its base because to do so would be to prompt them to abandon economic nationalism. To reindustrialize the American economy is not as simple as bringing the 'Computer Manufacturer' back within the borders of the U.S. It requires not only the development of the motherboards, CPUs, and monitors but also the nuts, bolts, and screws required to make them, the chips that must be extracted and refined, the machinery used in the factories that make all of these, the engineers, CAD, and construction workers that have to design and build the building including its electricity and plumbing, the extraction and refinement of the construction resources needed to make those factories, and the transportation necessary to connect each of these steps to one another. It is true that all of these create jobs, however, these jobs are tied to American labor standards, subject to worker protections and minimum wage laws, that will at every level of reindustrialization, increase the cost of production, which will inevitably be pushed onto the consumer. That is even assuming these industries could be constructed and running in time before sweeping tariffs raised and offset production costs onto the consumers. It's a foolish endeavor when one stops to think it through, but that is irrelevant because the entire point is that you are not supposed to think it through! It's a meaningless position held simply to help stoke nationalist sentiment among the masses away from class contradictions sharpened by capitalist development and onto the inter-factional bourgeois struggle within the state.

Like Tito in Yugoslavia, these many splintered factions can only be united under one entity so long as a strong, charismatic figure is there to bundle them into one movement united against a common enemy. In the context of the U.S., Donald Trump holds the position of the unitary figure that unites the isolated reactionary American tribes under the banner of Trumpism. Once that figure falls from power, whether it be a fall from grace or death, the 'heir' to the movement must recapture control of the tribes, or the movement will splinter and turn on itself. The problem with that is that quite often, 'Great Men' and celebrity narcissists, for that matter, have a hard time not buying into their own hype; the movement isn't bigger than them, THEY ARE the movement. On top of that, it is not often that the heir, whether well-groomed for the position or not, can capture the same unitary fire of their predecessor.

Regardless of the name, Trumpism is not unique to America. It is an all-encompassing term for the global resurgence of the reactionary right. Marine Le Pen, the current leader of the National Rally party in France, is close to taking power with stances starkly opposing immigration and the 'globalist' economic policies of the European Union in favor of economic nationalism. Her marginalized group to be 'othered,' like many in Europe, is the influx of Muslim immigrants seeking refuge from regions destabilized by the actions of the West. She referred to this immigration as an occupation, saying, "There are of course no tanks, there are no soldiers, but it is nevertheless an occupation and it weighs heavily on local residents." Giorgia Meloni, the current Prime Minister of Italy, was a member of the youth wing of the MSI, a neo-fascist organization founded directly after WW2 in 1946, and went on to be co-founder of the Brothers of Italy or FdI party, which is based on the principles of defending God, the fatherland, and family. If that isn't on the nose enough, she and her movement also favor economic nationalism as opposed to the European Union, with strong anti-immigrant and anti-LGBT sentiments. We see similar movements in Britain, with Nigel Farage and the newly founded Reform Party seeking to capitalize off of the collapse of the Tories and the dissatisfaction with the Labor Party after the ousting of Jeremy Corbyn. In the Netherlands, Geert Wilders, the leader of the Party for Freedom, is busy trying to wage a holy crusade against the 'Islamization' of Western civilization, stop immigration to protect the 'Dutch identity,' and leave the European Union to pursue Dutch economic nationalism. The list goes on and on, with more and more status-quo neoliberal regimes losing ground to reactionary conservative movements that run on nothing more than stoked fear and bigoted bumper sticker slogans.

Trumpism requires that it be ill-defined, collectivist to the interests of the personality cult, and polarizing to continue to expand its base by casting the widest net it possibly can among the increasing number of reactionaries within the masses. It must constantly appeal to emotion instead of making substantive arguments to keep up the facade of its political spectacle. It must demonize some marginalized groups to deflect class politics in place of identity politics. It must do this or the movement itself will stagnate and collapse within itself;, it must ride its momentum to the seizure of state power, but once it takes control of the state it is stuck. Returning to Bordiga's speech on fascism, he says, "Our analysis leads to the conclusion that fascism has added nothing to the traditional ideology and programme of bourgeois politics. All things considered, its superiority and its specificity consist of its organisation, discipline, and hierarchy. Aside from this exceptional and militaristic exterior, it possesses nothing but a reality full of difficulties that it is unable to overcome. The economic crisis will constantly renew the causes of revolution, while fascism will be unable to reorganise the social apparatus of the bourgeoisie. Fascism does not know how to go beyond the economic anarchy of the capitalist system. It has a different historical task, which lies in combating political anarchy and the organisational anarchy of political groupings of the bourgeois class."[78]

Like fascism, once this new reactionary conservative force comes into power, it has no program but the reorganization of the state. It utilizes the tools of state violence to viciously oppress those it deems as enemies of the 'people,' and by the people, it means the movement, and by the movement, it means the leadership. It has no economic program that can

[78] Bordiga, 1922

address the contradictions of capitalism that constantly concentrates and centralizes capital as well as growing and expanding into new markets. It may try to reindustrialize its economy, but the drop in the standard of living would radicalize the population against the government in mass, leading either to its ousting or the mass repression of the population by the police, military, courts, and surveillance agencies. The movement is doomed the moment it succeeds. It is doomed because it is inherently reactionary, not revolutionary! It seeks to change nothing but the reorganization of the status quo - the repurposing of the state for the same purposes; it is entirely pointless! So, what is to be done?

5

What Is To Be Done?

On Electoralism:

We must first deal with the most immediate question, whether or not to participate an electoral politics. The general answer would be that we do not participate in bourgeois elections, or at the very least not unless through the proxy of a workers' party. There are, however, two things to remember. One, societal change or revolution cannot be brought through electoral means alone, yet they can be used as a tool in building the conditions for one. And two, we must operate within our material reality. There is no relevant workers party and there is no active proletarian movement. Therefore, there is no electoral proxy, the only viable options are the bourgeois and the radical bourgeois. You can, of course, blame the lack of viability for more revolutionary parties on the people voting for the Democrats and Republicans, and you would be correct, but at the same time, you would be ignoring the material reality of the America we live in. You would be giving into idealism. Does this mean you should give into lesser evilism?

The answer is that it is entirely subjective. Your vote is not going to stop the genocide in Gaza, but it will sign your support to it by legitimizing the regime perpetrating it. We are stuck between a rock and a hard place but have no doubt in your mind that it can certainly get worse. There are things to consider. Would you prefer to organize and live under the political base of a neoliberal government or a radical conservative government?[79] How detrimental are the differences in social policy between the parties to you and your community? And what are you voting for? Are you voting to buy more time? If so then c'est la vie! As long as you recognize that electoralism is nothing more than a tool, you may use that tool however you see fit. To understand that you cannot vote out the rule of capital is to understand the falsity of reformist politics; so, vote for the lesser evil, toss a sympathy vote to a meaningless third party or 'socialist' party that is definitely not funded by oligarchs or foreign powers, or even abstain in protest and protect your integrity; it does not matter so long as the ballot box is not where your 'activism' stops.[80] There are many more pressing issues in building toward a revolution than shading in a bubble on a ballot! We can prolong our slow death and get to work laying the foundations for the future, or we can pretend that social media socialists are more prepared to lead a revolution today than Huey P. Newton and Bobby Seale in the 1960s and 70s, and if you want to do that you might as well just bite down on a cyanide capsule and save the redneck Gestapo the trouble.

Preliminary Recognitions:

Priority number one for the American revolutionary is survival. Recogniz-

[79] Although half the people who raise this question don't organize in any capacity at all!

[80] Those that spend all of their time advocating for people to abstain from voting are strange. These people seem to make the claim that they understand electoralism is unable to break the rule of capital, and that it is essentially a waste of time, but then proceed to waste their time lecturing people about the ineffectiveness of electoralism. Spending all your time convincing people not to vote, instead of agitating them to participate in politics outside of the voting booth is a strange tactic indeed. Especially because many who take this approach speak like they exist on a higher level of understanding. They speak down to people with a condescending authority, when half the time they are just advocating people to vote for completely nonviable third-party candidates. It is a true absurdity to speak down on others for voting for the lesser evil when your alternative is just voting for an even lesser evil. The problem isn't the party or the candidate, it is the system that the parties and candidates exist within; a system governed by capital! When we say your vote doesn't matter, that is what we're referring to.

ing that this is not a television show is of the utmost importance. There is no plot armor. The good guys don't just win in the end. There is no magical MacGuffin. The cavalry is not coming when hope is at its bleakest. If the time for revolution is thrust upon us and the proletariat is not unified, organized, and conscious then we literally just die! Fade to black. Story over. But before we can begin to build the foundations there are more things that must be recognized.

First, the American population is indoctrinated by American Exceptionalism on both sides of the aisle. This indoctrination is ingrained in the foundations of our society and can only be changed through a cultural shift or revolution.

Second, revolution is not simply being an activist. Participating in boycotts, strikes, and protests that are not organized in mass as specific targets is generally a waste of time because the population has been designed in such a way that if one side forms the opposition, the other will naturally take up the mantle of support. This is not of course a law. Issues can be valued differently by different groups, or in some cases, the majority of the total population may join one side of the issue. It is simply a general rule.

Third, a true proletarian revolution does not have a 'leader.' Naturally, people with leadership qualities will arise and help to organize the unconscious masses. When we say there will be no leader we mean to say there will be no singular authority figure. There is no great man, thought leader, or pope of the proletariat. Party organizers themselves must be thoroughly theoretically educated in order for the proletariat to have purpose, aim, and tactics. Theory is the shield of the proletariat and action its sword. Any movement that allows itself to be led or instructed by a singular person or group is not a movement of the people, but of the person or group. The only exception to this is in the case of the dictatorship of the proletariat. Under the DoTP, the proletariat as a class must lead and suppress the bourgeois as it transitions to socialism and abolishes class entirely.

Fourth, any movement that is able to begin organizing the proletariat as a class will be crushed by the reunion of the bourgeois class. The neoliberals and the fascists for as much infighting as they do will always collaborate together to crush a rising proletariat because the movement of the proletariat directly threatens their existence as a class. Socialist agitators will be arrested and others executed or assassinated. People will flee the movement in fear while others see the power vacuum and try to fill it. The last inter-party faction standing will be the one that swears fealty to the bourgeois and becomes their far-left puppet party; a Venus fly trap planted to catch the next generation of socialists to deradicalize them into social democrats. The party, therefore, should not become outright revolutionary until the culture has shifted enough to give the proletariat a fighting chance. If it plays its hand too soon, the movement collapses; and if it waits too long, it may miss the revolutionary window and be co-opted by reformists.

Fifth, the United States is massive! It is comprised of fifty states, most of which are larger than European countries. A revolution in Cuba, for example, while a tall task is not even comparable to the monstrosity of a task that is abolishing the present state of things in the U.S. In fact, it is quite possible that internal revolution is impossible in the U.S. as nowhere on earth are the conditions and power required for revolution more drastic than in America; but that will not stop us from theorizing possibilities! And sixth, the advent of socialism will be an international phenomenon. It is an international movement that has been in development long before you were born and it will likely still be developing after you die. We are all nothing more than cogs on the wheel of time. We emerge from the void in an environment shaped and molded by those who emerged before us, and it is our job to shape and mold the world for those who will emerge after us. The movement of history is long, but our lives are short. It is easy to get lost in your own head dreaming of the world you'll never get to see instead of dealing with your material reality. Learn from the past then alter the present, and you will change the future.

The Cultural Lever:

Before the proletariat can seize the economic and political levers of societal power it must first be organized, and in order for the proletariat to get organized, the culture of society must be indicative of achieving that end. Therefore, seizing the cultural lever of power is the first task in constructing the conditions required for a revolution. The problem is that the cultural lever of power has been in the hands of the bourgeois since the country's founding. The bourgeois may, of course, gatekeep who gets to hold the lever as done historically with the Native and enslaved African populations, however, as a bourgeois society's culture becomes more socially progressive it will make concessions and let members of minority groups hold the lever so long as they do so representing the bourgeois class. The cultural lever controls many different aspects of our society. For example, the media including both the news and entertainment are owned, managed, and directed by corporations - the wielder's of the political and economic levers. The curriculum of our public education system is shaped by state and local education boards that cooperate with the federal and state governments to indoctrinate the youth with the worldview of American Exceptionalism. The educational battle over 'wokeness' is a cultural battle, but it is just progressiveness versus conservatism; it is not over the class struggle between the bourgeois and the proletariat. This same struggle is occurring in the business world over diversity, equity, and inclusion (DEI) programs. The struggle is again between progressiveness and conservatism, but the programs are being instituted by corporations because of the increasingly more progressive culture of the American population. The neoliberal order adapts to the changing culture and the conservatives grow more reactionary because of it, leading to the situation we find ourselves in today. The institutions that influence cultural change are trending more progressive over time. Demographic changes, both by age and the steady increase of our multicultural society, are further accelerants for this progressive trend. Again, please note the country is on a collision course due to this slow cultural shift. If the status quo survives the collision the shift will continue, and if it dies then cultural conservatism becomes enforced with an iron fist. You should also here again be able to see the extreme reactionary nature of conservatism and fascism, because although they represent the same bourgeois class interests as the neoliberals, their regressive cultural ideology would rather destroy society before allowing the other or the 'out-group' into the decision-making room.

Culture is a tool used to control and subordinate the masses to the ruling class, but that is not all it is. Although culture is able to be shaped and influenced by the controllers of institutional power, it is not as a whole a manufactured product. Culture, like human nature, is shaped by the material conditions of the society a population lives in; and one of the most important factors that effects a societies material conditions is its mode of production. Therefore, we can conclude that politics is driven by culture, and culture is driven by economics. We appear to have found a contradiction. In order to liberate the minds of the workers so that they can organize as a class, the culture of the society they live in must be shifted. However, in order for the culture to radically shift, the mode of production would have to radically shift. For one to occur, the other would already have had to been completed, but we are starting from a point where neither requirements are fulfilled. This contradiction is solved by the introduction of the revolutionary, a force that stands outside of nature. The revolutionary is a conscious member of the oppressed class. They operate within the material conditions of their society, but they recognize the contradictions in the world around them and theorize ways to solve them. The revolutionary is the fish that swims against the school and discovers the vastness of the deep blue sea, and once they are free, they find those likeminded comrades who found their way out as well. It is these first revolutionaries who are able to step out of the constraints of culture, that must come together and organize the proletariat's weapon against the bourgeois class, the revolutionary party. It should also be noted that culture naturally shifts and evolves very slowly under the normal conditions of society - but when those normal conditions are drastically altered, particularly in times of political and economic strife, culture can shift radically. Under normal conditions, you will then find fewer revolutionaries, and under drastic conditions, you will find more revolutionaries, however, with that increase in socialist revolutionaries there will also be an increase in reactionary revolutionaries. Both groups looking to break the status quo, but for radically different purposes and ends, they are therefore natural enemies of one another.

Revolutionary Tactics:

We covered the role and structure of the party under socialism in the phases section of this work, so we can refrain from reiterating them here. Instead, we will theorize the revolutionary tactics of the party as it operates during the revolution itself. Of course we must remember that capitalism is an international system and therefore so too are socialism and revolution international. The workers of every nation must deal with their own national bourgeois, and the material conditions of the battlefields these struggles are fought on will vastly vary - but the underlying principles and relations to production are identical to all. Capitalism has created a global market in which its competitors are countries, and these countries are nothing more than corporations. Some are large, some are small. Some hold almost monopoly-like power over regional markets, and some specialize in specific areas of production, but they all fundamentally run on the same mode of production. We can then look at the U.S. as the largest, most powerful corporation on the planet today. The board of directors of U.S. Inc. are the oligarchs - the big capitalists. The state is the union of the bourgeois in that it collectively bargains on their behalf against the interests of the proletariat, and acts as the intermediary between bourgeois interclass conflicts. The political parties organized and funded by the oligarchs thanklessly allow the people or the workers to elect their leaders or managers from a preselected and vetted list of bourgeois candidates. The top leader, the president, is elected to the position of CEO of the company. They take their orders from the board and act as the country or company's spokesperson, and when things go wrong they take the fall! The revolutionary party must recognize this reality and concretely understand the goal is not to take over the company, but to set it ablaze and build something new. Trying to win state power instead of smashing it is what separates the reformists from the revolutionaries. The proletariat can never be liberated through reformism and participation in the bourgeois system.

Instead, the proletariat must operate outside the system. It may utilize the system to its advantage in furthering revolutionary action, but it must never compromise its character by pursuing reformism as the means to the end. However, recognizing that in its current state the U.S. is teetering on the edge of a bourgeois civil war, and that there is no socialist base ready to seize on this opportunity, we can acknowledge that a socialist revolution in the U.S. is for the foreseeable future impossible. Our current long term goal should thus switch from national proletarian revolution to supporting to growth of the international proletariat by sabotaging the world's biggest company, the U.S., from within. Both of these goals require us to take similar paths, but by focusing on attacking capital from within the imperial core, our ends feel much more achievable. Accelerationists might argue that we should not stand up to the fascist menace and instead allow the U.S. to destroy itself. That is a fools game. Firstly, because fascism does not attack capital - instead, it organizes it in a much more brutal fashion both domestically and internationally. And secondly, because we would be playing with not only our lives, but the lives of billions of people around the world should the U.S. return to military imperialism from economic imperialism. It may very well be the case that it is far too late for a socialist movement to rise in the U.S. in time to turn back the rise of fascism, but presuming the threat is temporarily pushed back, we must begin building immediately.

With the goal of sabotaging the empire from within, steadily shifting the culture and increasing the organization of the proletariat, we find our starting point. The last thing we must recognize (and I know we are asking you to recognize many things but bare with us) is that America nor any country that has reached the necessary level of development for socialist revolution will follow the paths of the revolutions in Russia, Cuba, China, Vietnam, etc. There are no major peasantry classes remaining so there is no need for class collaboration, nor is there a need to enter a stage of state capitalism or siege socialism. The material conditions that ignited those revolutions - bourgeois as they were (with exceptions to Russia) - simply no longer exist. That is why the idea that socialist revolution will come from the underdeveloped nations rather than the highest developed nations is flawed. Socialist revolution can only succeed from within the conditions of a developed nation, and therefore international socialist revolution can only succeed when the vast majority of the nations of the world are more equally developed.

With the many recognitions out of the way, the first step becomes clear - the scattered revolutionary socialists must come together as a united collective to form the revolutionary socialist party. The party can be newly established or conquered from within. Both come with advantages and disadvantages, but it matters not which path is taken. Theoretical disagreements are completely fine and should be actively encouraged, however, the revolutionary character of the party must serve as the movements foundational premise that must not be allowed to be compromised by any means necessary. Therefore, the only 'purity' test to being admitted to the party should be unyielding belief in the abolition of the present state of things for the establishment of the association of free and equal producers. This 'golden rule' will ensure that while their may be vicious factionalism and ruthless critique, the infighting will be over tactics, not the revolutionary socialist character of the movement. While quantity is of great importance to the revolutionary movement, 10,000 revolutionary socialists will always be more valuable than 100,000 reformists. The proletariat is one class and it must be politically represented by one united party. The revolutionary socialists must see this fact, set their petty squabbles aside and collectivize as the movement demands. We call for a mass merger, or alternatively, a mass abandonment of the current parties for the establishment of a singular revolutionary party.

The basic tenets of the revolutionary party are as follows: First, the base line of the party must be maintained and defended as revolutionary socialism. Second, all party members are given an equal vote and are allowed to vote on electing party leadership and ratifying resolutions. Third, under the policy of democratic centralism, factionalism and debate will be encouraged and all viewpoints and ideas should be throughly heard and discussed. However, once the debate is finished, the democratic decision of the party will set the official party line that must be upheld by all members. The issues can be revisited and revised later, but in the immediate the party must conform to the democratic decision. Fourth, the party must be entirely independent from the bourgeois parties and their puppeteers. The party cannot take the path of the CPUSA and subordinate itself to being the 'left wing' of the Democratic Party, nor should it totally ignore electoralism in favor of endorsing social democrats as is the current policy of the DSA. The political independence of the party means a commitment to quality over quantity. It means members, a program, and tactics, that are suited towards the interest of the liberation of the proletariat and not the maintenance of the status quo. Again, while we are inherently anti-fascist, it is not our sole purpose to fight fascism. An ideology of pure anti-fascism bends to the whims of the status quo. It demands you immediately deal with the infestation by 'killing' the fascists, but never asks you to figure out why the infestation occurred in the first place. The anti-fascist clears one infestation and another pops up, it's an endless cycle because the root of the infestation is never accounted for. The revolutionary socialists and the party must be able to recognize this cycle and the part both factions of the bourgeois play in its continued existence; and it can only do that so long as it is independent of bourgeois influence. Fifth, the party must make itself and its actions known to the public, and it therefore should run electoral candidates that will represent the socialist line and actively and loudly protest the bourgeois institutions from within its most sacred halls. Sixth, it can only win elections and build a true power base by focusing and consolidating its power in specific locations. The DSA, while having around 100k members, is so spread out across the nation that its influence (even if entirely filled by revolutionary members) is entirely diminished. Back to quantity over quality debate, 100k votes across 50 states is very little compared to 10k votes in a single state. By building a power base starting from a single city and spreading across a single state, control and political power can be won locally and leveraged to win a seat or two in the House of Representatives. This condensed power, if based in an electoral swing state, could also serve as an anchor forcing the neoliberal democrats to make concessions left instead of to the right-wing moderates. Seventh and finally, the party must associate with and embed members in local unions.

We would now like to delve a bit deeper into participation in electoral politics and union association. It is fine to participate in electoral politics as long as it is looked at as a tool or a game instead of a path to realizing socialist construction. While socialism cannot be implemented through congressional policy, a socialist agitator in the public eye of the halls of Congress can serve as a great tool of propaganda for the movement. The role allows both the positions of and the party itself to be represented and broadcasted nationally. The elected official would be given time to publicly rebuke the bourgeois system and its corruption and imperialism, and with the ability to vote on policy, the party could now directly claim credit for cultural victories; and with the ability to draft policy, we can force the Democratic Party to support the policies they claim to support or show their hand as controlled opposition. The best part is that all of this is possible through the legal framework of the U.S. system. The ultimate goal of electoral participation would be to land a socialist agitator on the presidential debate stage, where every news station would be forced to broadcast the propaganda to every viewer in America. We are not trying to win the presidency, instead, we are using the political apparatus as a broadcasting tool, and to uplift the poor and working class as best we can. That is the other point to remember, we want to agitate the public to question the system they live under, we do not want to agitate them into hating us! The elected official should and must have redlines they will not cross when it comes to voting on bills, but that does not mean they should protest every bill just because it is sponsored by a bourgeois party. If a policy truthfully helps the working class, the agitator should support it whole heartedly and become its most prominent champion. If there is an interview they should do it, if there is a debate they should be the first one to the podium, and where there is corruption they should be the loudest voice calling it out.[81]

With a strong power base at home, the agitator is protected from the threat of being primaried by the bourgeois parties, and the socialist party is protected from rogue agitators by turning the local election base against them. However, no federal candidates should be run until the local power base is secured. The socialist movement will never have the funding to match the bourgeois parties so we must pick our battles and battlegrounds much more strategically. The small victories will only snowball into bigger victories and thus the movement will continue to grow in power and number, but if we jump the gun and chase a big victory without any prior support built up, we will experience a most humiliating defeat. For every defeat we suffer, the movement for socialism is postponed and the reactionary bourgeois face a smaller and weaker threat.

While participating in electoral politics is technically optional, associating with unions is not. In order to organize the proletariat the party must reach out to and directly organize the proletariat. Renting a plane to airdrop leaflets across the country is not going to get the workers to revolt. Direct action must be made, and that direct action is building and organizing union power. The goal here is to build a symbiotic relationship between the unions and the revolutionary socialist party through the establishment of a proletarian or class union. The class union ignores the divisions of the workers between individual factory, industry, and state by collectivizing them into one union with one purpose - class war. It is a union for all wage laborers, public or private, blue collar or white collar, productive or nonproductive, for the disabled, and for the intelligentsia. In other words, it is one union to rule them all. The word "rule" here is representative of the rule of the proletariat, not the party. The class union will not be subordinated to the party and nor will the party be subordinated to the union. As we said, it is an association of the two - two symbiotic and inseparable

[81] There are also positions a socialist agitator could push for that would help foreign nations further develop their economies and thus their proletarian class. This could include things like ending economic embargoes and sanctions, pushing for an end to trade tariffs, and promoting anti-imperialist and anti-war action among the masses.

halves that when combined, form the foundation of the revolutionary movement.

Following the idea of starting small, so too will our movement to associate with unions. Though there are different types of unions, it can be said a business is either unionized or it isn't. Our first goal is to simultaneously reach out to the already existing unions in an attempt to form association and assist the workers of non-unionized businesses in starting the process of unionizing. From the outset, many party members should attempt to join both types of these businesses depending on how their skill sets align. For example, a scrawny, socially awkward geeky guy would be better suited in helping to unionize a coffee shop than a construction company, although that is just a generalization. You may be asking why would a union or a unionizing business want to form any association with a small socialist party, and the answer is simple; we offer soldiers! 500 socialists voting for a random third party presidential candidate is small and insignificant, but 500 socialists on a picket line (especially locally) is both large and incredibly impactful. Size is relative. And we do not use the word 'soldier' to LARP as some battle hardened militia, it is simply an acknowledgement of the class war. Every strike is a battle and every picket line is a formation of soldiers in the war between the bourgeois and proletariat. These battles may be small and insignificant now, and they may grow to be larger but still completely legal and peaceful; but once they grow large enough to start seriously threatening the status quo, liberalism will show its true face and utilize its monopoly on state violence to wage a war of annihilation on the class union. But to get to that point, we must continue to tie in more and more individual unions for the construction of the class union. So, in return for the bodies we offer to bolster the union's efforts, we ask they accept the platform or constitution of the class union (which we will discuss shortly) and send an agreed-upon number of delegates to regularly meet with the party. On these terms, the symbiotic association between the individual union and party is formed, and with it, another link is added to the class union.

The platform of the class union should in many respects be a 'watered down' version of the party platform. The emphasis should be on creating an environment of cohesion between the unions regardless of industry and general solidarity amongst all workers. A decent general outline could be similar to the ICP's class union principles outlined in the article *Towards the Rebirth of the Working Class Trade Union*,

"PRINCIPLES of the class union:

a) To aim for solidarity amongst workers of every category in order to oppose the disadvantageous divisions imposed on workers by bourgeois society;

b) It isn't the job of the class union to defend the national economy or finances of the bourgeois State, nor to propose alternative solutions to their crisis such as a "fair taxation system", which in this society is unimaginable. If the State is constrained to attack the petty bourgeoisie, let IT take the blame: the position on which class union lines up is the intransigent defence of the working class;

c) Struggle for normative and wage equality for the same job, regardless of age, race, sex, nationality, religion or language;

d) its objective is international workers' solidarity, understood not in a sentimental or abstract sense, but as a prospect based on common goals, struggles and organisation;

e) It considers that the de facto capacity to strike and organise derives not from rights enshrined in laws or constitutions, but depends on which way the balance of power between the classes is tipped: a legal strike being forbidden is just as likely to happen as an illegal trade union establishing itself. To accept strike-limiting laws in order to obtain recognition by the State is a serious mistake since the bosses and the State will never recognise a truly combative union unless constrained to do so by force; the union will only be able acquire true representation when it is backed by the workers and is able to mobilise them around an intransigent class line;

f) The trade-union organisation must be separate from, and opposed to, the various forms of organisation and internal structures set in place by the employers within the workplace and must be funded by workers alone. The delegating of the collection of dues to the bosses is to be decisively rejected since it involves the handing over of a list of members to the class enemy and transferring the means of financing the union into their hands;

g) In its best tradition, militating in the union is carried out by ordinary workers, after work and at their own expense. The excessive use of paid officials, of official absence from work for union reasons, of meetings in working hours, conducted under the eye of the boss and his spies, only make things easier for the organisation in a superficial way, and are often used as a form of corruption, of intimidation and blackmail;

h) The class union, having rejected prejudices and erroneous explanations of the causes of the degeneration of the regime unions, must aim to eventually become a centralised unitary organism, organised on a national scale, which proletarians join voluntarily with a view to taking part in coordinated actions in pursuit of common objectives. In order to function properly, permanent executive organs are an indispensable requirement since only these can ensure the requisite speed and unity of decision-making when it comes to taking practical action. The necessary monitoring of the leaders to ensure they are firm in their commitment to the class interest, and selecting the best political line for the trade union, is a capacity which the class will need to develop. They are problems which cannot be sidestepped by adopting the suicidal conclusion that the class can do without its indispensable organisational instruments;

i) The class union holds on to the fact that the exploited will experience real and lasting relief from suffering only by fully emancipating itself from the condition of wage labour, and this is the general objective which it pursues."[82]

The specifics of the platform would have to be debated and written by the party, but the ICP has provided us with a valuable outline to work with. While naturally empowering the workers through strengthening the unions, the class union can move past the individualism that plagues the isolated unions. It allows for wide-ranging solidarity among all workers and thus in turn increases the class consciousness of the individual workers. As an added benefit to us, members operating within the unions themselves and those standing in solidarity on the picket lines will be able to recruit members from the masses into the revolutionary cause of the party, and it is from here that the party grows in quantity without sacrificing on quality!

The isolated union represents a small group of collectivized workers who remain cut off from the masses and thus they themselves will in general still be unconscious. Through the process of associating with the party, these isolated unions find comradery in every direction. The movement will likely start in a few targeted industries at first. Already established unions of an industry come together to support each other and to support the unionization of others in their field alongside the numerical support of the party. Once a local industry has been by the majority unionized we can begin to implement the economic apparatus detailed in the section *Foundations of Cooperative Federocracy.* The once isolated unions of an industry now bound together in solidarity with one another can form an Industry Syndicate - a body representing the collective interests of all workers of the local industry, regardless of which capitalist they work for. Although each individual union is dealing with different working conditions, different management, and different capitalists, by uniting together as an industry their collective bargaining power drastically increases; more importantly, it gives them the ability to shut down the entire local industry at the blow of a whistle. Once two or more of these Industry Syndicates have been formed and solidified, a cross-industry local union body can be established. We referred to this in foundations as the Local Economic Chamber, at this time it would probably

---

[82] ICP 1992

go by a different name as it would still be serving as a union in direct conflict with the capitalist class, instead of an organization of economic management and control. Regardless of the name, this cross-industry union provides the same benefit as the Industry Union or Syndicate, as it increases the collective bargaining power of the workers and now allows them to shut down an entire local economy at the blow of a whistle. This model can be expanded from local city to local city until enough Local Economic Unions are established to form a State Economic Union which can scale across the states to form a National Economic Union; and if this were to occur across several countries at the same time an International Economic Union could be formed as well! From this expansion process, you can see how the vision laid out in foundations can come to rise from within the bourgeois capitalist society. However, in reality, the state will begin to violently crack down on this class union long before it reaches the formation of a singular State Economic Union. We should expect violent crackdowns from the militarized police and strikebreakers, attempts to paint the movement for workers' rights as evil communism coming to take people's toothbrushes in the media, bribery and infiltration of both the unions and the party, and if all that fails, outright imprisonment or assassination of key members to sow fear and discord in the movement.

Economics is governed by land, labor, and capital. The capitalist controls land and capital, and although they can rent or purchase labor, it is the workers themselves who own their labor. If the workers refuse to sell their labor then the production process comes to a grinding halt. That is the purpose of striking and that is why striking is one of the proletariat's strongest weapons. As individuals refusing to work causes no damage to the system, your labor will be thrown onto your co-workers until you return or are replaced; but if nobody shows up to work then no work is done. Others can be hired to replace those who strike, but if the number of people striking outnumbers the reserve labor army then the replacements are not sufficient to continue the production process. Through the organization of the class union, we can use labor as a weapon against the controller of land and capital to force concessions to the working class. Once the bourgeois grow tired of making concessions and turn to using state violence, we should expect to suffer a serious blow. Up to this point, the movement could be compared tactically similar to that of Dr. Martin Luther King Jr. The workers are loud and disruptive in their stand against economic injustice, but they do so peacefully. The workers at this point are mainly interested in bettering their own conditions, not fundamentally changing society; but they do not know that by their simple act of unionizing on a major scale, they have already begun fundamentally changing society. When the first violence comes they will be unprepared. They will be bloodied, beaten, and bruised. Many will flee, some temporary, some for good. At this point the movement will face its toughest test. There will be members who want to take their victories and go home and there will be those who call to bomb the Whitehouse - the answer lies in the middle. For those that remain steadfast in their aim and solidarity with one another, the state has shown its hand, and so they must adjust to the changing rules of the game. As the violence continues, the workers discontent with the system will grow as will their discontent with the members who seemingly seek to surrender to the bourgeois. When this contention reaches its boiling point, the unions must be transformed into workers' councils. This act is the revolution! The union's purpose is to shield the workers from the horrors of capitalism and to collectively bargain on their behalf. As the movement becomes more revolutionary, the unions naturally lose their purpose. The workers no longer need a shield, they need a sword! The union leadership will not go quietly in the night. They will try and suppress and contain the revolutionary fervor of the workers because their very existence relies on the stalemate of class struggle, but proletarian liberation requires the end of class struggle through the destruction of the bourgeoise. At this stage the proletariat no longer needs an organ of capitalist production and thus the union leaders are ousted and the unions themselves transformed into organs of revolution. The transformation of union into council takes place when the workers no longer bargain with their labor against the controller of land and capital, but instead seize control of land and capital from the capitalist. Or in a much more well known phrase, the workers seize the means of production! Instead of refusing to work, they take over the work. They oust the individual capitalists and take total control over production. The class union, already structured and organized, immediately unites every conquered business through the same federated system as before. This action gives control of the economic lever of power to the proletariat. If successful, the bourgeois can launch as vicious of an assault as it wishes, and cut off from production its defeat becomes an imminent reality. The proletariats initial victory will be challenged by domestic counterrevolution and foreign intervention on behalf of the fallen national bourgeoise, which is why international support is vital in securing the victory of proletarian revolution. If victory is secured and defended, the period known as the revolutionary dictatorship of the proletariat will have been reached. At this point, society will begin transitioning from capitalism to socialism. A model of this can be seen in foundations through phase one and two. Until phase two is reached and socialist relations to production are established, the revolution has not constructed or reached socialism and should not be referred to as such. The gap between the formation of the class union and the transformation to councils is a long and tenuous road, and victory is not guaranteed. We can only theorize about possible tactics ranging from spontaneous action, to the mass strike, to armed struggle; but the actual tactics that will be used cannot be planned out, they must arise from the proletariats analysis of its ever changing material conditions and then put into practice.

6

Three Sector Model

Introduction:

As the furthest developed nations reach the peak of their industrialization, their productive forces become as vast and efficient as the nation has ever known. However, this peak comes with a cost. The double-edged sword of industrialization for the capitalist lies in the fact that in order for their nation to reach its peak industrial strength, so must the working class reach its peak strength through the organizational power of their unions. As industrial power develops, so too does working class solidarity and collectivization. In other words, by nature of its economic development, capitalism strengthens its direct antagonist - the proletariat. Fortunately for the capitalists, there is a way out. The key to the survival of the capitalists of the furthest developed nations is the process of deindustrialization. We should be more specific as to say modified deindustrialization because the nation is not receding to mercantilism, but transforming itself into a higher stage of capitalism. To deindustrialize would be to dismantle the national industry. The modified form of this is more so a transfer or pawning off of industry than a dismantlement. Through modified deindustrialization, riding the wave of wealth and power afforded to them by their newfound industrial might, the furthest developed nations transform their economies into primarily service-based economies instead of their former industrially based economies. This would also be known as a transformation away from the secondary sector to the tertiary sector. Now, of course, the national economy still requires the power of industry and resource extraction, but it does not necessarily need it domestically (at least not at the same capacity as before the transformation). Capitalism's greatest achievement is that it has united the world into one global economic system, although it still keeps them divided, the process of socializing the entire world is already in development. This global economy allows the furthest developed nations to buy themselves more time from the menace of their domestic proletariat by transferring or outsourcing large portions of their nation's industrial sectors to the less developed nations around the globe. In doing so, the power of the domestic working class and their unions becomes crippled and slowly dies off as workers move from factories into the social alienation of offices and desk jobs. The working class of the less developed nations without established unions and worker solidarity is left to be heavily exploited because of a lack of workers' rights that had already been won by the workers in the furthest developed nations. The capitalists of the less developed nations therefore inherit the now old problem of the further developed capitalists, that being that their nation is quickly industrializing, but so too is their working class and unions growing in number and power. Once these nations reach their industrial peak, they too will seek to pawn off their industrial sector onto even lesser developed nations. This process of industrializing and deindustrializing will continue until there are no countries undeveloped enough to pawn off the industrial sector to. Once that occurs, nations will be forced to slowly but steadily increase their industrial and possibly their primary or resource sectors over time, once again leading to a rise in worker and union power. This time, however, there will be no countries to exploit in order to stifle the growing antagonism of the working class. It is at this point that the level of global unequal development between the most and least developed countries becomes so diminished that an international socialist revolution becomes possible! With the rise of worker and union power across the globe, social democratic movements will flair up and we will see a wave of fascism sweep the world that makes the 1930s look like child's play. Through the violent fascist reaction to this global social democratic movement, the workers will become radicalized that no ideologue nor work of theory need tell them the phrase 'revolution over reform,' because they will know it for themselves. And on the day the majority of the workers of the world hear the cry for revolution in their own minds, that day will be known as the eve of proletarian revolution!

Sector Data:

GDP, current prices (Billions of U.S. dollars)	2017	%	%2	%3
Major Advanced Countries: (G7)	Total GDP	Primary	Secondary	Tertiary
U.S.A.	19477.35	0.90%	19.10%	80%
Germany	3689.547	0.70%	30.70%	68.60%
Japan	4930.837	1.10%	30.10%	68.70%
U.K.	2685.637	0.70%	20.20%	79.20%
France	2594.235	1.70%	19.50%	78.80%
Italy	1961.104	2.10%	23.90%	73.90%
Canada	1649.266	1.60%	28.20%	70.20%
Developing Countries:				
China	12265.327	7.90%	40.50%	51.60%
India	2651.474	15.40%	23%	61.50%
Mexico	1190.721	3.60%	31.90%	64.50%
Nigeria	375.745	21.10%	22.50%	56.40%
Iran	486.829	9.60%	35.30%	55%
Columbia	311.89	7.20%	30.80%	62.10%
Venezuela	115.883	4.70%	40.40%	54.90%
Least Developed Countries (U.N.)				
Myanmar	61.267	24.10%	35.60%	40.30%
D.R. Congo	39.461	19.70%	43.60%	36.70%
Cambodia	22.206	25.30%	32.80%	41.90%
Burkina Faso	14.176	31%	23.90%	44.90%
Niger	11.181	41.60%	19.50%	38.70%
Chad	10.079	52.30%	14.70%	33.10%
Central African Republic	2.072	43.20%	16%	40.80%

Data collected from the IMF Datamapping Tool and CIA World Fact Book.

For our analysis we used the G7 countries to represent the strongest and most developed nations, a random selection of nations listed as developing by the IMF, and a random selection of nations listed as least developed by the U.N. The choice to use data from 2017 was simply for ease of access, as the sector data available to use for the chosen countries was easiest to secure up to the year 2017. Data around 2019-2021 is drastically affected by the COVID-19 pandemic, but from a brief view of the data not much differs in regards to the economic sectors from 2017 to 2024. The economies have grown of course, but the sector percentages themselves have remained relatively the same. A more thorough investigation would be interesting, but we are not here to prove the three-sector model, we just want to analyze the relationship between economic growth and sector growth and depreciation. We discarded small islands and nations that rely on tourism as their service economies are almost always over 95% and by their nature they serve as more of an outlier. We also avoided nations with outdated or no data. The findings hold true to the theory of the three-sector model. The most developed nations have minuscule primary sectors, small secondary sectors, and massive tertiary sectors. The developing countries had small to medium-sized primary sectors (all of which were larger than the most developed nations) and medium to large secondary sectors. The industrial nature of these nations was as predicted large, but in all cases, they were still slightly smaller than the tertiary sectors. Interestingly, the least developed nations had the most balanced sectors of all the nations due to larger primary sectors than the more developed nations. Perhaps the most interesting point is that even though China has the second-largest economy in the world it is still very clearly a developing country. It has built its economy by being the outsourcing center or the industrial center of the world with 40% of its enormous economy dedicated to the industrial sector. In the new Cold War for global hegemony, this could very well be to China's advantage as it has more space to develop as opposed to the U.S. which has an enormous tertiary economy, but we will save that for our later forecast.

Magic Money and the Falling Rate of Profit:

Money (as an evolution of currency) is a foundational pillar of capitalist economics. As briefly mentioned in 'Phase Two,' money has constantly evolved and adapted as capitalism has developed and gone through constant expansions and contractions, or boom-bust cycles. Metallic currency's value depreciated as chunks of their metal chipped away naturally in circulation. This led to the metallic currencies taking on a more symbolic role with fixed values set by their sovereign or minter. Over time, banks began issuing slips of paper called IOUs, allowing merchants to expand business across areas with different currencies. Paul Mattick describes the significance of these early IOUs in his book *The Return of Inflation,*

"Since not everyone reclaims the money they've deposited at the same time, and the money lent by banks is returned at different times, the same money can be loaned to more than one borrower: the bank attempts to keep enough money in reserve to pay out whatever claims are likely over time. The money can be loaned as a note... or in the form of a new deposit, in the borrower's name, in the loaning bank; thus the original money lent to the bank can appear in two or more different deposits, each of which can be used to make payments by banknote. In this way, as with bills of exchange, banks enlarge the money supply."[83]

As the populations of nations grow, more money must be injected into circulation otherwise economic growth will slow or stagnate, and many people will lack the means to purchase goods. The market economy requires circulation to continue. Goods being produced and consumed, capital being accumulated and reinvested, and competition attempting to drive prices to equilibrium. The market is the self-propelling engine of capitalism, but that engine can go bad when wacky things happen to its money supply. The rise of symbolic money allowed nations to implement paper money (commodity money). Historically, the supply of these banknotes would be backed in full by a direct convertibility to an equal amount of gold bullion, this method became known as the gold standard. But the days of the gold standard are over. Some gold bullion is still held in reserve to back the value of money,

[83] 2023 Mattick, p. 22-23

however, it can no longer serve as the main reserve because our demand to increase the money supply has far exceeded our gold reserves. Following the Bretton Woods agreement that laid the foundation for staking the U.S. Dollar as the asset of monetary reserve globally, and the U.S. complete severance from the gold standard in 1971, Mattick writes,

"Thanks both to the U.S. trade deficit and to the dollar's role as reserve currency, American money accumulated internationally, increasing the monetary bases of other countries without reducing that of the USA. Today, the world's currencies consist of paper (or electronic) central bank credit money, backed in all countries by reserves of dollars and a few other currencies, and still... some gold."[84]

The post-war recovery at home and in Europe, as well as the intensity of the Cold War was all backed by increased government spending. Whether that spending is to provide healthcare, education, and housing to one's citizens, or to bomb the hospitals, schools, and homes of foreigners doesn't really make a difference. All that matters is economic growth! Borrowing money and increasing debt to promote the expansion of the global economy is much more favorable than the alternative of a balanced budget with economic stagnation. This is why regular inflation is widely regarded as preferable to deflation because it signals economic growth as opposed to stagnation. Mattick explains how the Federal Reserve influences the amount of currency in circulation by purchasing treasury bonds with Federal Reserve Notes (the paper money in your wallet) and how they set the interest rates at which banks can borrow money from them. He further says,

"That all money is produced today by banks and other financial institutions tells us that the banking system, essential to the functioning of a capitalist economy, has acquired a governmental character."

The evolution of industrial capitalism to finance capitalism is a major moment in the history of our world that has led to a mass increase in economic growth, development, and for many, prosperity. However, this

---

[84] 2023 Mattick, p. 35-36

evolution is not distinct from one another in a way that alters class struggle as a whole. For example, although feudalism and capitalism co-existed for a time, one eventually had to trounce the other. The two systems' internal contradictions demanded mutual exclusivity as the top dog over society at large. This holds true for capitalism and socialism. The two are antithetical to each other and so both cannot co-exist or collaborate in tandem as the global economic system. In the case of industrial and finance capitalism, both are simply developments of the same economic base. Capitalism can develop past industrialism, but it cannot sever itself from it completely, because the basis of finance capital is built upon the foundation of industrial capitalism. The evolution to finance capitalism was necessitated by the self-propelled engine of growth, expansion, and ultimately, profit. There is no 'going back' to the way things were before because to do that would be to contradict capitalism's basic principles. Government intervention in the economy and monetary policy, the replacement of commodity money with credit money, and the staking of the U.S. debt as the chief reserve currency are the natural evolutions of capitalism. Through boom and through bust, the wheel of historical progression will continue to turn. Ride with it or be crushed.

Falling Rate of Profit:

Here we must tie in Marx's argument in *Capital Volume III* that as capitalism develops, there is a tendency for the rate of profit to fall. The claim is that the eternal competition between capitalists in the chase of profit will continue to grow and expand industries. As these industries grow, the capitalists will seek out and deploy labor-saving technologies (automation and innovation) to increase the output of commodities through an increased productivity of labor. Abstractly, an increase in the productivity of labor would increase the rate of surplus value extraction, because (labor hours remaining the same) the increased productivity reduces the labor hours required to reproduce the value of the living labor (the worker) and increases the labor hours of unpaid labor (surplus). This increase in productivity would theoretically increase the rate of profit due to increasing the rate of surplus extraction, however, it neglects the integral nature of dead and living labor or constant and variable capital. As labor becomes more productive its output per hour increases, but this increase in output necessitates an increase in inputs to take advantage of said increase in productivity. To put it more clearly, if workers normally produce 100 widgets in a working day and a new machine allows them to produce widgets twice as fast, it does not benefit the capitalist if the workers produce 100 widgets in half the working day and then go home. Instead, the capitalist derives his gain through the workers producing 200 widgets in the full working day. The machine allows the capitalist to increase the productivity of his laborers, but he must also increase the materials used by those laborers in order to take advantage of their new capabilities.

Therefore, an increase in the productivity of variable capital demands an increase in constant capital. As surplus value can only be extracted from variable capital, the rate of surplus value (or profit) depends on the proportion of variable capital in production. If the proportion of constant capital to variable capital increases, then the rate of profit should decrease. It's important to remember we are dealing with proportions and rates, not totalities. The variable capital or workforce population can increase, but so long as the growth of tools and materials used by it exceeds its own, the proportion of variable capital used in production will decrease. As the productivity of labor increases, the proportion of surplus value to necessary labor increases, however, it decreases in proportion to the proportion of constant capital advanced in the production process. This difference in proportion will only widen as automation and innovation continue. So, while the business may continue to grow and reap more profits than ever before, the profit per unit sold will decrease. Thus, the rate of profit will tend to fall over time.[85]

Conclusion:

[85] The tendency of the rate of profit to fall is hotly contested not just by economists, but among Marxists as well.

If our projection that capitalist development will inevitably lead to a diminished level of development inequality between the most and least developed nations comes to fruition, we would expect to see a general equaling out of the sectors to something around 10% primary, 30% secondary, and 40% tertiary, give or take 3-5% per sector. Some nations will always have large primary sectors due to an abundance of natural resources and island nations will always have vastly tertiary economies, but the bulk of nations should have more comparable economic sectors. The path to this stage would likely be one of the greatest eras of human prosperity ever known, but an even greater contraction would be well on the way.

As the level of unequal development flattens due to the development of global capitalism, the rate of profit should also tend to fall as the productivity of labor increases alongside innovation and automation. A falling rate of profit would lead to a slowing of economic growth and thus less attraction for investments. Labor-saving technologies would continue to decrease the demand for workers in comparison to constant capital across most industries continuing the decrease in the rate of surplus value extraction and thus the rate of profit. This lower demand for workers would throw more bodies onto the labor market further who will chase high wages until wages decrease to near equilibrium across the board. From here, the unemployed population, or industrial reserve army as Marx referred to them, would further act as reverse pressure on increasing wages, and falling wages are a great catalyst for mass unionization movements!

Once this equality in development is reached, the strength of the financial economy will waiver because there will be nowhere for the capitalists to dump their industrial base. The falling rate of profit and the organization of the real economy across all nations will reveal the conditions for socialist revolution unfolding across the world rather quickly, but that does not mean socialism will just come into existence. The revolutionaries must be ready with their organizations and foundations already constructed and ready to organize the working class to realize their ultimate liberation. If they fail and an era of fascism reigns, many nations will be economically destroyed and it will take many years for development to equalize again, therefore, we should strive to get it right this go around![86]

[86] As Paul Mattick puts it on p. 138, "Though the stock and bond values vaporized in periodic crashes can be replenished by central banks, capitalist society cannot keep going without the steady production of goods and services that can be sold to yield returns reinvested in plant, equipment, and labor able to generate yet more value and profit. That is, the 'real economy' and money are... indissoluble aspects of one system... If capitalists can't make enough money to pay their workers enough to afford the rents or mortgages of their homes... mortgage-based bonds and venture-capital investments will not turn a profit. Housing prices will eventually collapse... and the money invested in them will disappear. Every period of prosperity involves the extension of credit a point in which it outstrips the ability of profit production to support repayment... This is why business-cycle downturns appear as banking and stock-market crashes as well as the sudden appearance of unsalable goods and unemployable workers."

7

On Violence

Is It Necessary?

With many people witnessing an armed resistance against a colonial force for the first time, the debate between violent and nonviolent resistance is heating up once again. There is no debate to be had. Liberation and revolution inherently require violence. That is not to say that nonviolent demonstrations cannot be very powerful tools in liberation movements, as demonstrated by Dr. Martin Luther King Jr. in the American Civil Rights movement. But unlike American schools would have you believe today, Dr. King's nonviolent demonstrations were just one part of the larger Civil Rights movement. Alongside him were armed revolutionaries like the members of the Black Panther Party, and those who did not actively use violence but recognized that the struggle had to be won by any means necessary, like Malcolm X. The armed defense of communities, and the riots demanding change alongside Dr. King demonstrating nonviolent solidarity in the face of state violence, were all key factors in achieving a successful liberation struggle. While Dr. King himself considered riots to be an indefensible form of resistance, he understood the conditions that stirred the masses to take to the streets. People often quote this small excerpt from his speech *The Other America, "... a riot is the language of the unheard."* But let's take a look at the full quote to understand his full point.

"But it is not enough for me to stand before you tonight and condemn riots. It would be morally irresponsible for me to do that without, at the same time, condemning the contingent, intolerable conditions that exist in our society. These conditions are the things that cause individuals to feel that they have no other alternative than to engage in violent rebellions to get attention. And I must say tonight that a riot is the language of the unheard. And what is it America has failed to hear? It has failed to hear that the plight of the negro poor has worsened over the last twelve or fifteen years. It has failed to hear that the promises of freedom and justice have not been met. And it has failed to hear that large segments of white society are more concerned about tranquility and the status quo than about justice and humanity."[87]

While against the violent nature of riots, he would not condemn them without addressing their cause. For him, their cause was the helplessness of the Black people of America in their quest to achieve true equality and justice, but this applies to all liberation struggles and very prominently to the way the media has covered the current Israel-Palestine conflict. Whenever a Palestinian voice has been brought on the news to discuss the plight of their people, any attempt to shine a light on the 75-year occupation of their people is cut off in favor of the question, "Do you condemn Hamas?" The interview is hijacked from the very beginning. The media wishes for the oppressed to condemn the riot, but will never let them condemn the conditions that caused the riot to start. To the media members, the rioters woke up on the wrong side of the bed and decided to commit indiscriminate random violence. All context is stripped and the violence itself is put under the microscope. They are obsessed with the effect but never the cause. This can be observed through the end of his quote where he explains that the white liberal, no matter how big an ally they portray themselves to be, is more concerned with defending the status quo than achieving true justice and

---

[87] King Jr. 1968

equality. We see this today when liberals and many so-called progressives are quick to abandon their false platitudes for the oppressed as soon as they 'riot' against the conditions brought upon them by their oppressors. It seems that for many, it is easy to stand up for the oppressed when they resign themselves to take the beating, but when the oppressed suffer enough bruises and decide to punch back, their allies creep back to the fence and call for 'peace.' But what is peace to the oppressed? Peace without victory is a call for a return to normalcy, a return to the status quo, a return to suffering in silence. As Kwame Ture put it, *"There's a difference between peace and liberation... You can have injustice and have peace... So peace isn't the answer. Liberation is the answer... that's the white man's word: Peace. Liberation is our word."*[88] Calls for peace without solving the conditions that bring war are nothing more than advocating for further oppression with a smile. It's modern progressivism (liberalism) at its finest. As Dr. King wrote in *Where Do We Go From Here, "Freedom is not won by a passive acceptance of suffering. Freedom is won by a struggle against suffering."*[89]

National Liberation

However, a struggle for civil rights is quite different than a struggle for national liberation or decolonization. While in a sense both are seeking justice and equality, a national liberation struggle will inherently be more violent than a civil rights struggle because the movement is not demanding change from the state, it is itself replacing the state by abolishing the current state of things. Nowhere is this inherently violent struggle better detailed than in the pages of Franz Fanon's *The Wretched of the Earth*. He opens his text with the statement, *"...decolonization is always a violent event... decolonization is quite simply the substitution of one 'species' of mankind by another. The substitution is unconditional, absolute, total, and seamless."*[90] No matter the

[88] Tell Me Lies (A Film About London), 1968

[89] King Jr. 2010, Ch. 1 p. 20

[90] Fanon 2022, p. 1

internal struggles or factions within a colonial nation, the society is divided into two inherently antagonistic forces - the colonizer and the colonized. They are inherently antagonistic like the bourgeoisie and the proletariat, because one cannot exist without the other. The colonized without their colonizer is just a native population with self-determination, the colonizer deprived them of this. Fanon explains that this division in society is secured because *"frequent, direct intervention by the police and the military ensure the colonized are kept under close scrutiny."*[91] In other words, the colonized are subjugated by the state violence of the colonizer. Fanon further describes how the colonizers dehumanize the native population, *"The native is declared impervious to ethics, representing not only the absence of values but also the negation of values. He is, dare we say it, the enemy of values. And other words, absolute evil."*[92] We can see this use of dehumanization domestically, and in foreign imperial and colonial actions to justify the use of state violence. Domestically we often see the media used to decry Black people and immigrants as 'thugs' and criminals, and through the whitewashing of Dr. Martin Luther King Jr., anyone who breaks from the nonviolent approach is deemed as a radical for betraying the peaceful legacy of Dr. King. Most notably abroad, the Arab world and Muslims in particular have been actively dehumanized by the media for decades now to justify foreign intervention to secure resources, topple governments, and secure the Zionist state of Israel.

Furthermore, Fanon described the driver for revolution, *"The colonist's world is a hostile world, a world which excludes yet at the same time incites envy. We have seen how the colonized always dream of taking the colonist's place. Not of becoming a colonist, but of replacing him. This hostile, oppressive and aggressive world, bulldozing the colonized masses, represents not only the hell they would like to escape as quickly as possible but a paradise within arm's reach guarded by ferocious watchdogs."*[93] He then explains that *"The colonized subject discovers*

[91] Fanon 2022, p. 4

[92] Fanon 2022, p. 6

[93] Fanon 2022, p. 16

reality and transforms it through his praxis, his deployment of violence and his agenda for liberation... The challenge now is to seize this violence as it realigns itself. Whereas it once reveled in myths and contrived ways to commit collective suicide, a fresh set of circumstances will now enable it to change directions."[94] It should become clear that colonialism is a violent process that attacks the colonized both physically and mentally. It cuts them off from the world, dehumanizes them, and beats them down with force. The contradiction, however, is that the harder the boot is pressed against the oppressed, the more the need for violent struggle arises. Because of the violent nature of colonialism, it can almost always only be dismantled through the violent struggle of the oppressed. Peace movements and reformists may win temporary reforms, but increasingly more reactionary elements of the colonial government will work tirelessly to repeal said reforms, and in truth, further worsen the condition of the colonized. Violence is most definitely the answer; the question, however, is how to organize the violence into a movement that can achieve not just national liberation, but a better society. It is probably wishful thinking that the liberation movement, in abolishing their colonial government, does not then subjugate itself to the domination of the world market by establishing itself as a petty capitalist nation, but as a united class of workers producing for their common good. Nevertheless, the removal of the colonial government, unless somehow replaced by feudalism, can be considered a historically progressive movement.

Conclusion:

While non-violent tactics are of vital importance to revolutionary movements, especially in the movement's infancy when it does not yet possess the power or numbers to violently resist its oppressors, a denial or flat-out refusal to adopt violent tactics is the most infantile idea imaginable. Acknowledging the necessity of violence does not mean the adoption of all forms of violence or indiscriminate violence for that matter, it simply means

---

[94] Fanon 2022, p. 21

one realizes that reform can only go so far before it can either be transformed into a revolutionary movement or be snuffed out along with all its gains. The necessity of violence is of the utmost importance to national liberation movements as Frantz Fanon so passionately described in the pages of *The Wretched of the Earth,* however, that does not necessarily mean that national liberation is still a part of Marxist ideology. The feudal governments have all been overthrown and the capitalist mode of production reigns supreme across the globe. Some argue that because of this, any national liberation movements today are simply bourgeois wars. There is truth to this, of course, but we believe that even if these movements are not inherently Marxist, they still provide a great benefit to developing the necessary global conditions required for an international socialist revolution. The multi-polar world we are heading toward through the new Cold War between the U.S. and China will allow many nations to attempt to secure more of their economic and political sovereignty. As capitalist competition forces corporations to compete for control of the consumer market, so too does a multi-polar world force the two global superpowers to compete for control of global hegemony by winning the influence of the smaller nations. We hope that as this competition and general development of global capitalism continues, all nations reach a certain level of development that they no longer have to take orders from the global powers. To do this, they will of course need support from their neighbors, which can be achieved through regional alliances and trading blocs. As all of this occurs and the three-sector model balances out, the international proletariat should be organizing and building the power they need to launch the revolt for their future.

8

Forecasting Revolution

Introduction:

The burning debate between socialism in one country and international proletarian revolution should have been settled before it even began. Nearly two centuries ago in his pamphlet *The Principles of Communism,* Friedrich Engels answered the question of if it would be possible for revolution to occur in one singular nation. He wrote,

"No. By creating the world market, big industry has already brought all the peoples of the Earth, and especially the civilized peoples, into such close relation with one another that none is independent of what happens to the others. Further, it has co-ordinated the social development of the civilized countries to such an extent that, in all of them, bourgeoisie and proletariat have become the decisive classes, and the struggle between them the great struggle of the day. It follows that the communist revolution will not merely be a national phenomenon but must take place simultaneously in all civilized countries — that is to say, at least in England, America, France, and Germany. It will develop in each of these countries more or less rapidly, according as one country or the other has a more developed industry, greater wealth, a more significant mass of productive forces. Hence, it will go slowest and will meet most obstacles in Germany, most rapidly and with the fewest difficulties in England. It will have a powerful impact on the other countries of the world, and will radically alter the course of development which they have followed up to now, while greatly stepping up its pace. It is a universal revolution and will, accordingly, have a universal range."[95]

In order for the conditions to be right for a global proletarian revolution, the difference between first and third world nations must be as diminished as possible. This means a world where the vast majority of nations have total economic and political self-determination alongside a developed capitalist mode of production. There has been no point in human history where this condition has been met, therefore, never before has a successful implementation of socialism been possible. In our brief analysis of the Soviet and Chinese revolutions we explained that while they contributed to historical progression, they could not lead the world into the next era of humanity - the era of socialism - because the global conditions were not sufficiently developed to that end.[96]

A lot of time has gone by since the revolutions of the past. The USSR collapsed into a corporatist oligarchy by the end of the Cold War, and China today is arguably better at using the capitalist mode of production than the United States. As we now understand it, these revolutions were more akin to bourgeois revolutions in that they overthrew backward governmental and economic structures, along with developing both capitalism and therefore the proletariat of their nations; although we would use the term bourgeois revolution much more loosely when regarding the USSR as it was practically the first real attempt at a socialist revolution (Dual revolution would be a better term). But the fact remains the same, no matter what a country labels itself or what American 'journalists' label their opposition, there are no communist nor socialist nations on earth. For one, because every nation operates a capitalist economy based upon generalized commodity production/wage labor, private property, and value-form economics. More importantly, it's not possible to have socialism in one country and survive long enough to have any semblance of relevancy, because once again,

[95] Engels 1914, "Principles of Communism"

[96] (Pt. I, Ch. 2, 'Role of the Party')

revolution is an international or global phenomenon. It is shortsighted to expect that we will see the toppling of capitalism and the rise of socialist production in our lifetimes because history tells us otherwise. Economic systems mark eras of human history. They span centuries and their rise and fall are not singular events that we can point to in a history book; they rise and fall out of a series of events relating to the natural contradictions between the preceding mode of production and the succeeding mode of production. That period of transformation will obviously be marked by a series of failed revolutions, a rise and fall of varying theories and figures, and death and destruction. One should not be confused by any of this or question why changing the order of the world requires violence for it always has.

Let's take a look at our present age and attempt to forecast a possible future. The three global powers today remain the USA, China, and in a distant third place, Russia. Since the end of WW2 and the collapse of the USSR, the USA has held firm control of global hegemony - the world runs on the US Dollar, Europe/NATO is subsidized by the US, leveraging its power over the ruins of the world post-WW2, the vast majority of the new United Nations became powerless in proportion to the US, there are American military bases all over the world, and the Middle East has been under constant military and economic siege for over a century. Russia following the collapse of the USSR has been able to remain a global power and a dominant force in Europe through the consolidation of power under Vladimir Putin. They are in an ongoing proto-proxy war with the United States via the Russo-Ukrainian War that restarted in 2022. We say proto-proxy war as the U.S. is not currently actively engaging the Russian army on the ground, but supplying the Ukrainian military with money, supplies, and weaponry. As for who is in the 'right' and 'wrong' in this conflict is not of any real relevance. One can acknowledge that Russia is very obviously on the wrong side by invading and butchering a nation over the bruised ego of a despotic oligarch, while at the same time not wishing to prolong a war and the bloody destruction that comes with it inevitably. The Ukrainian people are absolutely in the right to defend themselves from yet another territorial land grab from Russia, but the question that only they can answer is for how long they are willing to see their friends, family, sons, and daughters throw their lives away over national pride and soil. If against all odds Ukraine can defend its sovereignty and even win back its lost land, the nation will be dredged in political and economic turmoil for the next century! Internal strife, devastated infrastructure, and debts to the nations that funded their defense will either lead to internal coups or national subservience to its new masters. The price of victory is steep, and what Ukraine is willing to pay can only be determined by its people.

China on the other hand has been busy studying from the past. They have been developing at a rapid rate through a symbiotic relationship with capitalist nations. The great powers of the West require the labor of underdeveloped nations to cheapen production costs in the unending race for profit and expansion. China just so happened to have a lot of cheap labor to offer, to the point that today the global market is extremely reliant on China for industry and production. This over-reliance has allowed China under the oversight of the CPC to grow the country into not only a regional power, but a global economic and military power second only to the United States, and that point is arguable. It is very obvious that we are in a second Cold War, there are however a few major differences between this Cold War and the last. Firstly, Russia is not one of the major powers. This Cold War is between the United States and China with the end goal once again being control of global hegemony. Secondly, in the first Cold War, both the US and the USSR were rapidly developing powers; this time around, the US is not in a state of mass expansion or development. Instead, it has reached a higher stage of development at the expense of its industrial might. The American economy is still strong and growing, but domestically and politically, the nation is incredibly strained. Its political leaders should be playing sudoku in a retirement home instead of drafting policy, and the political realm itself slides further into right-wing radicalism every election cycle to the point that people are being asked to vote for their favorite flavor of genocide at the ballot box. Rising wealth inequality, a lower standard of living compared to the size of its economy, and the power of the internet are all factors that are steadily radicalizing the American population and ever so slowly tearing down the propaganda instilled into generations of Americans during the Red Scare (access to the internet has also led to increased reactionary radicalization, though traditional media has bolstered it as well). These factors mark the beginning of the decline of the American Empire just as its Cold War with a rapidly developing power in China is escalating. With America divided over funding Ukraine's defensive war against Russia, the shocking display of large numbers of Americans (especially the American youth protesting in support of Palestine against the genocidal apartheid state of Israel), a massive increase in both the numerical and political power of reactionary republicans and large swathes of the population dissatisfied with their government, the foundation of American indoctrination appears to be slipping out from underneath the ruling class.

The lesson that China learned from studying the past is that trying to match the US militarily is a fool's errand. They need a large and modernized military of course, but they do not need to allocate nearly as much government spending to their military and proxy conflicts as their economy, a lesson learned from the failure of the USSR. China plans to compete with the U.S. economically and through foreign policy, both very winnable fronts due to the fact that the U.S. is overextended, declining, and does not have many friends outside of Western Europe. Ironically in this competition for control of global hegemony, China's strongest tactic is to do nothing. So long as they continue to manage and develop their economy while offering underdeveloped nations another alternative, the contradictions of the U.S.'s own development will unravel itself. To simplify this conflict to sports terms, the aging champion (USA) in their overconfidence is stepping into the ring with a hungry underdog (China) - an underdog that they themselves sold PEDs to earlier in their career. Without bias, a betting man would put all their chips on the underdog. The only thing keeping the betting line close is the champion's historic reign, but fight after fight it's becoming more and more clear that the champion isn't what they once were. There are three possible conclusions to this Cold War. First, the USA manages to hang on to global hegemony most likely due to a collapse of China's economy. The collapse of the Asian market would send economic tidal waves across the globe, but the over billion population of China would again become subservient to Western capitalist influence. Secondly, China succeeds in supplanting the U.S. as the controller of global hegemony. It's vital to understand that a Chinese victory over the U.S. does not mean a victory for socialism. This victory would only mean the swapping of global control from a Western capitalist superpower to an Eastern capitalist superpower. The part we take interest in is the effects that swap will have on the world through foreign policy both internationally and regionally. Lastly, it is technically possible that the conflict will stalemate, leaving us with a multi-polar world with two global capitalist superpowers. This competition can be preferable as it forces the global powers to compete for influence across the world which can lead to better development of the global south, but it can also lead to a lot of unneeded bloodshed. While the Cold War will lead to multi-polarity, it is likely this will only be temporary until scenario one or two takes place. We foresee the most likely scenario to be option two.

What does this dawn of a new global hegemony have in store for the rest of the world? Let's take a look. The U.S. was able to build its economic might off the back of supplying Europe through two world wars and taking advantage of the weakened Western colonial empires in the following years of reconstruction. While it's able to convince its citizens that the free market won over the evil of 'communism,' the citizens of the global south know a different story. They know a story of colonialism, subjugation, deprivation, maldevelopment, death and dismay. This story cannot be edited through press releases or state visits, it can only be mended through actual actions. Actions that the U.S. and Western powers are unable to make. China is not some hero for the underdeveloped nations, they too deal in economic colonialism and the creation of spheres of influence, however, there is a stark difference that favors them. The countries in Africa, Latin America, and the Middle-East did not suffer through a history of brutal military occupation turned to brutal economic colonialism by China. In fact, many of these countries have good relations with China, especially because of initiatives like the Belt & Road. China has shown an ability to expand its spheres of influence with a smile and a handshake, through economic and developmental partnerships, not through warships, assassinations, and coup d'états'. It is for this reason that we can predict a world under Chinese control will be a somewhat better alternative for the nations of the third world. Debt trapping will still be an issue, but these nations will have a far easier time developing their national economies and therefore also their proletariat because of a stronger sense of stability. The scars of Western imperialism and colonialism will begin to fade as they no longer have to predominantly deal with their historic oppressors. In tandem this will lead to politically and economically stronger nations, helping to diminish the gap between first and third world. However, this will also breed strong national characters in these regions, leading to conflicts and wars for control of regional hegemony. Let's take a closer look at these regional zones.

North America:

North America is one of the more straightforward regional zones. While we predict the collapse of the American Empire, it is highly unlikely foreign tanks will ever roll through Washington D.C. and plant a flag on the White House lawn. The collapse of the empire means the U.S. will be left as a major regional power and still a sizable world power, probably comparable to Russia today, only economically stronger. The majority of its bases across the world, particularly in East Asia and the Middle East, will be evacuated and with it a diminishment of the strength of their spheres of influence in the region. They will likely hold on to influence in Europe, South & North America, Oceania, and some parts of Africa. Their direct neighbors Canada and Mexico are not political, economic, or military threats, not even after the collapse of the empire. The biggest threat the U.S. will face is internal strife and the power vacuum that follows. The increasing radicalism of liberal politics in the U.S. since the election of Ronald Reagan laid the red carpet out for the Trump presidency. This steady road to right-wing extremism in America is an unavoidable consequence of its pseudo-duopoly political structure. Because both parties share the same structural views on the economy and foreign policy, all they disagree on is social issues, or as they are commonly referred to, culture wars. These culture wars are the method of the political radicalization of the common citizen. Although voters love to talk about the economy, the vast majority of them have no idea what the economy is, or why Politician D's ideas are any Different than Politician R's ideas. People vote based on what is important to them and what they find important to them is decided by the media they consume, it is no longer a personal choice, if it ever was. If a viewer tunes into 'mainstream' media like CNN or MSNBC, they will be spun in a Neo-liberal, borderline socially progressive narrative; and if they tune into Fox News, they will be radicalized against their own interests in favor of those of reactionary actors. This radicalism will inevitably come to a head and either come out victorious or decimated, and if it hasn't spilled over into violence before the empire collapses it certainly will after. It's impossible to foresee what the conditions will look like when this 'second civil war' occurs, but if things follow as they have been we can make a few inferences. First, historically the true left wing of the United States has been demonized and dismantled through the ruling class's interest in dismantling communism both domestically and abroad. Leaders have been imprisoned and assassinated, citizens witch-hunted through the era of McCarthyism, and the Communist Party (CPUSA) co-opted and subjugated by the Democratic Party. The 'lesser evilism' of the past few decades has led people to the choice of voting for Candidate Genocide or Candidate Genocide Jr., and any who vote against genocide are lambasted by the others for not supporting their favorite genocidal leader. People feel stuck and the conditions are only worsening. The largest left-leaning organization in the U.S. is the DSA with just under 100,000 members, and it is one with next to zero revolutionary potential. To say it plainly, in the event of a political revolution in the U.S., the reactionaries on the right wing are in a much more advantageous position than those on the left. The regular liberal, or in this case the Democratic Party, would be completely ineffective in the face of a true insurrection. They would be too busy trying to file court proceedings to stop the hangman from tying the noose around their neck. The only force capable of stopping conservative radicalism once it has reached the point of no return is a large, organized force of revolutionary leftists (Socialists/Communists), and unfortunately at this stage, there is no organized force ready to stand in their way. Fortunately, however, historical progression waits for no man. Whether the reactionaries, leftists, or Neo-liberals hold power, history will progress all the same. While it would of course be preferred that the leftists take control of the U.S., it is most likely that they will fail and temporarily put both the U.S. and its neighbors under the sphere of radical social conservatism. Though this time period will be terrible for the people who live through it and many atrocities will likely be committed, it will be temporary. In this scenario, it is possible the surrounding nations, particularly those in Central and South America, could form a coalition against the U.S. Together or individually, they may also seek protection from China in return for greater Chinese influence in the region.

Latin America:

However the U.S. turns out, Latin America will remain a vitally important theater for international socialist revolution. Before we move to the mainland, there is a small island in the Caribbean that could play an important role: Cuba! While not achieving socialism, Cuba remains a shining example of anti-imperialism. Through sanctions, invasions, assassination attempts, and an ongoing embargo, the Cuban government has remained both stable and functioning. While there are concerns about the economy drifting further and further away from building towards socialism and general economic turmoil, the nation's success in winning and securing its independence and sovereignty serves as a bastion of liberation for all anti-imperial struggles in the present and future. If able to renew itself to the cause of building socialism, Cuba could leverage its history of anti-imperialism to support the growth of revolutionary consciousness throughout North and South America, especially in places like Mexico, Bolivia, and Panama, which would set the groundwork for a possible future socialist bloc! Now let us move back to the continent and take a brief look at a few more countries, including those previously listed.

Mexico is a large nation with a large economy, and it is currently the U.S.'s top trading partner. It is, of course, not without its internal strife. The nation is riddled with political corruption and powerful criminal cartels, however, there is a far more interesting group that holds some power within Mexico - the Zapatistas. The Zapatistas are a left-wing militant group that has successfully held control of nearly 10,000 miles of land in Chiapas to this day. It is not in the scope of our current investigation to deeply analyze the Zapatistas and their theoretical basis; our interest is with Mexico as a whole. And in the event that the U.S. does fall into the hands of reactionary right-wing extremists, it is a high probability that Mexico will bear the brunt of their assault. The seeds of this have been set over the raging debate over immigration and drug flow into the U.S. to the point that candidates for President in the Republican primary were competing to see who had the most radical plan to militarily attack Mexico to 'secure the border' and 'destroy the cartels.' Under the control of a reactionary leader and population, these campaign promises could very likely be put into effect and an invasion of northern Mexico and a country-wide bombing campaign could take place. It is for that reason Mexico, unless able to join a coalition of nations, would be more likely to face a war for national sovereignty than a class war.

South America is another very turbulent area with no true dominant regional power. It could be argued that Brazil is the regional power, but all of these nations have tense political climates with histories full of foreign intervention, coups, and dictatorships. Venezuela has been posturing towards intervention in Guyana, Argentina is trying to implement libertarian economics, and there was allegedly another attempted coup in Bolivia. There is nothing right now that can lead to any definite predictions for the future outlook of South America, but we are hopeful that the workers of these nations can eventually come together and form a strong regional power bloc.

The Middle East:

The Middle East is a fascinating theater because for the past century, it has been one of the major focal points for both political and economic imperialism, military occupation, and modern colonialism styled like that of the preindustrial era. The major players in the region are currently Iran, Saudi Arabia, Israel, Egypt, and Turkey if you include them. As with every country we mention, the controllers of regional power are always subject to change as history unfolds. For example, Iraq was a major player with one of the largest militaries in the world until the U.S. invaded and destabilized the nation in 2003. Afghanistan is a nation of interest due to its title earned through blood, 'The Graveyard of Empires." However, it is not of interest to us because the reason it was able to survive and win its conflicts with the USSR and the U.S. was due to its extreme economic underdevelopment and guerrilla tactics - great for defensive measures, but not so great for securing regional hegemonic power. There are of course other smaller nations like Jordan, Qatar, Yemen, Lebanon, and Syria, but these nations are either too small to compete or are themselves political pawns of the larger regional powers. Of the major players, the three truly competing for regional hegemony are Israel, Saudi Arabia, and Iran. All three of these nations are abysmal and their rule would be less than satisfactory for the region, but one must win. On one end you have Israel, the *'beacon of democracy and Western values in the region of darkness,'* as a Zionist would lead you to believe, masking the truth of a genocidal theocratic ethnostate. On the other end, you have the *'great anti-imperialist force'* in the Islamic Republic of Iran. A nation led by the Ayatollahs - high-ranking Muslim clerics - who came to power after co-opting a coup against the Western-backed Shah of Imperial Iran, Mohammad Reza Pahlavi. And with their power, they repress the people, deprive them of human dignity, and persecute and execute many. Between these two poles of evil lies Saudi Arabia, a theocratic monarchy rich off of its desert of oil and migrant labor,[97] whose leaders cannot decide whether they want to exchange their 'king' for a 'pawn' of the U.S. or China. These three give us the perfect trifecta of ugly stupidity. Iran was able to stabilize itself from internal revolution by uniting its people in their defense from Iraq's invasion in 1980, an invasion the U.S. funded with military and economic aid. Their successful defense and new ability to blame Iraqi expansion on the U.S., or more notably Western imperialism, gave Iran the tool to ensure continued stability for the years to come. Defending the Middle East, including its Arab neighbors from Western expansion is the Iranian battle cry; it is the tool that is used to stifle and subjugate its people. And the main force of Western imperialism they decry is not the vast American military base, it is the 'unsinkable aircraft carrier,' the 'only democracy in the Middle East,' the State of Israel. Here we will quote in long form our article, *The West Cheers for Genocide,* following the October 7th attack on Israel originally published on October 12th, 2023.

"On October 7th, 2023 the world awoke to the news that Israel was under attack by Hamas-led terrorists from Palestine. The news came in rapidly across social media and the misinformation was and is still running rampant currently. From reports of ISIS flags to mass rape and the decapitation of forty infant babies, everyone without personal stakes or interest in the conflict will only know what the media tells them, and the media has not been this united on an issue in my lifetime. From solely projecting the point of view of the Israeli government and its supporters abroad and downplaying the immense damage done to the people of Gaza as "self-defense," the Western media is actively manufacturing consent. Consent for what? To further demonize the Palestinian people as savage animals of a barbaric religion to help further the goal of Israel, their great ally in the Middle East, the complete ethnic cleansing of the Palestinian people. Genocide.

The State of Israel brought upon the region by the British mandate and

---

[97] CIA World Fact Book: Approximately 40% of Saudi Arabia's population is comprised of non-citizens

the Zionist movement is the disease that withholds the region from peace. Before its creation, the Palestinians were as they are today a multicultural group of indigenous people, Jews and Arabs of all Abrahamic faiths lived together. One must understand Palestinian doesn't mean Arab, nor does it mean Muslim, there are Palestinians of various races, colors, and creeds. The issue started when a Zionist state, a state for the Jewish people was established on this land disenfranchising a large portion of the population. Jewish people fleeing persecution from the Holocaust in Europe and the rest of the world came in droves taking land promised to them by those who had no right to promise it. In doing so these immigrants to Palestine became settlers, and so the state of Israel from its foundation was a state of settler colonialism and apartheid. Facing a force backed by foreign powers, the resistance of the Palestinians was futile, and more and more land was taken, embruing further discontent, hatred, and violence between settlers and natives. As this process has gone on the Palestinian Territories have been split into the Gaza Strip and the West Bank. While the West Bank faces its own threats, especially with settlers, when the Palestinian struggle reaches the mainstream news it is almost always because of Gaza. The Gaza Strip is one of the most densely populated regions in the world. It is approximately 140 square miles and home to over 2.2 million people. Of these 2.2 million people, half are children, half are women and young girls, 50% are unemployed, and about 90% have inadequate access to clean drinking water. While Hamas is the representative organization of Gaza, it is Israel that on a whim can blockade the strip and deprive it of food, water, power, and gasoline, that is the definition of control. The Gaza Strip is beholden to Israel. It is walled in and pinned against the sea, the roads to Egypt have been blockaded and bombed, and Israel has threatened to bombard any trucks bringing supplies and aid across the border, they cannot build an airport or coastal ports. It is without question the largest open-air prison on earth. It is said to be born in Gaza is to be born dead. And unfortunately for the people of Gaza, death is all they've ever known. Bombings, invasions, kidnappings, and cold-blooded murders conducted by the IDF have been the status quo of Gaza for its entire modern history.

And those that survive live a life of extreme poverty sitting in the dark with their family praying a bomb doesn't level their entire street.

Hamas while without a doubt an organization with terroristic elements (initially supported by the State of Israel to further fracture the PLO no less), is not the cause of these conflicts, it is merely a symptom of the Israeli regime. When you continue to pack and condense 2 million people into a strip of land six times smaller than the city of Jacksonville, and you starve them, poison their water, bulldoze their streets and farms, slaughter their families, and bomb their homes, schools, mosques, and hospitals, you are radicalizing a generation of people who have nothing to lose. When you suffer in silence and the world ignores you, when you protest peacefully and are shot, men, women, and children alike, what are you to do? When you're locked in a prison where all you know is death, when the prison gates open all you will find is death. We should condemn the killing of the innocent Israeli people and the foreign nationals at the music festival no matter how distasteful the event was, but we must not condemn the Palestinians for fighting back, for what else are they to do? There are no tears to be shed for the dead members of the IDF or active settlers who stand their ground. The world turns a blind eye to the crimes of Israel and the IDF but immediately demands condemnation from the oppressed when they fight back. The constant calls for condemnation of the Palestinian resistance are nothing more than an attempt to deflect the blame for the history of violence from the State of Israel onto its victims. When a Palestinian Ambassador attends an interview hours after the IDF killed six members of his family, the first question he is asked is if he condemns the violence brought by Hamas. It's a disgrace. Nobody is cheering on the death of innocent children; the environment that led to the death of these people has been manufactured by Israel for over 75 years now.

The Gaza Coalition is doing the only thing it can do, the only thing it's been conditioned to do by Israel, fight for its survival. And we can never condemn them for resisting. However, we must also understand that for every Israeli who dies innocent or otherwise, several Palestinians will die in response. It is an absolute tragedy that seemingly cannot be avoided. If they do nothing they die, if they protest they die, if they fight back they die. There is no end. There is no peace. There are seemingly only a few possible endings to this conflict. The complete subjugation and assimilation of all Palestinians under Israeli apartheid or a victorious violent struggle that topples the state of Israel and establishes a secular state for all Palestinians to live equally, but as long as the West backs the state of Israel, the Palestinians will be helpless to win an armed struggle no matter how much domestic or international support it has. They are simply outgunned and outmanned. Until the fall of Western hegemony, a victorious armed struggle to liberate Palestine can only come from a coalition of Israelis and Palestinians united by class and humanity, not by ethno-nationalism, religion, or hatred. But this seems as far away as ever. We are witnessing an unprecedented siege of Gaza. Power and water have been completely shut off and the strip has been under constant bombardment. Hospitals, mosques, refugee camps, schools, and residential buildings have all been leveled, a precursor to a full-scale ground invasion by the IDF. In an attempt to starve out and target Hamas the 2.2 million residents of Gaza will suffer and die. The death toll from this will be near incalculable and the bodies they pull from the rubble won't be 'terrorists,' but families, men, women, children, and babies, all sent to their death in the 'self-defense' of an apartheid state. All while the Western media stumble over each other to proclaim themselves the most ardent supporters of Israel. They preach to their audience the necessity of Israel's invasion of Gaza and so they coax their viewers into supporting genocide. Any dissent from supporting the State of Israel is blasted as anti-Semitic, pro-terrorist, pro-baby-murdering, apologia. Protesters are thrown in jail, the Palestinian flag has been branded a symbol of terror, and dissidents are silenced and fired for daring to speak up in defense of the voiceless in Gaza. So-called progressives and liberals who have put the Palestinian flag and hashtags in their social media bios have seemingly overnight become war-hawking conservatives. The truth is that's what they always were. These so-called progressives obsess themselves with standing up for the little guy, the oppressed people who cannot defend themselves because it makes them feel good; like they're standing on the right side of history. But when faced with oppressed people standing up for themselves and taking the fight to their oppressors, their true colors come to light. The mask comes off so to speak and they reveal themselves to be what liberals are, the moderate wing of fascism!"[98]

We would like to take the time here to walk back absolutely none of this. In the days following the October 7th attack, it was claimed that Hamas slaughtered 1,400 innocent civilians and went on a mass raping, beheading, and burning campaign across southern Israel. As of February 2024, the casualty report from the October 7th attack was revised to 1,163 dead of which approximately 770 were innocent civilians including 36 children.[99] That is of course a tragedy, but it tells a very different story than the one continuing to be spun in the media. From 1,400 to 770 innocents and 393 non-civilian targets, that is approximately a 2:1 ratio between civilians and non-civilians. The 36 children include anybody under 18, which puts the still circulating claim of 40 beheaded babies in the dirt, and every claim of mass rape has either been debunked, unsubstantiated, or written by active or former members of the IDF. It is entirely possible that victims of the attack may have been raped or sexually assaulted, however, no evidence at this time has been brought forward to support the claim of a mass raping campaign. In response to the October 7th attack, Israel has proceeded with its bombing and siege of Gaza and skirmishes into the West Bank. They have systematically leveled Gaza, sparing no mosque, school, or hospital. They have bombed people in their homes, ambulances, refugee camps, journalists, and even members of the United Nations. The death toll in Gaza is rising every day and currently sits at just over 29,000.[100] This number includes approximately 12,500 children, 8,500 women, 200 journalists, 150 UN members, and 300 healthcare workers.[101] This is an underestimate compared to that of U.S. Secretary of Defense Lloyd Austin, who claims

---

[98] King 2023, The West Cheers for Genocide

[99] AFP 2024

[100] Shurafa & Magdy 2024

[101] PaliInfo 2024

25,000 women and children have been killed in Gaza,[102] though that was of course expeditiously walked back by the Pentagon. The current projections from the U.S. claim that Israel has only killed somewhere between 6,000-9,000 Gazan militants.[103] What is clear is that Israel is killing at a much more indiscriminate rate than the militants who attacked Israel on October 7th. And after all of this, the West still struggles to do the bare minimum and call for a ceasefire. Israel has been taken to the Hague and accused of genocide, and still, the U.S. vetoes four UN general assembly resolutions for a ceasefire. It can no longer be denied that the West and the U.S. in particular are more than complicit in the genocide of the Palestinian people.

We wrote in our article *The Road to Peace,*

"While peace seems further away now than ever, it is ever-important that peace not become a distant dream. Peace is possible. In fact, it is mandatory for that area of the world to progress into the future. It is of course hard to imagine, after all this conflict has raged on for over one hundred years, from the writings of the father of Zionism, Theodor Herzl, to the Jewish people seeking refuge in Palestine following the Holocaust and anti-semitism in Europe, through the Nakba of 1948 and the cycle of violence that followed.

The main barrier to peace today is the State of Israel. There is of course bad and corrupt leadership that has plagued the Palestinian side, however, that must never distract from the reality of the situation of Israel being an occupying, settler-colonial force. If this were the 1700s, Israel wouldn't face any problems in ethnically cleansing the local Palestinian populations to create their ethnostate, but unfortunately for the Zionists, we're in the 21st century. Colonial states have fallen and continue to fall. The British Empire has been contained to its rock, the French driven out of Asia, apartheid in South Africa (for the most part) ended by Nelson Mandela and the ANC, and Rhodesia left a footnote in history following the Bush War. The era of boots-on-the-ground colonialism has long ended in favor of economic colonialism/imperialism. What does this mean for Israel? Time is ticking.

---

[102] AlJazeera 2024

[103] WSJ 2024

From its inception, the Zionist movement has always required external support. First, it was the British Empire, and following 1948 to the present, it's been the American Empire. Empires rise and fall, and the American Empire is on the decline. When that fall happens and the U.S. is left as a major regional power instead of the premier global superpower, Israel will be left without foreign support for the first time in its existence, while still surrounded by enemies fueled by one hundred years of hate.

While the State of Israel and the Zionist movement must be destroyed, there is a way out of this for the people of Israel. The road to peace for Israel is taking the path of love and charity. It is the only way to secure the safety of Jewish people in the Middle East. To abandon the politics of the Likud, to end the occupation, to end the apartheid, and to love thy neighbor; this is the only way forward. For the Israelis, this may be a hard pill to swallow. For all the wrong the State of Israel has done in the name of Zionism, its citizens still have the right to live as a people and a community, and with that comes the right to mourn and feel anger for the damage caused by this seemingly eternal conflict. Indeed, Hamas and the coalition of Palestinian Resistance are actively 'damaging' the ability for peace, but that is because they see no other option to achieve peace but through the might of the sword, and why is that? Because of the actions of the State of Israel! You cannot end resistance by leveling entire neighborhoods, schools, mosques, churches, hospitals, and ambulances. Nor will you win supporters on the other side by air-striking journalists, and UN workers, or by burying thousands of children under burning rubble! The way to 'destroy' Hamas and Palestinian Resistance is by creating conditions that the Palestinians have no reason to resist." [104]

This was, of course, a futile dream. Despite all the death and destruction in Gaza, all the families completely eradicated from the face of the earth, the people being slaughtered trying to get aid from convoys, the man zip-tied and slowly crushed under a tank, and the little girl's mutilated corpse hung from rubble like a Christmas stocking; the greatest wound of this conflict

[104] King 2023

is that it spells the definitive end of a peaceful end to this conflict. It no longer matters if Israel succeeds in fully ethnically cleansing Gaza and the West Bank and assimilating those who remain. Their actions following October 7th, even without taking into account the 75 years of colonialism, apartheid, and brutal occupation, have flipped the hourglass on the State of Israel. Presuming Israel continues its actions and completes its genocidal rampage, this does not solve its underlying problem - that problem being it stands alone surrounded by enemies. The relations it was working to build have been torched. Its reliance on the West needed now nearly as much as it did during its initial colonial founding. The American Empire, while strong, will not last forever. Once it collapses and loses its grasp of its global hegemony, the Israeli government in its current state, even if it extends its borders to encompass 'greater' Israel, will be left to drown in water where the sharks are already circling. The only way to protect Jewish people in the Middle East is to give up on establishing a new 'Kingdom of the Jews' and instead make concessions and live alongside their neighbors, specifically the Palestinians. Israel has chosen time and time again not to make these concessions and instead chooses to stand steadfast in their mission to take up the mantle of the Nazis. It is a wolf in sheep's clothing that yet still cries wolf! Because of this, when the American Empire collapses and there is no one left to protect the Zionist project, the chances of another genocide of the Jewish people rapidly increases. A reality we hope never to see again.[105]

The point of all this is that the collapse of the State of Israel will coincide with the collapse of American and Western influence in the Middle East; and with that, the weapon of anti-imperialism used by Iran to subjugate and repress its people vanishes. The stagnation of development in the Middle East is of course not only the fault of the West and Israel, but with their end so are the excuses of the totalitarian regimes of the oil barons and extreme religious fundamentalists. The development that has stagnated for over a century due to direct military, economic, and political intervention, along with colonial occupation, will finally begin to start again. The people of these nations will be forced to confront the direct contradictions of their rulers, cultures, and religions (just as all people must do when their national rulers take up the mantle of foreign rulers), and through this new domestic struggle, the rise of the proletariat and progressive values will intrinsically develop in these nations. While we view the collapse of the State of Israel as a necessity for progress in the region, this in no way implies that Israel is on the back foot and at a point of collapse. It is likely that once the Grand Ayatollah Khamenei dies, Iran will suffer an internal collapse akin to that of the Soviet Union where borders, leadership, and messaging largely remain the same while the internal character of the ruling regime fundamentally changes in favor of reformist neoliberalism in the charge of figures like

---

[105] It must be noted that the rise of anti-semitism should not be ignored, especially by those who support Palestinian liberation. While we acknowledge Israel was founded on the ethnic cleansing of the local population for the establishment of a theocratic ethnostate, we can also acknowledge why so many Jewish people felt and still feel the need to have their own state for security. From their original diaspora from the region to their discrimination and persecution in Europe and around the globe, leading to the height of Jewish hatred during the holocaust, the Jewish people have faced foreign attacks for seemingly their entire history. The U.S. cannot be said to be a safe haven for the same reason Germany was not a safe haven for Jews before the Nazi party took power. Just because they are not being persecuted now does not mean they won't be in the future, especially in nations where half the country is leaning into fascism. With that being said, the answer is not to turn that persecution and murder onto an innocent group of people to establish a safe haven. The Palestinians should not be told to pay for the crimes of the fascists in Europe. The true answer is a global revolution that ends the conditions for the rise of fascism!

Masoud Pezeshkian. Whomever wins the short-term battle for control of regional hegemony, the Ayatollahs of Iran, along with the oil barons, religious fundamentalists, and monarchs of the Arab world, without any foreign forces to blame will be forced into an unwinnable war with the proletarians of the Middle East.

Africa:

The final theater of interest is Africa. We will keep this section brief as the continent is far too volatile to make any comfortable predictions. The main reason for this is that Africa is by far the least developed of the inhabited continents. You can read ten thousand books as to why that is, but a major part of its underdevelopment, or maldevelopment if you will, is its history of being raped, pillaged, and colonized for going on centuries now. Even when the militant boots-on-the-ground colonialism ended, it was simply replaced by political and economic colonialism or imperialism. Historically, anti-imperialist movements have been put down, strong leaders like Thomas Sankara assassinated, and apartheid states like South Africa and Rhodesia had to be actively overthrown by the local populations. The unfortunate reality is that the continent of Africa is one of the most fertile battlegrounds for the struggle over global hegemony. That is not to deny that the nations and people of Africa have free will and agency, they certainly do, however the deck is stacked against them. The strongest tool available to the nations of Africa today is the choice of their foreign oppressor as we covered earlier. They can choose to deal with the West which has historically treated them in the most brutal fashion, or they may deal with the 'nice businessman' in China. We may expect Northern Africa to be more Western-friendly, and South and Central Africa to be more Eastern-friendly. This split could lead to large multi-country conflicts that vastly change the shape of Africa's future, and again that is something impossible to predict. The best case for the nations of Africa is that as the new Cold War rages, they can continue to develop their economies to the point that regional blocks strong enough to resist foreign intervention can be established. Socialism, due to its international nature, is only as strong as its weakest link, and Africa, through the struggle that lies ahead of the continent, will grow as solid and strong as tungsten.

Conclusion:

A lot has changed since the original publication of this essay. As of December 8th, 2024, both Hassan Nasrallah and Yahya Sinwar have been martyred in their struggle against the Zionist state, Hezbollah and Israel have signed a ceasefire that is holding for the time being, Hamas continues their struggle as Palestinians continue to be slaughtered in droves, and Turkey has finally flexed its muscles to oust the butcher Bashar al-Assad out of Syria. The fall of Assad was marked by the rapid collapse of his forces in an eleven-day struggle that saw the country turned over to Abu Mohammad al-Julani, the former leader of a branch of Al-Qaeda. What the future holds for Syria is unknown, but for better or for worse, the era of the Assad family is over, and with them, Ba'athism fades into the dustbin of history. The 'Axis of Resistance' has been isolated and defanged. Donald Trump won re-election to the Oval Office as social conservatism continues to spread like a cancer through the Western world, and it seems like every week a new theater of conflict rears its head. Trump's victory and the increasing rise of supporters of economic nationalism due to the austerity inherent in neoliberal economic policy may bring about a global realignment of alliances. Trump and the surging European nationalists are bound to be more favorable to Russia, and as a consequence weakening NATO and the European Union. The Trump regime will likely be attempting to sever China's diplomatic gains by threatening the weaker nations on the Belt & Road that reside within their immediate sphere of influence and by trying to tether Russia to the U.S.[106] If a reshuffling of the global order is in the works, it's also possible a hydra alliance of the U.S., Russia, and China, could be formed, even if only temporary. That would necessitate a deeper investigation into Kautsky's theory of 'Ultraimperialism', but for now, that's further speculation than need be. However, through all of these changes, our analysis remains unchanged.

The two global superpowers remain the U.S and China, with Russia becoming an even more distant third every day that they remain embroiled in their pointless war in Ukraine. It also holds that China has ingrained the lessons of the USSR's failure in militarily challenging the U.S, because, through all that has transpired in the past two years, China has not lifted a finger to get involved on any side. The power of doing nothing cannot be understated. Time is on their side, and so long as they do not allow themselves to be goaded into joining irrelevant bourgeois infighting in proxy conflicts or in dealing aggressively with Taiwan, they are on track to be the U.S.'s toughest match yet.

With that being said, although we are trending towards a more multi-polar world, that polarity is between two capitalist superpowers, not two clashing economic systems. There is no true principled anti-imperialist axis on the global stage. There are of course states fighting against imperialist powers,

---

[106] Recent events as of March 1st, 2025 show this strategy of attempting to strong arm nations away from China is likely in effect. The Trump regime has attacked Panama over their relationship with China, going so far as to threaten to reclaim the Panama Canal. Posturing has been made once again at purchasing Greenland, a move that would be massively beneficial to the U.S. as a strategic air defense system over the Arctic. Trade wars and sweeping tariffs of up to 25% have been threatened against the EU at the same time that Trump and Vice President Vance verbally ambushed and berated the Ukrainian President Volodymyr Zelenskyy in the Oval Office over his refusal to commit to 'peace' (this coming days after Trump put out a statement calling Zelenskyy an unelected dictator). If the regime sees Russia as a more beneficial bulwark against China than Western Europe, this 'strongman' diplomacy is simply a means to an end. In any case, any new major wars are unlikely. If a conflict is to break out within the next four years, Iran may be the target as Trump continues to tighten ties with the far-right in Israel. Such a move would likely be the end of the 'Islamic Republic' in its current form, giving way to Turkish and Israeli hegemony in the Middle-East (observed by the U.S.) for the foreseeable future.

but just because one lacks the ability to enact imperialist policy themselves doesn't make them anti-imperialist; it makes them an imperialist without a crown. While their struggle against an imperial power is in the immediate sense progressive, their victory does not necessitate an end to imperialism any more than it would necessitate an end to capitalism; it is simply the shift of power from one camp to another. To be truly anti-imperialist is to be anti-capitalist, and to be truly anti-capitalist is to be communist. That is the key takeaway.

The struggle for a multi-polar world is the natural movement of a global world under the capitalist system. It is nothing more than the struggle for monopoly power which will often leave us with an oligopoly or duopoly of nations vying for the top seat. To challenge the monopolist for his throne is to wage war, whether it be cold or hot, economically or militarily, through the pen or the sword. A war that, through any means, will lead to conflict and which incentivizes the monopolist to keep large swathes of nations in a state of constant destabilization to prolong the time it takes them to ready themselves to challenge for the throne. A destabilized region is both dependent on and subservient to superpowers and, in many cases, faces perpetual events arising out of the unstable societal conditions around it that further insecurity. Ultimately, it will be up to the workers of the world to end the cycles of barbarism by forming a revolutionary organization that directly intervenes across the globe to create a multi-polar struggle between the two classes - the bourgeois and the proletariat. Revolution is not inevitable; it is forged out of class struggle. Dare to struggle. Dare to win.

III

Topics on the International

9

The Tie That Binds

Introduction:

The transition from Phase One to Phase Two marks the period of the dictatorship of the proletariat and the ongoing struggle for the global liberation of workers. This is the period when the infant proletarian nations fight to supplant the capitalist mode of production and the bourgeois class internationally. This is when class struggle evolves into class war. The nature of the international revolution's infancy would indicate that a large part, if not the vast majority, of the world remains in the hands of the bourgeois. To attempt to stand alone against the entire bourgeois class - to enter the protective state of 'siege socialism' or state capitalism - is to concede the international revolt before it even begins. While historically, entering a state of siege socialism/state capitalism was necessary due to underdeveloped productive forces and failed neighboring revolts, the productive forces today are developed! Feudal production has been abolished. The bourgeois class is in power in every country on Earth, and so in every country, there is also an exploitated branch of the proletariat. Once one domino falls, the time for delay is over. There will never be a time more fragile for the revolution than its first days when only a few subsections of the international proletariat have seized the levers of power. It is in these infant stages that these loose and isolated revolutionaries must bind their struggles together to form one cohesive struggle. Appeals to nationalism, religion, etc., may be well enough to knock over one domino, but to start the chain reaction, one must appeal to the antagonism that transcends all social constructs of the superstructure - class. Failure to form this international union of class struggle is the death of proletarian revolution. Class is the tie that binds, but what might this bind look like in action? In the next chapter, we will make the argument that adopting a system of international federalism in tandem with the model detailed in Phases One and Two provides a workable foundation for the next era of human history. To do so, we will analyze two federations, one successful and one failure - the U.S. and Yugoslavia - and we will address an alternative system put forward by Abdullah Ocalan of the PKK - Democratic Confederalism.

On 'The Federalist Papers':

During a break from writing a series of essays titled 'Captured Culture,' my attention was drawn back to 'Freedom Road' as I considered the question of how to scale the system of Cooperative Federocracy to the international level. As the system already established a proletarian federal democracy, international federalism was the natural next step in my analysis. As an American, this left me to first ponder the struggle for a federal republic in the still-infantile United States; and in doing so I penned the following thesis:

"The American Revolution was a two-phased bourgeois revolt starting in 1776 with the break away from the British monarchy and the establishment of the first nation founded on liberal ideals. The second phase of the revolt spanned nearly a century through the struggle between Federalists and Anti-Federalists and, by proxy, industrial capitalists and the petty-bourgeois or Utopian socialists. The prominent struggle that started between characters like Alexander Hamilton and Thomas Jefferson over the balance between a strong central government and states' rights would eventually culminate in the U.S. Civil War, a war over the rights of the southern states to own and run a slave economy. So while it is correct that the war was fought over the issue of slavery, it is also true to say that slavery was merely the striking point of the much larger issue of Federalism.

The reason that slavery served as the striking point that set the nation ablaze was that the Federal government, with the election of Abraham Lincoln, was positioning itself to abolish the economic mode of production of the South. The abolition of the decentralized, agrarian slave economy of the South in favor of an increasingly concentrated, industrializing economy like in the North, was a tremendously progressive move framed through the lens of class struggle. This historically progressive move, however, was seen by the petty-bourgeois leaders of the South as an existential threat to their existence; a plot by the North to subjugate the South, because after all, how could the Southern states survive without the free labor of enslaved Africans? And so, in 1861, the Southern states seceded from the union and formed the Confederacy, which began the war not simply over the abolition of slavery, but bigger than all, the final battle (at least for now) between the Federalists and Anti-Federalists, and industrial capitalism and Utopian socialism.

When the dust settled in 1865, the North had won. The Confederate states disbanded and were subsumed back into the Union, where they remain over 150 years later. With the North's triumph, the South's regressive mode of production was abolished, and the Anti-Federalists were crushed, marking the end of the American Bourgeois Revolution. Though remnants of Anti-Federalist thought still permeate the minds of libertarians, it is little more than a bumper stick slogan for the modern-day Republican Party, which is wholly uninterested in dismantling the Union no matter what rhetorical devices they use to garner support. The American Union is now fully united behind the interests of capital, seeing its development from industrial capitalism to finance capitalism and the imperialist exportation of capital abroad. Today's civil strife is always related to the political superstructure of society and not its economic base because both wings of the political sphere are so firmly planted in its economic foundations."

I intend to write on that topic in the future, although the scope of the argument whether it be a simple article or a full-length text escapes me for the time being. However, in my brief investigation into the topic, I picked up and read through a copy of Penguin Books' selection of 'The Federalist Papers' by Alexander Hamilton, James Madison, and John Jay. I found the essays intriguing, if not a little rambly- though I'm sure the same will be said of my essays. Regardless, their arguments are useful enough to respond to and adapt to the context of international proletarian federalism.

For context, on the 4th of July, 1776, the thirteen colonies declared themselves independent of the British crown, and on November 15, 1777, the first guiding documents for the nation, the Articles of Confederation, were adopted by the Continental Congress. Gregg Jarrett summarizes this period as such, "Following the Revolutionary War, the thirteen colonies operated under a loose and ill-defined structure of government outlined in the Articles of Confederation. It brought some temporary stability but little practical organization to just how the new nation would function effectively and in unison amid competing political and economic interests among the respective states that clung to their own sense of sovereignty. If the goal was to create a 'more perfect union,' the Articles were woefully inadequate."[107] It is because of the inadequacy of the Articles of Confederation, particularly in its inability to allow Congress to levy taxes, regulate commerce, enforce treaties, and maintain a standing army, that led the delegates of the Constitutional Convention of 1787 to push for a radically new federalist constitution in place of revising the existing Articles. It was in this struggle for the new constitution that Hamilton, Madison, and Jay penned their 85 essays arguing in favor of federalism, and they would ultimately succeed as the U.S. Constitution would be ratified in June of 1788. We are obviously not seeking to join the long-dead debate over federalism in America. The purpose of our investigation is to one, point out the bourgeois hypocrisy in the original articles, and two, adapt these aged arguments to defend international proletarian federalism within the context of the system of Cooperative Federocracy. With that out of the way, let's begin!

Before we can begin to adapt 'The Federalist Papers,' we must point

---

[107] Jarrett, 2023

out that the authors of these papers were Enlightenment Era Liberals, arguing on behalf of a federal government predicated on the defense of bourgeois right. This is quite evident as early as The Federalist No. 1, where Hamilton writes, "I propose, in a series of papers, to discuss the following interesting particulars: The utility of the UNION to your political prosperity- The insufficiency of the present Confederation to preserve that Union- The necessity of a government at least equally energetic with the one proposed, to the attainment of this object- The conformity of the proposed Constitution to the true principles of republican government- Its analogy to your own State constitution- and lastly, The additional security which its adoption will afford to the preservation of that species of government to *liberty*, and to *property*." Anyone with the slightest interest in the Enlightenment period or American history will be familiar with John Locke's famous phrase, "Life, liberty, and estate [property]," or as Thomas Jefferson would change it in the U.S. Declaration of Independence, "Life, liberty, and the pursuit of happiness." You will find many historians arguing over why he made this alteration, but you will find none who seriously claim it was a rejection of ownership of estates or property. The basis of my point here is that Federalists or Anti-Federalists, the vast majority of the United States' founding fathers, were a part of the propertied class and thus were the political representatives of bourgeois right- the legal rights regarding property ownership. There was no dissension on that front. The introduction by Hamilton lays the foundations of the essays that follow, 84 essays detailing the need to strengthen the central government for the express purpose of regulating commerce, negotiating and enforcing treaties, and maintaining a national military; all vitally important attributes for an emerging mercantile and soon to be industrial capitalist nation. Although not divided by strict lines, the Federalists were far more predominant and powerful in the North, and consequently, the Anti-Federalists held more sway in the South. It is arguable that the geographic regions of the North and South predisposed the Northern states to expand industry and commerce much earlier than the Southern states due to their poorer soil.

The bourgeois nature of the Constitution can be further studied through

James Madison's The Federalist No. 10. In this essay; Madison argues that factionalism is a necessary byproduct of liberty and that to fight it would be to subvert liberty itself. Instead, he argues, we should work to control the power of factions once they seize power. "There are again two methods of removing the causes of faction: the one, by destroying the liberty which is essential to its existence; the other, by giving to every citizen the same opinions, the same passions, and the same interests. It could never be more truly said than of the first remedy, that it was worse than the disease... The second expedient is as impracticable as the first would be unwise. As long as the reason of man continues fallible, and he is at liberty to exercise it, different opinions will be formed... The diversity in the faculties of men, from which the rights of property originate, is not less an insuperable obstacle to a uniformity of interests. The protection of these faculties is the first object of government. From the protection of different and unequal faculties of acquiring property, the possession of different degrees and kinds of property immediately results; and from the influence of these on the sentiments and views of the respective proprietors, ensues a division of the society into different interests and parties. The latent causes of faction are thus sown in the nature of man..."

We should take a keen interest in examining the second portion of this quote. "The diversity in the faculties of man, from which the rights of property originate, is not less an insuperable obstacle to a uniformity of interests." This means that because people have naturally unequal physical and mental characteristics, it would logically follow that there will be an unequal acquisition of property, which will necessarily lead to a conflict of interests between the propertied and the propertyless as well as the small property owners and large property owners. Because of this, he gives credence to the idea of "the nature of man" or human nature as is so often spouted. He goes on to write, "But the most common and durable source of factions has been the various and unequal distribution of property. Those who hold and those who are without property have ever formed distinct interests in society." He later recognizes these as different classes formed from divisions in civilized societies, which is true! If we deem civilized societies to be societies where class exists, so excluding primitive communal societies, then it is entirely correct to say that differing class interests necessitate class conflict. His examples, "Those who hold and those who are without property... Those who are creditors, and those who are debtors..." go a step further to demonstrate that these differing classes are in direct antagonism to one another. In each, one class holds power and control over the other. They are not two equal factions with differing interests; they are two conflicting factions in which one's existence depends on the repression of the other. Human nature, in the way non-materialists describe it, is asinine. Humans, regardless of time point in history, have the intrinsic need for food, water, and shelter. Once those are satisfied, we manufacture new needs or wants that are shaped by the material world that we live in. Throughout all eras of human history, the time to acquire our basic needs has shifted. As class struggle has taken us through feudalism, slave societies, and mercantile and industrial capitalism, the time to meet these basic needs has gotten progressively and drastically shortened. Through each era and, in particular, through industrialization, the productivity of labor has increased, and thus, our leisure time has grown. The more time we have to leisure, the more vast and unique our artificial needs become. Along with these shifts between eras of human history comes the subjugation of one class by another. Each class, through the contradictions innate to class society- the mere conflicting interests, as Madison put it- reaches a point at which the strife wrought by said contradictions becomes too much to bear, and class struggle evolves into class war. Under feudalism, the nobility weaponized the church to use religion and tradition to woo the peasantry into submission, with the promise of eternal paradise in the Kingdom of God if they accepted their lot on the Earthly plane. That was until the mercantile middle class grew in number, power, and education, armed with enough Enlightenment ideals to weaponize the dormant peasantry against their oppressive manor lords and kings. Being humble and content were natural characteristics of the peasantry because that is what was ingrained in them by the ruling class of society that they lived in. The rising middle class was able to weaponize the peasantry by embodying antagonistic characteristics like arrogance and selfishness and demonstrating that a better life was possible when one broke tradition and challenged their lot! 'Human nature' evolves with class struggle, and class struggle evolves through the clash of contradictory economic modes of production. Madison can recognize that the "unequal distribution of property," or simply, private property, is the leading cause of class antagonism and 'factionalism' in society; but to abolish that inequality is, to him, the abolition of liberty because he and his class relate to the ownership of property in the exact same way that the very nobility he fought against related to their crowns! The factions he saw back in the late 1700s were in actuality the seeds of a far deeper contradiction, the next stage in the history of humanity, the struggle between the bourgeois and the proletariat. Inter-class factionalism will exist so long as classes exist, which may not be abolished, but it is unequivocally false that 'factionalism' between classes cannot be abolished. It has before, and it will again. Madison sees it as an impossibility because it necessitates the destruction of his own class - his very extinction - but it should come as a surprise to no one that a ruler would never abolish the seat of their power without being strong-armed by their subjects.

With their idealistic notions of class aside, we should further analyze the authors' plan to control bourgeois factionalism under the new federal government. The framework of their plan - the separation of powers and checks and balances - is detailed by Madison in The Federalist No. 47, "...the preservation of liberty requires that the three great departments of power should be separate and distinct." He briefly expands on this in The Federalist No. 48, "It is agreed on all sides, that the powers properly belonging to one of the departments ought not to be directly and completely administered by either of the other departments. It is equally evident, that none of them ought to possess, directly or indirectly, an overruling influence over the others, in the administration of their respective powers. It will not be denied, that power is of an encroaching nature, and that it ought to be effectually restrained from passing the limits assigned to it." We will not go into depth with quotations on the outline as, to a certain extent, this is just high school civics. They argued for three branches of government: a legislative branch split between representatives of the 'people' and the individual states, a small yet energetic executive, and the judiciary serving during good behavior to ensure the other branches respect the constitution. As a way of mediating factionalism within the bourgeois class, their system was and is successful, but that is all it is. The separation of powers, these checks and balances, are nothing more than a way to obfuscate the state's role as the union of the bourgeois class and its instrument of class domination while providing a stable, hard-to-change foundation for bourgeois society to flourish.

The state is the apparatus of violence one class uses to subjugate others to its will. In our world, the state is controlled by the dictatorship of capital or the bourgeois class. That dictatorship exists no matter how many people get to vote and regardless of how numerous the inter-class factions of the state are. Socialism is only reached when the proletariat seizes the means of production and the state apparatus to simultaneously suppress the bourgeois class and transform production relations from the value form to social production; and the state can begin to wither away.[108]

The key is that it withers away. It is not a policy choice to be enacted, it is simply the natural evolution of a society where class struggle is coming to a close. The bourgeois as a class cease to exist as their relations to production are abolished and their access to state violence is suppressed. Thus, only one class remains - the proletariat. The one class whose relation to production is non-exploitative and who, through directly intervening in the class struggle, has finally brought the notion of class to an end. The proletariat stands alone with no class to oppress, and so the apparatus of state violence loses its purpose. The state thus withers from human existence, but the tasks of administration remain. It is entirely possible that during the Dictatorship of the Proletariat, ideas like the separation of powers and checks and balances should be adopted and adapted to better fit the frame of proletarian internationalism. That adaptation may hold little in common with the ideas detailed in 'The Federalist Papers,' but its underlying purpose remains the same: controlling inter-class factionalism; only this time, the

[108] This period being the Dictatorship of the Proletariat (DotP)

class in control of the state is the proletariat!

While federalism has both survived and thrived in the United States, its success can also be attributed to the homogeneous population of its ruling class. While we may regard the fifty separate states as one nation today, none of these territories were uninhabited at the time of their settlement. The creation of U.S. federalism was possible because the states seeking to form a union were formed by the bourgeois of a white nation that had colonized, committed genocide against, and subjugated entire nations that had previously inhabited the land. Although the surviving nations have, to a certain extent, become Americanized, e.g., Native Americans and Black Americans, that does not erase their domestic oppression. While it is true that by nature of being Americans, these groups benefit from the exploitation of capital abroad and serve as agents of imperialism by joining the military, they still face the oppression baked into the very foundations of their society. An actionable plan to combine the workers of the world must reconcile with the fact that any such international federation will not be built from homogeneous nationalities and cultures. Entire histories of discrimination, religious tensions, oppression, bitter rivalries, hatred, and general alienation stand in the way of a united international. To weave our way through these obstacles, we must bring our investigation to the failed federation of Yugoslavia.

On Yugoslavian Federalism:

The story of Yugoslavia was threaded over centuries of different oppressed nationalities trying to find and define their identities while under the boot of empires and dealing with religious, ethnic, political, and economic tensions. A struggle to unite these downtrodden nations under one identity, not Croat, Serb, Slovene, Bosniak, etc., but Yugoslavian. A struggle against a monarchy for autonomy. A struggle against the fascist wave in Europe. A struggle that tried to light a fire in a world that grew oh-so-cold. And a struggle that would ultimately end in death, destruction, and disintegration. It is, above all else, a tragedy.

The failures and contradictions of Yugoslavia, from its foundation to its collapse, will provide us with vital lessons concerning international proletarian federalism and the balancing of national autonomy with class solidarity. I am far from an expert on its history. However, the subject matter is far too important to be left out of our investigation. Our analysis will be largely shaped by Professor Harold Lydall's 'Yugoslav Socialism Theory & Practice' and Richard West's 'Tito and the Rise and Fall of Yugoslavia.'

While Lydall begins, "The state of Yugoslavia came into existence in 1918 under the name... of the Kingdom of the Serbs, Croats, and Slovenes. It was a creation of the Versailles peace settlement, bringing together the hitherto independent Kingdoms of Serbia and Montenegro with four parts of the former Austro-Hungarian Empire: Slovenia, Croatia, Vojvodina, and Bosnia and Herzegovina." Richard West would remind us that "Modern political commentators too often try to explain human conflict in sociological terms such as class struggle..." while ignoring "the human heart of history, myth and religion." While we disagree with West on that front, his contribution to documenting the history of the South Slavs is invaluable. Where Lydall starts from the 'founding' of Yugoslavia in 1918, West walks the reader through a history starting in the early 1000s, traversing from the schism in Christianity to the influx of Islam through encroachment by the Turks, the constant struggle for power between Christendom and the Ottomans, a series of crusades (some targeting Christian heretics), inspiration from Napoleon and the French Revolution and the many political revolutions of 1848. All of this came to a head with the Central Powers losing the Great War and the Austro-Hungarian and Ottoman Empires collapsing, leaving the door open for change in a rapidly transforming Europe. Lydall explains the early period of the new Kingdom, "Although... at first greeted with general enthusiasm... the Croats in particular began to have second thoughts... The new state inherited the Serbian king, the Serbian capital, and the Serbian military and civilian bureaucracy. Moreover, in the 1921 elections... all parties except the Communists were organized on national lines, and the Serbian parties... were able to disregard the Croat Peasant Party's demand for a federal constitution." Here, we can see early on that the foundation of the merger of these nationalities was heavily fortified by ethnic nationalism. Besides the mentioned Communists, all political parties in the Kingdom were organizations interested in pursuing national identity politics. We can predict that the Communists were not organizing on national lines because they saw the issue of class as the primary contradiction that could unite the proletarians of the conflicting nationalities. The Communists, being a large minority, did not win the elections, and the ethnic tensions continued to fester due to the unbalanced power of the Serbs, leading to the King suspending the constitution and ruling as an absolute monarch. Lydall explains how this period of dictatorship led to mass repression and alienation of minority nationalities and the outright ban of the Communist Party. This ruthless suppression would lead to the King's assassination in 1934. Prince Paul, the regent who ascended the throne, collaborated with the fascists in Germany, Italy, and Japan by signing the Tripartite Pact which led to a coup just two days later. "Within two weeks" Lydall writes, "The Yugoslav armies had collapsed and the King and his government had fled. The state of Yugoslavia was temporarily at an end." It is evident that the main driver in the original formation of Yugoslavia was national politics, and in particular, the national politics of the Serbs, who held the greatest influence among the Southern Slavs at the time. Although the idea of Pan-Slavism spread as a means to counteract the dominance of foreign imperial powers, the denial of federalism in favor of a centralized unitary government laid bare the inevitability of a national divorce, as was seen during the outbreak of WW2.

With the government in collapse and the Axis powers invading and annexing territory, the shattered kingdom split into three main factions: the Chetniks led by Dragoljub 'Draža' Mihailović - a Serbian nationalist, the Ustaše - a group of ultra-nationalist Catholic Croatian fascist collaborators, and the Partisans - a communist resistance force led by Josip Broz 'Tito.' While the collapse of the monarchy and the Axis invasion caused the struggle between these factions, the core of their issues dates back, as Richard West insisted, to the Middle Ages. The Serbian Chetniks knew what it was like to live under the boot of foreign powers, and with the horrors of the Great War still in their psyche, their necessity to preserve and defend their national identity drove their resistance. The Ustaše were appointed the ruling party of the Independent State of Croatia (NDH), which was under Axis occupation. West describes the NDH as follows, "Far from being a docile puppet regime subservient to its Axis allies, the NDH was incomparably more ambitious and more independent than Mussolini's Italy, and more violent than Hitler's Reich," he continues to describe their policy of 'converting a third, expelling a third, and killing a third' towards the approximate two million Orthodox Serbs. Lastly, the Yugoslav Partisans stood against them all and came out triumphant because of the ace, not up their sleeve but rather down face up on the table for all to see. Lydall explains this advantage of theirs as such, "the Communists were not tied to any one national or religious group, but could stand forth as champions of all-Yugoslav 'brotherhood and unity' in the common struggle against the fascist invaders." The differences between these factions laid out the inevitability of the Partisan's victory, but the differences were not as distinct as one might see at first glance. While the Chetniks and Ustaše were outwardly nationalist, so too were the Partisans. Although the Partisans were outwardly Communist, they did not wage a proletarian revolt; they waged a struggle for national liberation. Not liberation for Serbs. Not liberation for Croats. Not liberation for Catholics, Orthodox, or Muslims. They waged a struggle for the liberation of all people within the former kingdom, regardless of ethnicity or religion. The partisans waged a struggle for the liberation of Yugoslavia. Liberation from the fascist incursion, the centralized rule of the monarchy, and the tension of the divided nationalities. Brotherhood and unity was the slogan of this liberation struggle, and it was the catalyst that united these historically tense national and religious groups under one banner, and in truth, one man - Tito.

Following the war, the Communist Party took over leadership of the new nation. The triumph of the Partisans instilled, at least for a time, a positive increase in Yugoslavian nationalism. After initially following in the footsteps of Stalin's Soviet Union, a quarrel between Tito and Stalin would lead to Yugoslavia's expulsion from the Cominform[109] and a theoretical shift in Yugoslavian 'socialism' from centralization and collectivization to a federation of worker self-managed businesses.[110] Throughout the years, Tito and the party would continue to struggle with the internal contradiction of the nationalities problem. Many federal constitutions were written, transforming and changing both the political and economic structures in the country. Keeping with the theme of brotherhood and unity, national autonomy was key to many of these changes. The six republics, Serbia, Croatia, Slovenia, Bosnia and Herzegovina, Montenegro, and Macedonia, had their own governments and constitutions, and alongside them, there were two autonomous provinces within Serbia, Kosovo and Vojvodina. As time went on, the Cold War heated up and cooled down again, competition between the republics festered, the centralization of power continued to diminish, and with the opening up of trade to the West, economic disparities between the richer and poorer regions exasperated leading to a two-fold increase in nationalism. The better-off republics felt as though they were being penalized to subsidize the struggling republics, and those worse-off felt abandoned and increasingly oppressed within the federation. In all of history, there may be no better case to claim the Great Man theory than in Yugoslavia. It is a testament to the character and charismatic nature of Tito that the federation and the suppression of national division lasted for as long as they did, but in the same breath, it is Tito's failures, particularly in preparing his succession, that left the leadership of the party too weak to ward off the resurging issue of the nationalities following his death in 1980. Weak leadership combined with further economic decline continued to exasperate the nationalities' problem, which eventually led to the collapse of Yugoslavia in 1991 and a series of wars that took the lives of over 100,000

[109] An international communist agency

[110] If this sounds familiar to the system detailed in this book, you'd be correct! Yugoslav 'socialism' was foundational to my conception of a socialist economy. The problem for Yugoslavia theoretically was its inability to break from the market and balance worker autonomy with centralization. Whether any of that was practically possible is extraordinarily doubtful.

people.

The collapse of Yugoslavia shows us the threat of nationalism to an international project. The difference between the original thirteen United States and the six republics of Yugoslavia could not be any more different, so it is imperative that we later examine the national question and how to successfully sublate the individual nationalities into one international identity. The true pitfall for Yugoslavia was out of its control. While led by a Communist Party, the system they implemented made no true breaks from capitalist production relations and formed a hybrid of free market/planned 'cooperatives.' It is impossible to permanently bury the nationalities problem without uniting them to intervene in the class struggle. While internally struggling with whether to follow the 'siege socialist' state capitalism of the Soviet Union or transform into their own hybrid self-management system, Yugoslav 'socialism' was always socialist in name only. Their economy continued to operate within a market system based on wage labor and commodity production, making any attempts to reconcile these relations with socialism entirely nominal. Again, there lies the massive contradiction within the Yugoslavian project: the impossibility of overcoming nationalism within the material world of capital.

The Yugoslavian experiment proves that proletarian federalism cannot simply balance national autonomy and class struggle; it must fundamentally transform the economic base of society. With history serving as our compass, the path forward becomes blindingly clear: the integration of all national identities into a shared project for proletarian liberation—one that unites the workers of all cultures, not in some abstract national identity, but in the concrete identity of class.

Democratic Confederalism:

Democratic Confederalism was the birthchild of one Abdullah Ocalan's response to the Kurdish question - but just who is this Abdullah Ocalan, and what is the Kurdish question? Ocalan can be defined by two words: militant theorist. He is a former Marxist-Leninist who helped found the Kurdistan

Workers' Party (PKK) in the 1970s, an organization born amidst the Cold War seeking to answer the Kurdish question, the question over the stateless Kurdish nation. He writes in the pamphlet 'Democratic Confederalism,' "The PKK never regarded the Kurdish question as a mere problem of ethnicity or nationhood. Rather, they believed, it was the project of liberating the society and democratizing it... They also recognized a causal link between the Kurdish question and the global domination of the modern capitalist system... there seemed to be only one viable solution: the creation of a nation-state."[111] Since 1999, he has been imprisoned in Turkey for the crimes of treason and separatism. However, this imprisonment allowed him to engage more with Western anarchists like Murray Bookchin, eventually leading to his abandonment of Marxism-Leninism in favor of his own theoretical concept of Democratic Confederalism.

Ocalan is highly critical of nation-states, calling them "a colony of the capital" and "an enemy of the peoples." In his writing, he consistently ties capitalist modernity and the patriarchy as the pillars of the nation-state, noting that "A resolution to the Kurdish question... can only be found in an approach that weakens the capitalist modernity." All of this leads to his summary of his ideology, "Democratic Confederalism is open towards other political groups and factions. It is flexible, multi-cultural, anti-monopolistic and consensus-oriented. Ecology and feminism are central pillars. This kind of self-administration will require an alternative economy to increase the resources of the society instead of exploiting them and to do justice to the versatile needs of the society." While this sounds great in theory, particularly in regard to the Middle East post the Sykes-Picot Agreement, it is social democratic at best and unwittingly sows the seeds of its own destruction.

This inevitable destruction will be caused by two critical theoretical failings of Ocalan's ideology: over-decentralization and the abandonment of the primacy of class struggle. The former is intrinsically tied to the latter but can be separated for the purpose of investigating Ocalan's misconception

---

[111] Ocalan, 2011, p. 7

of the state. He writes, "Due to its centralist orientation the state pursues the interests of the power monopolies, which in turn support the state. The state can only preserve its power by means of a strict centralism" and that "... capitalist modernity enforces the centralization of the state... in this respect, legal order and public peace only mean the class rule of the bourgeoisie." As we wrote earlier, the state is the apparatus of violence one class uses to subjugate other classes. It is indeed a monopoly - a monopoly on violence. While Ocalan is correct to point out that "the legal order and public peace" or, in other words, law and order are pillars of a bourgeois state, it is not quite right to make the absolute statement that the state cannot exist without strict centralization. Ocalan does not see the state as something that needs to be seized by the proletariat and turned against the bourgeois before it can wither away, instead, in a rather anarchistic approach, he advocates for a grassroots movement to establish the "cultural organization" of a democratic nation using his ideology as a blueprint. All power to local communes with direct democracy to empower "...all groups" and "all strata" of society "...for the formation of different and diverse political groups." Here, you should be able to see the link between his obsession with decentralization as a weapon against the 'state' and the lack of a strong class analysis. He recognizes the state represents bourgeois interests and is supported by power monopolies (the agents of law and order) and is thus only nominally democratic, but his solution is to simply dilute the centralized state power into many decentralized headquarters of bourgeois interests. Democracy for all strata of society is IDENTICAL to the policy he opposes. It's as Lenin wrote in 1918, "It is natural for a liberal to speak of 'democracy' in general; but a Marxist will never forget to ask: 'for what class?"[112] Of course, Ocalan, abandoning his Marxist roots, forgets to ask what class his democracy is for, for if one were to contemplate on it for even a moment, they would be forced to conclude that no matter if it's at the international, national, or local level, it's a democracy for the bourgeoisie.

His lack of a strong class analysis is further shown through his beliefs

[112] Lenin, 1918, 'The Proletarian Revolution and the Renegade Kautsky'

regarding revolution. He writes, "A revolution cannot create a new society. It can only influence the ethical and political web of a society." Ocalan's analysis reeks of idealism. A revolution doesn't influence the ethical and political web of a society, the relationship is entirely reversed! Revolutions arise due to civil strife within the ethical and political web of society! Whether it is a violent or peaceful revolution, the number and fervor of the revolutionaries are stoked by the external antagonisms of the society's superstructure. However, those external antagonisms arise from the internal contradictions of the society's mode of production. When the external antagonisms grow too heated, the civil strife becomes a revolt that either fizzles out through time or force, or succeeds in conquering the state apparatus. An inter-class revolt will merely reorganize the state apparatus which could be reasonably stated as merely influencing the superstructure, but a successful class revolt absolutely marks the creation of a new society. Whether that successful revolt stands the test of time and counterrevolution is another story entirely. However, Ocalan ignores all of this and claims that "The state will be overcome once democratic confederalism has proved its problem-solving capabilities with a view to social issues." This definition of overcoming the state puts Democratic Confederalism, the PKK, and the AANES[113] on the same track as Yugoslavia, a nationalist project cloaked in the aesthetics of socialism on a one-way track to self-destruction. The failure in Yugoslavia was marked by its inability to bury the nationalities problem due to its inability to truly unite the nationalities behind their common interest as working-class proletarians. It is the failure of Democratic Confederalism to bury the nationalities problem due to its inability to acknowledge the primacy of class struggle. Class is the primary contradiction. Holding class as a struggle equal to feminism, ecology, and pseudo-democracy, entirely dilutes its unitive power. While feminism is a vitally important struggle against patriarchy, and patriarchy indeed predates capitalism, that does not make it any less intertwined with the ever-flowing human history of class struggle. Without recognizing class

---

[113] Autonomous Administration of North and East Syria

as the primary contradiction, a movement will never form enough links to grow strong enough to supplant the ruling class.

Preliminary Conclusion:

From our investigation of the founding of American federalism, the failure of Yugoslavia, and the theoretical basis of the AANES, we have derived many important lessons to take into account in the context of constructing a system of international proletarian federalism. American federalism shows that a federal system can assimilate many different nations across massive territory under one identity and that checks and balances can manage inter-class factionalism. The collapse of Yugoslavia shows us that national autonomy is incredibly useful in mending tensions between nations but that without centering class struggle, the nationalities problem can never truly be buried. Abdullah Ocalan's theory of 'Democratic Confederalism' shows us that the abandonment of Marxist analysis in favor of an obsession with decentralization, democracy, and intersectionality dooms the movement for proletarian liberation from the starting line. These three struggles we chose to investigate differ in time period, location, ideological background, and purpose, but each demonstrates that only class is the tie that can bind the workers of the world together. It can do this because it is solely based on their relations to production. Regardless of religious, ethnic, national, sexual, or gendered tensions, all proletarians have the same relation to the means of production as one another. To not acknowledge this is suicidal.

10

The Gradient Scale

Introduction:

Having recognized that only class can bind the global proletariat together, we must cease the critiques and apply the lessons learned from 'The Tie That Binds' in scaling Cooperative Federocracy to the international level. We must scale both the model itself and its principles from the national level to the global stage, where problems like nationalism, religion, and social progressiveness rear their ugly heads at a level unachievable on the domestic level. The 'phase' detailed in this essay would encompass an indefinite amount of time between phases one and two, hence the use of gradient scale in the title. We will detail how the Economic Chambers and Assemblies change at the international level, the framework of an international constitution, the process of ratifying global laws, and the establishment of an International Labor Corps.

International Economic Chamber (IEC):

While the International Economic Chamber is part of the same federative structure as the Local, State , and National Chambers, its distinct responsibilities represent a significant break in the centralization of power. As detailed in 'Phase Two,' detailed planning - the precise allocation of resources - is predominately done locally through LECs and their encompassing Industry Syndicates; strategic planning - planning long-term economic projects - is debated and designed by the SECs and ultimately approved, tabled, or denied by the NEC; and macroeconomic planning - budget allocation and economic policy, is reserved to the NEC to oversee the national economy while leaving autonomy of action to the lower chambers. This scale of both shared and distinct powers and responsibilities is fine within the frame of a single nation, but when we tie not just two nations but the entire world together, the individual NECs must create a body above their own. However, keeping with the theme of our federative structure, this IEC will have its specific responsibilities on an even more macro scale. To the nation, the city is micro; to the international, the nation is micro. So, what are these responsibilities? One, the regulation of commerce and trade between nations both within and outside of the federation; and two, overseeing and directing large-scale multinational infrastructure projects like energy pipelines and grids, railways, ports, canals, dams, and communication networks.

Trade during the revolutionary period has two fronts - domestic and foreign. With the goal of abolishing capitalist production relations (including money) in mind, the federation must wain itself off the lifeblood of capitalist trade and investment in the pursuit of self-sustainability and ultimately complete autarky. Domestically, the IEC would utilize the detailed accounting reports collected from local enterprises throughout the federation and submitted to them by the NECs to get a clear picture of where resources are being allocated, total national inputs and outputs of both intermediate and final goods, efficient and inefficient domestic industries, and consumption trends across the federation.

With this information, the IEC can adapt comparative advantage - the idea that two countries can become more efficient by specializing production based on comparing opportunity costs - to fit within the economy of time. An opportunity cost is simply the benefits you miss out on by choosing one option over another. For example, going to college instead of immediately entering the workforce costs you two to four years of wages, even though that cost is not tangible to you. Traditionally, comparative advantage would compare the opportunity cost of two countries producing two specific goods. For example, if it costs Country A $100 to produce 1 unit of C and $50 to produce 1 unit of D, and it costs Country B $80 to produce 1 unit of C and $160 to produce 1 unit of D, then Country A should specialize in producing D, and Country B should specialize in producing C because they each have a comparative advantage or lower opportunity cost to produce those goods; and can thus be more efficient by simply trading their surpluses to one another instead of building industries for both C and D domestically. This can be adapted directly to the economy of time by measuring the allocation of necessary labor hours instead of price. Let's look at an example between two nations within the federation. If it takes Nation A 10 labor hours to produce 1 unit of C and 5 labor hours to produce 1 unit of D, and it takes Nation B 8 labor hours to produce 1 unit of C and 16 labor hours to produce 1 unit of D, then again, these nations should specialize production by their comparative advantages to be as efficient as possible. They would still trade the surplus product to one another, only it would be mediated by the IEC and measured through a transfer of labor hours. Trade is free within the bounds of the federation. The role of the IEC is that of mediator and accountant. When two or more national chambers wish to trade with one another, they will submit a trade request to the IEC, which will then note the type and quantity of goods being exchanged and the number of labor hours being exchanged. After processing this information, the IEC will approve the request and, if applicable, immediately update the total allocated labor hours of the national chambers to match their new surplus and deficit.

Trade between federation nations does not need to be balanced! Balanced trade would be importing and exporting goods embodied with an equal number of labor hours. Following the example above, it is entirely possible for Nation A to import 10 units of C from Nation B at the expense of 80 labor hours, and export 10 units of D to Nation B to the gain of 50 labor hours to produce a trade deficit of 30 labor hours for Nation A and a trade surplus of 30 labor hours for Nation B. All this means is that of their annual total allocated labor hours, Nation A expends 30 hours, and Nation B gains

30 hours. One's surplus is the other's deficit. Labor hours are not created or destroyed. Nor is being on the deficit side harmful, as the cost in labor hours to acquire the needed product is lesser compared to running that production domestically. While it costs Nation A 80 labor hours to import 10 units of C from Nation B, it would have cost 100 labor hours to produce those 10 units domestically. Those 100 labor hours would only be offset by the gain of 50 hours from exports, leaving behind a total loss of 50 labor hours for the same amount of product. Specialization across the federation will provide more efficient production, and more efficient production will provide more leisure time to the workers.

The goal is not to turn every part of the federation into a metropolis of industry and not every place can be New York City. Specialization is just as much influenced by geography as it is by comparative advantage. Extrapolating away from nation-states, we can view the Earth as one entity, one land of one people. Although today we may divide this entity between nearly 200 national corporations or 'countries,' the global nature of capitalist markets shows that, even while suppressed, the global economy requires the unity of the world's workers. As we examined through our analysis of the Three Sector Model, these national corporations exist at different levels of development, observable through the portions of their economies dedicated to resource extraction, industry and manufacturing, and service. The more service-oriented an economy (excluding tourist economies), the higher its development and the more power it wields, whereas the more resource-oriented an economy, the lower its development and the more dependent on the powerful corporations it becomes. Under the current order, incredibly weak national corporations may occupy a land abundant with natural wealth and a population ready to develop it, but because of their dependence on the more powerful corporations (through force or coercion), they sell the intermediate goods extracted from nature for cheap instead of refining them into final goods. However, once again, extrapolating away from the current ruling order, there will always be some inequality in the sectoring of regional economies, if not for any other reason than geography.

An incredibly resource-rich region will always have a sizable portion of its economy dedicated to its extraction, and a resource-starved region will always import resources they don't have access to in order to build industrial and manufacturing centers that the service sector relies on. The service sector itself is partially just the evolution of industrial capital, but portions of it, like administration, teaching, nursing, etc., will always exist. For example, it would be incredibly foolish, even in the context of our proletarian federation, to develop a large industrial center in an area of abundant fertile soil. The goal is not to develop all economies into large industrial centers; the goal is to create a single, self-sustainable economy of the federation, which will vary from region to region in purpose, while also removing the unequal and inequitable treatment these resource and manufacturing economies currently receive under the capitalist world order. The federation should seek to industrialize, regulate, and automate much of this hard labor, specifically starting in the least developed regions of the federation. This is not to suggest these regions should be prohibited from developing their industrial and services sectors, rather, both over-specialization and under-specialization are dangerous trajectories to take. Over-specialization can lead to vital sectors of the federation's entire economy collapsing due to sabotage or natural disasters, and under-specialization creates an inefficient economy. The federation has the ability to remove the vastly different levels of living standards between the resource and service economies of the capitalist world. It can provide safe working environments and conditions, adequate housing, healthcare, and education; and it will because it is not driven by a profit motive but by meeting societal needs, of which these are the most vital and basic.

Trade outside of the federation must be limited and strategic. Ideally, with every year that passes and with every nation that joins from the foundation of the Federation, less and less trade will be required with the capitalist bloc. Since it would be unlikely that capitalist nations would accept the federation's labor voucher, some form of money will have to be used as currency. If this trade occurs before the federation abolishes money, then trading with foreign nations would simply use the same money as inter-federation transactions. Contrarily, if the federation has abolished money, it is possible they could keep a large reserve of existing money either with the national chambers or entirely centralized with the IEC for the express purpose of using it in dealings with the capitalist bloc from trade to other negotiations. This money would, of course, be valued as nothing more than a fancy slip of paper within the bounds of the federation. Another alternative is to attempt to barter, offering a direct exchange of one quantity of goods for another. However trade with the capitalist bloc is done, its purpose should always be used to either advance progress towards self-sustainability through buying rare materials, industrial machinery, technologies, etc. or to mitigate disasters through buying food, water, medical supplies, construction materials, etc. If the federation has a large surplus of certain goods, it may be wise to export it to poor and maldeveloped capitalist countries at below market price to one, help the nation on a path to its sustainability, and two, as a means of pro-socialist propaganda and outreach to those proletarians on the periphery. Like a drug, reliance on the capitalist bloc will become addictive and, before long, destructive. If the federation is unable to wean off its reliance on the capitalists, it will become corrupted, shrivel up and die.

The other responsibility of the IEC is to discuss, debate, direct, and oversee multinational infrastructure projects throughout the federation. It will do this by 'taxing' a certain amount of labor from every nation within the federation. This 'tax' will be the appointment of a set number of workers and their annual labor hours from each nation to serve in the International Labor Corps (ILC), which will be detailed in its own section. It is the ILC and the total labor hours that encompass it that will be tasked to complete these multinational infrastructure projects approved by the IEC.

International Assembly (IA):

Keeping with the theme of respecting national autonomy while maintaining a federal system, the International Assembly also keeps its powers and responsibilities few and defined. As with the other levels of the assemblies, the IA also combines executive and legislative powers while maintaining the direct will of the workers as the executive head. The assembly is tasked with drafting, debating, and passing international laws that must be ratified by the workers in a process to be detailed later. These international laws, once passed, become binding and enforceable on all members of the Federation. The assembly will act as an arbiter for disputes between national assemblies, hearing the cases of both sides before collectively rendering a decision. Lastly, the assembly will examine data collected by the National Social Service Agencies to identify inefficiencies and areas of interest to focus efforts.

At the foundation of the federation, a constitution must be drafted, creating a basic set of laws that are binding to all members that are agreed upon. These laws must be short and not controversial enough to splinter these fragile and isolated proletarian movements; failure to unite these spontaneous revolts into one international movement will lead to each revolt's inevitable failure. And though it may be true that rights are not concretely reflected in nature, their existence as a social construct is real so long as the material world dictates that they hold significance. In this period of upheaval, society - while in the process of transforming - has not yet completed that transformation, and thus, rights still hold meaning at the individual and collective levels. We'll provide a skeleton draft of this constitution:

1. All powers left undefined remain with the various National Assemblies of the Federation. All international laws are binding and enforceable on all member nations.
2. The International Economic Chamber retains the sole right to regulate trade.
3. Only individuals of the working class retain the right to vote.[114]
4. All individuals have the right to free speech, expression, religion, assembly, and press.

---

[114] Includes the involuntarily unemployed, retirees, and those disabled with the inability to work.

5. No individual may be discriminated against based on their race, sex, religion, gender, or sexual identity (so long as it is between consenting adults).
6. All individuals have the right to a primary education, access to healthcare at the point of service, and the right to work if available.
7. The Assemblies at all levels of the federation must be secular, and no assembly may establish a primary religion.
8. All individuals have the right to free movement between member nations without facing barriers to entry, except in the case of individuals charged with bad behavior.[115]
9. All member nations commit to a permanent non-aggression pact and a mutual defense pact between all nations of the federation.
10. All member nations will make information and technology freely accessible to all individuals of society, dissolve all intellectual property laws and agreements, and enter a shared technology agreement with all member nations.
11. All member nations will recognize and respect individuals' cultural traditions so long as they do not infringe upon the international rights of others. No laws may be made targeting or suppressing the maintenance and preservation of these cultural traditions or languages.
12. All member nations agree to cooperate in sustaining the environment and in response to natural disasters.
13. No member nation retains the right to secede from the federation once admitted.
14. Constitutional amendments may be proposed by a simple majority vote of the International Assembly and ratified through the will of the workers.

Ratification Process:

---

[115] Criminals. However, the member nation may still permit a criminal in if they wish so long as said criminal is not fleeing from justice in another member state. The act of migrating between member states is unequivocally not a crime.

As with every level of the assembly system, the executive head remains the entirety of the working class. The assembly crafts and passes a law, and then the workers get to vote to ratify it. Simple. One worker, one vote. That is perfectly fine at the local, state, and national levels, but in the context of a federation of nations, it may fall short. More important than any singular right is the preservation of the proletarian federation. Without a united proletarian international, the liberation of humanity remains a utopic dream. While it would be easy to once again proclaim one worker, one vote, that is not a pragmatic approach to preserving the federation. While we can unite the workers behind their class interests, nobody wants to feel as though their fate is in the hands of others. Collectivism is the empowerment of the individual, but that individual must feel an equal part of the collective in order to believe that the group respects their own autonomy. To do that, we recommend an adaptation of the U.S. Electoral College system to handle the ratification process.

To start, each member nation will be allocated a number of votes, scaling based on population size with a set minimum threshold - the lowest possible being one. The larger a nation's population, the bigger portion of the working class it represents and thus the larger share of the votes it holds - and vice versa for the least populated nations. The weighting of votes is not to punish large nations nor is it to let 'land vote,' it is simply to ensure that the smaller member nations feel they are meaningful members of the collective with a voice that cannot be simply drowned out.

Once the International Assembly has debated and passed a new international law or policy, each National Assembly will hold a snap vote on the referendum open to all able voters. This referendum will be a simple popular vote that will determine the distribution of the nation's ratification votes. For example, if 70% of the population of Nation A votes in favor of the referendum and 30% of the population votes against the referendum, then 70% of Nation A's allocated ratification votes will be allocated in favor, and 30% allocated against. Taking the proportional votes from each nation instead of having a winner-takes-all approach ensures that the minority opinion in every nation, whether it be less than 1% or 49.99%, is taken into account. Once every member nation has completed its referendum and tallied its proportional votes, the International Assembly will compile the final ratification votes in favor and against. The federation must decide at the founding of the constitution to approve ratification by a simple majority or a predetermined threshold, like 66% approval (recommended). Whichever direction they choose, the ratification votes in favor must surpass the threshold in order to ratify the law or policy at the international level. A law that affects the globe should allow all voices of the globe to be heard, especially in a federation based on the unity and comradery of workers.

International Assembly Continued:

One of the International Assembly's key roles is to be the arbiter of disputes between National Assemblies. This responsibility does not give the IA unitary power over the lower assemblies. Disputes between National Assemblies should try every measure of recourse before submitting a formal hearing for a complaint with the International Assembly, and in order for a formal complaint to be filed, the dispute must be over the enforcement of an international law. In other words, the International Assembly may only arbitrate disputes when one nation claims another is in violation of international law. This would most likely be a violation of one of the agreed-upon pacts (disaster response, technology sharing, environmental protection, defense, etc.), in response to the creation of migration barriers, the refusal to extradite an individual fleeing justice in one nation, or violating trade agreements. A small committee within the IA will review the submitted complaint, and if they deem it valid, a formal hearing will be scheduled where a panel of 9 to 16 representatives will be drawn by lottery to hear the case from both sides and attempt to mediate a solution. If no solution can be found, the entirety of the International Assembly will hear the case, listen to both arguments, and render a decision in line with the international constitution. A decision will be reached by a simple majority vote, and the punishment will be handed down after 2/3 of the IA come to a consensus. This decision by the assembly is final, with no chance of appeal.

International Labor Corps (ILC):

As mentioned in the section on the International Economic Chamber, the International Labor Corps is the organization responsible for executing the tasks approved by the IEC. It is the force that will construct and maintain multinational infrastructure projects ranging from natural gas pipelines across continents, laying railways, digging canals, solar-paneling deserts, water management systems, communication networks, and more. It is the force that will be tasked with rapid response to crises like floods, earthquakes, droughts, pandemics, etc. It is the force that will take on global environmental restoration projects like mass reforestation and combating desertification of fertile soil. It is the force that will temporarily fill in labor shortages. And it is the force for blending the many diverse cultures of the federation into one cohesive unit with the sole task of fostering cooperation and bettering the federation and the world. It is not a military. It is a labor corps made up of volunteers, including construction, doctors, teachers, scientists, CAD, engineers, clerical, translators, and various other workers 'donated' by every member nation to take on the shared struggle of the proletarian federation.

Member nations will be required to donate workers to the ILC in proportion to their population and economic capacity. However, struggling nations may be given a temporary special exemption by the IEC to work out or recover from their stagnation. Once these volunteers are recruited, they will be matched to projects based on experience and skills; training will be provided to those who are inexperienced or whose skills do not align with available projects. Engineers, CAD, and construction workers are likely to be assigned to building infrastructure projects, whereas doctors and teachers may be sent to underdeveloped regions to help take the load off of Local Social Service Agencies. In most instances, a wide variety of positions will need to be filled, and clerical workers will always be needed to handle administration and communication between the IEC and the ILC.

Once the IEC decides on a multinational project and has calculated the approximate duration and number of labor hours required for its completion, it will tax those hours from the total allocated labor hours of the federation, which is found by taking the aggregate of every NECs budget. The budget for the ILC will include the labor of the workers, their necessary training, the equipment they'll need, their food, board, transportation, etc. Once their project is complete, the volunteers are free from their service and may return to their nation as regular workers. However, if they wish to continue their service and are in good standing, they are welcome to so long as their nation re-endorses them. It may be useful to establish a Central Command Committee attached to the IEC, filled with experienced workers, project managers, and clerical workers to handle communication between the ILC and IEC and manage deployment and execution. These positions should be full-time careers so that responses to malfunctions and crises are consistent and learned with time and experience. If utilized well, the ILC can bridge the gap in development between nations that join the federation having faced historical maldevelopment and those that haven't. It can also, if authorized, be used to help develop countries not in the federation, with no strings attached, no royalties, no loans, and no debt trapping.

Preliminary Conclusion:

In this follow-up essay to 'The Tie That Binds' and 'Foundations of Cooperative Federocracy,' we have modeled a scaled version of society laid out in phases one and two to the international level. We have detailed the powers and responsibilities of the International Economic Chamber and the International Assembly, the skeleton framework for an international constitution, and the International Labor Corps that will execute the multinational projects approved by the International Economic Chamber. From here, we must now address, in two further essays, two direct points: the national question and the religious question.

11

On The National Question

In this essay, we will discuss the national question as it relates to our model of international proletarian federalism. This is not meant to be a rigorous rehashing of the historical debate that critiques and synthesizes the ideas of other theorists; instead, we will be focusing on two points: the necessity of national autonomy and the right to political self-determination and the equal necessity that secession from the proletarian federation be prohibited in the strongest terms. Although we consistently critiqued the Yugoslavian and Rojavan experiments for their inability to truly subordinate the various nationalities and their identity politics to their united class interests in 'The Tie That Binds,' it is both possible to uphold the primacy of class struggle and promote national autonomy within the federation. Not only is it possible, but it is frankly a requirement to successfully mend the isolated proletarian masses into one collective force set to the task of achieving their liberation.

Nations will exist during the establishment of the international dictatorship of the proletariat and likely throughout the lower phase of socialism, where the principle of bourgeois right still remains. You may deny this claim by cracking open your dusty copy of the 'Communist Manifesto' and quoting the oft-quoted line, "The working men have no country. We cannot take from them what they have not got," but without proper context, this punchy polemic lacks substance. While it is true that Marx is outright repudiating bourgeois nationalism, he does not dismiss the utilization of nationalism wholesale. In the quote, Marx is laying the hook for his true argument that the development of capitalism, through its concentration and centralization of capital and connecting of global markets, dismantles the barriers isolating the workers of the world and simplifies class struggle to a one-front war between the bourgeois and the proletariat which in turn makes uniform the interests of each worker regardless of the national boundaries they reside in. Simply put, the worker in the United States has more in common and shared interests with the workers in Mexico, Japan, Kenya, etc., than the billionaire in their country. Shared class interests, for both the bourgeois and the proletariat, transcend national borders. The worker has no nation because the concrete identity of the 'worker' cannot be tied to an exclusive nationality, and conversely, the 'capitalist' identity also cannot be minimized to a national identity. The worker, regardless of their nation, derives their existence by selling their labor power to a capitalist and producing a good that enters the global supply chain as an intermediate or final good or provides a service that provides for some social necessity. Final goods cannot be created without the combined labor of workers across the world extracting and refining raw resources, constructing the intermediate goods, and finally producing the final goods ready for consumption. That is not even taking into account the workers transporting those goods from nation to nation and from business to business or all the other labor required to maintain the functioning society required for anyone to perform wage labor at all.

With this added context, however, it does not follow that simply because, from a class perspective, workers share an international relation to production that makes national distinctions obsolete, the nations themselves would simply cease to exist. The nation will undergo a transformative process that changes its internal character, which will cause the external shell or appearance of the nation to wither away into the emerging international proletarian identity. Marx makes this clear in the sentence immediately following the original quote by saying, "Since the proletariat must first of all acquire political supremacy, must rise to be the leading class of the nation, must constitute itself *the* nation, it is so far, itself national, though not in the bourgeois sense of the word." He clarifies this further in his Gothacritique by making the distinction between the substance and form of nationalism, "It is altogether self-evident that, to be able to fight at all, the working class must organize itself at home *as a class* and that its own country is the immediate arena of its struggle — insofar as its class struggle is national, not in substance, but... in form." This distinction is the most vital to comprehend when discussing 'proletarian' nationalism. A nation's form is its external shell, its name, cultural/ethnic makeup, languages, etc. - all aesthetics empty of concrete meaning. Its substance, however, is the internal content of which class controls the nation-state and, thus, which class's interests nationalism serves. The external shell in the context of class struggle and the emancipation of the proletariat is irrelevant outside of the reality of its existence.

Again, the 'Manifesto' solidifies this distinction, "Though not in substance, yet in form, the struggle of the proletariat with the bourgeoisie is at first a national struggle. The proletariat of each country must, of course, first of all settle matters with its own bourgeoisie." The domestic proletariat must seize the nation-state, which includes both the state apparatus and the national shell, from the bourgeois, replacing the bourgeois dictatorship with that of their own. Marx makes clear that the first front of the war for proletarian liberation resides within the individual countries themselves. He also makes clear that this war must be waged by the proletariat united by its class interests against their domestic bourgeois. Class collaboration and the degradation of the primacy of class struggle are both incompatible with 'nationalism' in the context of proletarian revolution. As we stated in the introduction, this essay will not delve into the debate over the national question in regard to decolonial/national liberation movements, outside of making the point that nationalism as a tool of national liberation is substantively bourgeois, whether or not that specific instance of bourgeois nationalism is progressive or not solely lies in whether it furthers the interests of the domestic proletariat in seizing control of the nation-state.

Those with a hard-line belief in the immediate abolition of the national shell are too preoccupied with trying to sound theoretically acute to make a point with any coherence. It's all well and good to stick your head in the sand and pretend that nations do not exist because granted, they are completely social constructions, so long as you recognize that this stance provides nothing for the emancipation of the international proletariat. This utopian outlook is just as infantile as those who conflate bourgeois national liberation movements as emancipatory for the proletariat with a premonition of doom and gloom rather than ignorant optimism.[116] Nations exist within capitalist society, and as Marx writes in the Gothacritique, "What we have to deal with here is a communist society, not as it has *developed* on its own foundations, but, on the contrary, just as it *emerges* from capitalist society; which is thus in every respect, economically, morally, and intellectually, still stamped with the birthmarks of the old society from whose womb it emerges." We cannot ignore the existence of nations, nor can we refuse to make the distinction between the substance and form of the nation and nationalism. 'Proletarian Nationalism' is substantively proletarian internationalism as it is the rejection and antithesis of bourgeois nationalism. We must recognize the initial fronts for proletarian liberation lie within the individual nations and that these early battles can only be won by these isolated nation-states falling into the hands of the isolated domestic proletarians. If these movements have truly unified behind their shared class interests, they will, without provocation, immediately begin seeking out and unifying with the newly found proletarian-controlled nations. It is here and only here, that an international proletarian federation can be formed.

Once this international proletarian federation is formed, however, it becomes paramount to answer the question of the right of a nation to secede from its ranks. While we strongly believe that the federation must uphold national autonomy by ensuring equal legal, political, and economic power among proletarians regardless of nation and by deferring the appointment of syndicate, economic chamber, and assembly representatives to the states, along with the rights to form their constitutions within the framework of

[116] Seriously, it's a fundamentally brain-dead position.

the international constitution and practice their own cultures and languages, we draw the line at the right to secession. The true question that needs to be answered is secession from what and to what end? If the federation has been formed through the voluntary linking of the isolated proletarian revolts and an internationally binding constitution has been ratified guaranteeing the rights to national autonomy detailed above, then for what possible reason could a nation be seeking secession? If some majority of the federation has thrown away all pretenses of class solidarity and has begun outright oppressing the minority, then what purpose does the right of secession serve? It is illogical to believe that an oppressed minority could lecture their oppressor into submission by pointing out their contradiction of legal codes. The right to secession in this instance, like all bourgeois rights, is entirely meaningless if one of the parties deems it nothing more than words on a sheet of paper. If conditions falter to this point, it would be an indictment on the federation's inability to uphold the primacy of class struggle in favor of seeping into bourgeois nationalism. At this stage, differences could only be settled through negotiations or the sword.

This outcome seems rather unlikely, given the roots of the federation's existence. For any other reason than an encroachment on autonomy, we can find no other reason for secession other than the splitting of the proletarian movement, which must be prevented by any means necessary. Factionalism and the most heated debate over the direction of the liberation movement are both expected and wholeheartedly welcomed, but so long as every nation has a voice and upholds the binding premise of democratic centralism within the assemblies, secession would only be sought after by the most bitter of babies. As the bourgeois and proletariat are both international identities and antagonists, they each form one specific polar end of the class war; they each embody one movement - a force on a collision course with the other. The bourgeois and proletariat are individual classes with contradictions that lead to their direct antagonism with one another. To attempt to divide the proletarian class into sectarian movements is to commit great treason against the cause of proletarian emancipation. The struggle for liberation finds itself embodied in the international. Isolated, it will be divided and conquered, and with its collapse, the world will fall into a new cycle of barbarism.

12

On The Religious Question

The Three Positions:

The question of religion's compatibility with socialism is an interesting, if not straightforward one. Particularly in recent times, this question has rerisen to the surface of debate. There are practically three sides with an answer to the religious question, which we will define here as the Left, Right, and Center.

The Right's position is that socialism and religion are compatible with one another. The Center's position believes socialism and religion to be incompatible, but on a personal level, it is a person's choice whether or not to follow a religion without facing retaliation from the state. The Left's position is that religion is not only incompatible, but antithetical to socialism, and therefore should be rooted out of society in its totality. On its own, this stance is the correct line. Working from the definition of religion being a belief in a higher power or god-like entity, being religious would be antithetical to Marxism at a minimum because religion is entirely metaphysical. It's idealistic in nature, as it is a theory that holds no basis in material reality. Religion serves as a way for humans to explain away the world's unanswerable problems as opposed to science, which seeks to solve the unanswerable questions. Through the synthesis of dialectics and historical materialism, Marxism leans far closer to a social science than idealism. It examines the history of the world and humankind as they have developed through the ages of man, studying the rise and fall of political and economic systems through an unending chain of class struggles. This analysis defines the lens of Marxism and lays bare for all to see the struggle for socialism against capitalism. To believe in religion is to completely subscribe to an idealist lens of the world and humanity. The idea that human nature cannot develop out of the material conditions in which human societies live, that our being is embedded in us by a god, is unquestionably incompatible and antithetical to Marxism and socialism. The problem with the Left's position is that it abandons the Center's view of personal religious freedom in favor of the position of militant atheism or, as a policy, State Atheism.

As opposed to the more libertarian secularism espoused by the Center, the Left's position creates a policy of authoritarian secularism, imposing authority where it is not needed. While elements of socialist revolution are authoritarian by nature, a militant stance on personal religious orientation is more harmful than progressive. We must stress the separation of personal and institutional religion. On the question of institutional religion, the only correct stance can be the militancy of the Left's position. Religion and its leaders and dogma cannot be allowed to accumulate political and economic power, decide law and policy, or receive special privileges like tax exemptions (there may be exceptions in cases of religious holidays and conscientious objections from military service). However, the liberation of the proletariat from religion, a theory that has been wrapped in human society since the dawn of man, cannot be done by force. Outlawing religion, burning texts, raiding houses of worship, and arresting religious leaders is nothing more than blind oppression. Such action would not excise religion from the masses in the same way you cannot eradicate hope by banning dreams! The proletariat can only be liberated from the opiate of religion when the material conditions of the society they live in deem religion obsolete.

Just as man's taming and domineering nature to his will has led to the gradual obsolescence of nature-based religions, it coincidingly led to a rise in polytheistic trade-based faiths where there were gods of specific occupatio ns/administrative duties that would take the human form; which as the development of class struggle led to the constantly increasing centralization of tribes, clans, and small republics, into unified kingdoms and empires, would itself be replaced by monotheistic faiths. As religion has transformed and been co-opted by state power throughout the evolution of human history, its purpose as a tool for societal control and as a coping mechanism for the individual has transformed as well. Today, the vast majority of people living in economically developed regions do not pray for rainfall to provide them with bountiful harvests, nor do they pray to the gods of wine and music before hosting their friends over for dinner. Modern religion is still a tool for social control, but its grasp on society gradually decreases with an increasingly educated and alienated population. We have brought nature to heel and transformed the world in the image of man, but the true question to be asked is, what is this image of man? Throughout any era of post-primitive human society, religion has been co-opted by the ruling class to serve the interests of the ruling class. As individuals, the oppressor and oppressed may believe in their faith with equal fervor, but their faith comes from completely different understandings of religion. It is the ruler's burden that God ordained him with the responsibility to govern His kingdom on Earth, and it is because of that burden that he may live lavishly while, on the other hand, the peasant is blessed to live a life of toil and sweat because the simplicity of his existence will earn him an eternal paradise in the Kingdom of Heaven. Did the crusades ever end, or do we just take a broad brush and apply moral and ideological systems to billions of people's belief systems to label them subhuman? And who is it that holds that brush? Is it you? Your neighbor? Maybe the barista at the coffee shop? Unlikely.

The image of man, at any point in time, always reflects the class that sits atop the hierarchy. The small tribes and clans tamed nature but conquered one another, and just as one clan claimed another, so too did one set of gods subsume another until they eventually merged and meshed into singular entities. The contradictions within these feudal and religiously bound societies spawned the struggle of the capitalists armed with the ideas of science and the Enlightenment. A struggle that once won began the capitalist era of humanity we live in today, which completed the subjugation of nature to humanity by unleashing the forces of production - connecting the world's economy, and increasing the standard of living and literacy level for the vast majority of humanity. However, in order to solve the contradictions of feudal rule and liberate the world from its natural chain, capitalism had to unleash a force of its own. The anarchic natural force of nature was conquered by the anarchy of market forces that came with contradictions of its own. These contradictions have led to death and destruction across the globe, but even in lands far from wars and artificial scarcity, people still struggle with the effects of alienation. As time moves on, this alienation only seems to grow. The internet, connecting people across the globe with the push of a button, not only hasn't helped solve the problem of alienation, it seems to have made it worse. This increasing social alienation works in tandem with the alienation of the worker from their work, the degradation of skill and admiration for their craft. It is this alienation that is so integral to the development of capitalism that causes mass depression and a loss of purpose within the populations of the most economically advanced societies! It is this alienation that serves as one of the primary pillars of contemporary religion, particularly among people who turn to religion later in life (not being indoctrinated into it from childhood). That is why the only path to true liberation is not through force or oppression but rather through the individual choosing to leave their religion behind despite familial tradition or the personal path that led them to seek a god.

The Religion of Liberation:

While the institution of religion is incompatible with Marxism and socialism, there is the argument that it has its uses in struggles for national liberation. Here, we must distinguish that national liberation movements are not, by their nature of being anti-colonial, automatically in line with Marxism or socialism. Many proclaim nations that have led successful national liberation movements as states of already existing socialism (AES); this is farcical, to say the least. A few notable characters of this claim are Fidel Castro in Cuba, Ho Chi Minh in Vietnam, Thomas Sankara in Burkina Faso, and Mao Zedong in China. While it is true these men did lead successful national liberation movements as well as taking on the aesthetics of Marxism, none of them came remotely close to establishing a socialist state (not necessarily by fault of their own) as the conditions for such a state were impossible, both domestically and internationally. These national liberation movements were equally bourgeois movements, but that fact should not be felt like a slur! As historical progression demands, these nations must develop their domestic proletariat, and they cannot do so while being subjugated by a foreign power. Only by overthrowing the foreign bourgeois overlord for the domestic bourgeois overlord (i.e., national liberation) can the nation begin developing toward the conditions for establishing socialism![117] It is in this period of national liberation that revolutionary socialists should not fear the influences of religion or united fronts on the proletariat. These influences can be tolerated with the understanding that they are in no way indicative of establishing socialism. They are a part of the bourgeois revolution, which may be critically supported by revolutionary socialists so long as they do not mistake the bourgeois revolution for that of their own. It is merely a necessary precursor to a socialist revolution, and if the socialist loses sight of that, they will find themselves facing the firing wall courtesy of their former comrades!

This distinction is important! Some struggle with the idea of a ruthless critique of all religions. Parts of this struggle are surely connected to the conflation of national liberation with proletarian liberation. For example, most leftists have no problems in taking a hard line against the Abrahamic faiths, Judaism, Christianity, and Islam. Although, in regards to national

[117] The development we're describing here is not regarding industrialization or economic growth; it is rather about the domestic bourgeoisie's use of the foreign bourgeoisie as a scapegoat to keep the domestic proletariat united under their shared national identity instead of combating both forces as their true class enemies. Once the foreign threat is removed, internal class conflict rekindles into a burning flame.

liberation struggles, particularly in places in the Middle East, some are far more lenient with Islam as compared to Judaism and Christianity because they see it as a means of uniting and empowering the local population into forces for national liberation. Outside of the context of critical support of the liberation struggle to accelerate historical progression, this stance holds no water!

Along with this, we see also a sort of sympathy for indigenous religions and spirituality on the basis of anti-colonial struggle. While it is a permanent stain on human history that colonialism exterminated vast swathes of peoples and cultures and further assimilated those that remained into the culture and values of the colonizer, that does not put the indigenous faith on a separate plane from the faith of the colonizer. The act of being colonized or oppressed does not grant one eternal righteousness, nor does it mean one cannot also be an oppressor. For example, in the case of national liberation, the domestic bourgeois is oppressed by the foreign bourgeois but remains an oppressor of the domestic proletariat! The same holds for religion. While a religion may be oppressed or suppressed by a colonizing force, domestically, it still oppresses the population through its nature as a tool of social control and its entirely metaphysical lens of analyzing the world! It is possible to respect a person's or a culture's religious beliefs and traditions and to vehemently defend their ability to practice them without abandoning one's materialist analysis because of guilt over historical and contemporary atrocities. We can do both, and we must do both. We must respect and defend the religious practices of individuals in so far as they are not being weaponized as tools of oppression, however, we must also be steadfast in protecting the materialist ideological framework of the party and its organs. To take a hard-line stance against religion and go so far as to purge religious members from the party is a foolish endeavor that seeks extreme purity at the expense of antagonizing and alienating nearly six billion people. Contrarily, if there is no ideological purity and religion's antithetical relationship with Marxian materialism is ignored in favor of mass appeal, the movement itself will become muddied and lose its revolutionary edge in favor of the reformist tendencies of liberation theology.

It is evident that religion can be revolutionary in a literal sense, but it can and has been revolutionary within class struggle as well. However, religion transforms similarly to modes of production, meaning, as they utilize their revolutionary potential to 'better' society by supplanting their oppressive force, that revolutionary potential dissipates into a suppressive force. It pulls the ladder up behind it so to speak. Once religion becomes institutionalized, it becomes a tool of state control; this is why at the institutional level it is impossible to separate religion from politics. On the level of the individual, religion and politics are separable as people participate in religions in different ways, for different reasons, and from different perspectives. The institution may have internal factionalism, as does the bourgeois state, but radical or revolutionary change cannot come from within its bounds no matter how progressive the faction appears. In the same way, social democrats provide the people with better working conditions and better social welfare than their neoliberal counterparts but still uphold the institution of imperialism and exploitation, liberation theologists may wholeheartedly believe in political and economic liberation for the poor and marginalized. They may even go so far as to be blatantly anti-capitalist, but because their ideological framework is steeped in a conflict between idealism and materialism, their means will lead to reformist ends. Religion is a powerful tool for connecting people, and liberation theology, in particular, is a great pathway to introduce anti-capitalist sentiment into the masses. However, liberation theology as the central pillar of a movement lacks the necessary class analysis to provide the revolutionary bond necessary for proletarian revolution. Liberation theology must yield to historical materialism, or the movement will be damned to the hellfire of reformism.

Religion Within the International:

Regarding the international, the question of how to handle religion develops alongside the struggle. The two key points of interest for us in this essay are the lead-up to the revolution and the structuring of proletarian federalism. For this section, we will assume the party has taken the Center's position of combating the institution of religion while respecting religious freedom; and that it has subordinated liberation theology to a tool equivalent to electoralism, rather than holding it as a central pillar of proletarian liberation. The internal struggle between progressive and conservative elements of religious institutions can provide the same entry point for radicalization, as does the internal struggle between progressive and conservative elements within the halls of congresses and parliaments. Social democrats cannot liberate the proletariat because they are blind to the internal contradictions of bourgeois rule, but through their failures or inevitable compromises, their voters become increasingly disillusioned with the institution of bourgeois politics itself. In the same way, the progressive elements of the church may appeal directly to the marginalized masses and provide them with food, shelter, medicine, and political education, but they cannot liberate the masses because the holy cloth they wrap around the leaking pipe of capitalism fails to address the foundational causes of the leak itself. Their critique of capitalism is superficial and surface-level. It's a critique wrapped in moralism rather than contradiction. Again, while both the progressives within the political and religious institutions cannot provide the solution to their internal turmoil, the masses' increasing disillusionment with the institutions and their novice political education can lead them into the arms of the revolutionary party, in so far as the party is organized and ready to meet them.

Regardless of your stance on national liberation movements and the significance of decolonial struggles in the 21st century, it cannot be denied that religion has and will continue to play a pivotal role in those struggles and, as a generality, nearly all political struggles. Islam heavily influenced both nationalist revolutions in Iran and Algeria's independence struggle against France, and Islam and Hinduism were major factors in driving British colonialism out of India and eventually partitioning the freed land into separate nations. The religious and political tensions between Catholics and Protestants had a heavy hand in influencing Irish nationalism and 'The Troubles.' Its influence does not wane in the context of social movements, as can be seen through Christianity's, and in particular, the Black church's influence on the Civil Rights movement in the United States, the rise of liberation theology throughout Latin America, and in standing against apartheid in South Africa. Religious identity will not disappear so long as class society and nationalism exist and to a certain extent, it can be compared closer to pan-nationalism, as religion and its struggles often exceed individual national borders.

In the process of building towards a revolution, the progressive elements of religious institutions should not be actively combated and, in strategic instances, should be worked with. Churches often have deep-rooted connections to their communities, and many of these communities are marginalized by society at large. Acknowledging that a large portion of the working class is reactionary, we can assume that a large portion of the religious workers support or attend conservative religious institutions. We cannot ignore these workers, and it is a most rigid tenet of being a revolutionary that we must work to combat their reactionary tendencies. To do that, we must not compromise with the conservative institution but rather critically support the institutional progressive's internal struggle against the conservatives. It may be possible to sink an initial hook into these reactionary religious workers by first interacting with them in the context of religion. Not in an antagonistic way but simply as a critique of the institution and its inseparability from the state and politics. From that foundation, we can work to lift the veil of propaganda that has been laid over their eyes, slowly over time interweaving class concepts and political/economic critiques as a rapport is established, working to combat their most reactionary tendencies and turning their frustration from the victims of class rule onto the bourgeoisie itself. Taking the compassion and comradery preached to the masses by the religious institutions and arming them with socialist political and organizational education lays the very framework for the eventual withering of religion as they discover compassion and comradery can be found not just at the pulpit, but within the struggle for their liberation itself. When the religious proletarian comes to realize they and their comrades don't have to follow the good book, grow old, and die for their salvation, but that they themselves already possess the means to achieve their salvation from the heavy chains wrought by the external antagonisms of class struggle, their religion loses its purpose. This lack of faith isn't externally suppressed; it is internally deconstructed; it is the self-excision of idealism.

As isolated proletarian revolts seize state power, religion will still exist throughout society and within the ranks of the party. Furthermore, the religious groups in one isolated region may be historically antagonistic to those within the bounds of another revolt. In order for these isolated revolutions to survive and successfully transform production relations, these religious differences must be carefully suppressed. The primary tool of suppression is the defanging of religious institutions via the abolition of their special privileges and the severing of their ties to the state and the levers of power. Secondarily, which of the three positions the party chooses to approach the religious question will heavily influence both the number and the fervor of the institutions, and their flock's resistance to the dictatorship of the proletariat. If the party cannot walk the line, these religious institutions will be supported by the foreign capitalist bloc as agents of destabilization and counterrevolution. It must defang the institutions with a soft hand and respect the individual's religious practices in order to preserve the integrity and stability of the movement. Assuming both isolated revolts come to this analysis, it should not be a headache to put the antagonisms of old aside to sign a constitution agreeing to both secular governance and the freedom of religion. This agreement is a necessity. The proletarian movement cannot allow itself to be splintered into different religious blocs. Class must remain the tie that binds, and that is why it must at all times remain the sole (primary) pillar on which the movement stands.

The Poverty of Ideology:

For all of human history, faith has been integrally tied to man. To summarize what Anton Pannekoek writes in greater detail in his text Socialism and Religion, primitive societies by their pre-industrial, agrarian economic systems, developed gods and spirits to explain the anarchy of nature. A bad crop or a long drought was the cause of angered spirits, and the eventual rain was reprieval from said anger. The Industrial Revolution and the era of Enlightenment were based on a turn from religion to science and philosophy. Interestingly, this turn from religion to science reverses once more as the proletariat, and forces of progression develop because the bourgeois state in an act of self-preservation will turn from the liberalism of the Enlightenment to that of reactionary conservatism[118] - a radical form of liberalism.

There is also a small movement of anti-deity religions, although practitioners may not claim to be religious. This includes staunch believers in astrology and tarot cards. While astrology may feign to be based on astronomy, it is no less idealistic than standard religion. Whether it be a moon phase, cool-looking rock, or tarot card, anything that holds no basis in reality that bestows upon a person a set of characteristics or morals is taking the place of a god; it itself becomes the deity! When the proletariat has seized control of the political and economic powers of the world and has constructed the new world order, religion like the state will wither away! It is here however that godless religions will supplant the god-fearing religions of old. By godless we do not mean atheism, but the anti-deity religions mentioned earlier. While star signs and tarot cards will most likely not become the new face of religion, they are an embryonic stage of what may come.

The new higher power will become philosophy - its many sects, its different schools, its deities' cults of personalities formed around long-dead men, its dogma century-old books read by few and understood by less! These dead philosophers who studied the world and analyzed the past and present to hypothesize about the human condition and future will be turned into deities. With the endless open interpretation allowed by philosophy, opportunists will spin the ideas of dead men into a web of their own ideology and the naive intellectuals will gather around these opportunists, making them into the new prophets - the messiahs of a new

---

[118] Pannekoek 1907

age. In the past, leaving development aside, being an atheist was not much of a choice. Religion was embedded in society by both law and social control. The king was given the divine right to rule by God, and the word of God was spread to the peasantry by the preachers of the church. To question the king was to question God, and to question God was to stand against the preacher and by extension the community, it was to become a scorned outcast. This example is altered, yet structurally unchanged under the religion of philosophy. The opportunist is given the right to rule through their oratorical ability to interpret the philosophy of the past age. In the same way, politicians call back to the founding fathers or the 'glorious' past to solidify or justify their rule. The naive intellectual flocks to the opportunist. Bound to their ideology like a holy cleric, they recite their theories like religious dogma. The naive intellectual doesn't preach to the masses from an altar, but from the podium, through media, through debate, etc. It is the naive intellectual more so than the opportunist who solidifies the ideology and spreads it to the masses through their uncritical and blind devotion to their newfound historical character and ideology. Unlike in the past, it's to be expected that people change religions or ideologies quite often, bouncing from position to position, from historical character to historical character, until they come to the realization that they are not the intellectual they once thought themselves to be! Once they realize this and they too join the ranks of the new 'atheists,' those who read and analyze philosophy themselves instead of letting it be planted in them by the ranks of the opportunists, they will be labeled as the ones acting religiously! That's the absurdity! To interpret from the source itself instead of listening to the interpretations of those born centuries later is considered dogmatic and ultraist, and for the crime of breaking free from the chains of aesthetic philosophy, these people now become the scorned outsiders! That is the religion of the new world, and that is the poverty of ideology!

Elementary Socialist Reading List

Principles of Communism - Engles

Wage Labor & Capital - Marx

Value, Price, & Profit - Marx

Socialism Utopian & Scientific - Engles

The Manifesto - Marx & Engles

Capital Vol: 1 - Marx

State & Revolution - Lenin

Imperialism - Lenin

Reform or Revolution - Luxemburg

Workers' Councils - Pannekoek

Democratic Principle - Bordiga

Socialism & Commodity Production - Chattopadhyay

References

Bordiga, Amadeo. *Dialogue with Stalin by Bordiga 1952,* www.marxists.org

Bordiga, Amadeo. "Report on Fascism." *Report on Fascism by Amadeo Bordiga 1922,* www.marxists.org

Bordiga, Amadeo. "The Democratic Principle." *The Democratic Principle by Amadeo Bordiga 1922,* www.marxists.org

Bordiga, Amadeo. "The Fundamentals of Revolutionary Communism." *Bordiga: The Fundamentals of Revolutionary Communism,* www.marxists.org

Bordiga, Amadeo. *The Lyons Theses, Amadeo Bordiga 1926,* www.marxists.org

Chattopadhyay, Paresh. *Socialism and Commodity Production: Essay in Marx Revival.* HAYMARKET Books, 2019.

Central Intelligence Agency, www.cia.gov/the-world-factbook/countries/saudi-arabia/#people-and-society.

Cockshott, William Paul, and Allin Cottrell. *Towards a New Socialism.* Spokesman, 1993.

Einstein, Albert. *Why Socialism?* Monthly Review, 1960.

Engels, Friedrich. *Anti-Durhing.* Editions Sociales, 1950.

Engels, Frederick. "Chapter 6 The Peasant War in Thuringia, Alsace and Austria." *Marxists Internet Archive,* www.marxists.org

IMF 2023, www.imf.org/external/datamapper

The Fundamentals of Revolutionary Communism. ICP, 1972.

King, Kelton. "The West Cheers for Genocide!" *The West Cheers For Genocide!,* Sweeney Tarik Press, 13 Oct. 2023, sweeneytarikpress.substack.com/p/regarding-palestine.

King, Kelton. "The Road to Peace." *The Road To Peace - by Kelton King,* Sweeney Tarik Press, 20 Dec. 2023, sweeneytarikpress.substack.com/p/the-road-to-peace.

Fanon, Frantz, et al. *The Wretched of the Earth.* Grove Press, 2022.

King, Martin Luther. *The Other America,* gphistorical.org/mlk/mlkspeech/mlk-gp-speech.pdf.

King, Martin Luther. *Where Do We Go from Here: Chaos or Community?* Beacon, 2010.

Lenin, V.I. *Lenin: 1917/Congpeas: Speech on the Agrarian Question May 22 (June 4), 1917,* www.marxists.org

Lenin, Vladimir. *The Tax in Kind,* www.marxists.org

Lenin, Vladimir. "The New Economic Policy." *The New Economic Policy And The Tasks Of The Political Education Departments,* www.marxists.org

Luxemburg, Rosa. *Reform or Revolution and Other Writings.* Dover Publications, 2006.

Marx, Engels. *The Communist Manifesto*. Penguin Books, 1967.

Marx, Karl Heinrich. *The Poverty of Philosophy*. Foreign Languages Pub. House, 1956.

Marx, Karl, and Karl Marx. *Critique of the Gotha Program*. Foreign Languages Publ. House, 1947.

Marx, Karl. *Wage-Labour and Capital & Value, Price, and Profit*. International Publishers, 2006.

Marx, Karl. *Capital, Volume 1 / a Critique of Political Economy*. International Publishers Co., Inc, 1977.

Pannekoek, Anton. *The Party and Class,* www.marxists.org

Pannekoek, Anton. *Workers' Councils*. AK Press, 2003.

Party, International Communist. *The Communist Party in the Tradition of the Left, 1974,* www.international-communist-party.org

Party, International Communist. *Towards the Rebirth of the Working Class Trade Union, 1992,* www.international-communist-party.org

Schweickart, David. *After Capitalism*. Rowman & Littlefield Publishers, 2017.

Stalin, Joseph. *History of the Communist Party of the Soviet Union (Bolsheviks),* www.marxists.org

Gilens, Martin, and Benjamin I. Page. "Testing Theories of American Politics: Elites, Interest Groups, and Average Citizens." *Perspectives on Politics* 12.3 (2014): 564–581. Web.

McCarthy, Justin. "Record-High 70% in U.S. Support Same-Sex Marriage." *Gallup.Com,* Gallup, 7 Feb. 2024, news.gallup.com/poll/350486/record-high-support-same-sex-marriage.aspx.

Saad, Lydia. "'pro-Choice' Identification Rises to near Record High in U.S." *Gallup.Com,* Gallup, 7 Feb. 2024, news.gallup.com/poll/393104/pro-choice-identification-rises-near-record-high.aspx.

Saad, Lydia. "Grassroots Support for Legalizing Marijuana Hits Record 70%." *Gallup.Com,* Gallup, 7 Feb. 2024, news.gallup.com/poll/514007/grassroots-support-legalizing-marijuana-hits-record.aspx.

Group of International Communists. *Fundamental Principles of Communist Production and Distribution.* Red & Black Books, 2020.

Mao's China, Certified Copy of the Bourgeois Capitalist Society, www.quinterna.org/lingue/english/historical_en/maos_china_certified_copy.htm.

"Hamas Toll Thus Far Falls Short of Israel's War Aims, U.S. …" *Wallstreet Journal,* www.wsj.com

"Over 25,000 Women and Children Killed in Gaza, Says US Defence Secretary." *Al Jazeera,* Al Jazeera, 1 Mar. 2024, www.aljazeera.com

Presse, AFP - Agence France. "New Tally Puts October 7 Attack Dead in Israel at 1,163." *Barron's,* Barrons, 1 Feb. 2024, www.barrons.com

Shurafa, Wafaa, and Samy Magdy. "More than 29,000 Palestinians Have Been Killed in Israel-Hamas War, Gaza Health Ministry Says." *AP News,* AP News, 20 Feb. 2024, apnews.com

Tell Me Lies (A Film About London), 1968

Central Intelligence Agency, Central Intelligence Agency, www.cia.gov/the-world-factbook/field/gdp-composition-by-sector-of-origin/.

List of Least Developed Countries (as of 18 December 2023), www.un.org

"World Economic Outlook Database April 2022 — WEO Groups and Aggregates Information." *International Monetary Fund*, www.imf.org

"الإعلام الحكومي بغزة يناشد العالم التدخل لوقف الكارثة الإنسانية بغزة." المركز الفلسطيني للإعلام - أخبار فلسطين - أخبار القدس, 8 Jan. 2024, palinfo.com

Hamilton, Alexander, et al. *The Federalist Papers*. Penguin Books, 2012.

Lydall, Harold. *Yugoslav Socialism: Theory and Practice*. Clarendon Press; Oxford University Press, 1986.

West, Richard. *Tito and the Rise and Fall of Yugoslavia*. Carroll & Graf, 1995.

Öcalan, Abdullah. *Democratic Confederalism*. Transmedia Publishing, 2014.

Made in the USA
Monee, IL
12 November 2026

e0a1cb76-6e5b-4a74-a879-9beb05ad5e9eR01